DO·IT·YOURSELF
DESIGNER FURNITURE

Richard Entwistle

DO·IT·YOURSELF
DESIGNER FURNITURE

Ebury Press
London

Published by Ebury Press
National Magazine House
72 Broadwick Street
London W1V 2BP

First impression 1986

ISBN 0 85223 560 7

Do-It-Yourself Designer Furniture
was conceived, edited and designed by
Grub Street, 4 Kingly Street,
London W1R 5LF

Plans and diagrams by Nigel Jones
Step by step illustrations by Robert Jones
Photography by Simon Battensby

Typeset by Witwell Ltd, Liverpool
Printed and bound in Italy by New Interlitho

Dedication
For Karen

Acknowledgements
My thanks are due to Jenny Doutré for
typing the manuscript, to Ian Dunn,
Dominic Neville and Ted Rainbow for
making the prototypes, and to The
Design Group for allowing me to write
the book in my spare time.

The designs in this book were
originally created using metric
measurements. The closest workable
imperial equivalents are given in all
cases, and a conversion chart is
supplied on page 160 should you wish
to check for yourself.

The designs in this book are intended for
those with basic woodworking skills. The
author and publisher respectfully wish to
point out that they cannot be held
responsible for errors or costs incurred
during manufacture.

Introduction

Creating Designer Furniture

We professional furniture designers owe much to the Italians, who have been the strongest influence on furniture design since the 1970s. And much has been done to bring Italian designers to the forefront by Italian manufacturers, who have appreciated what design can do for them in a commercial sense. This has earned Italy worldwide respect, although it has been left to the retailers to discover this style and import it to other countries. For me, 'designer' to a great extent means 'Italian', because the Italians have led the world during the last 20 years.

I have always been aware, however, that few books on making furniture at home reflect the current styles and trends seen in shops and magazines. Many D-I-Y magazines and books would not inspire those interested in modern design, and so discourage us from making our own furniture. I believe that, given a fashionable and stylish design and an easy way of making it, D-I-Y furniture transforms itself into an attractive proposition.

It is the purpose of this book to provide others with the know-how to produce furniture that is modern in design, inexpensive and created in materials that are readily available from reputable suppliers. *Do It Yourself Designer Furniture* presents a series of projects, conceived by a professional furniture designer, to be valued as much as pieces of modern design as personal achievements in D-I-Y craft. I hope it will appeal to those who want to achieve good results quickly — it is certainly not just a book for D-I-Y buffs or repressed cabinet makers!

Richard Entwistle

Contents

6

Before you Begin

Most furniture stores will add an 80-100% mark-up to the cost of a product in order to cover their costs and profit. Do-it-yourself shops and wood suppliers must also cover costs and make profits, so you can similarly expect to pay double for all your materials compared with the ordinary furniture manufacturer who pays for materials in bulk.

The materials for these projects have been carefully chosen so that the final cost is always less than the price of an equivalent article in a shop. You will find that most of the designs use either board or pre-prepared wood. Softwood (pine) is referred to by the woodwork trade as PAR (planed all round). Some designs, though very few, require hardwood. Your local suppliers will usually stock it, although they may have to machine it up especially for you.

You will also notice the extensive use of MDF (medium density fibreboard). This is the most interesting development in board material during the last 10 years and basically means that we now have board with both a good surface finish ideal for paint and a good core structure. When cut and shaped, a satisfying finish can easily be obtained by sanding; no filling is needed, as would be the case with chipboard. The main drawback is that of weight (and, for the moment, price) but for our purposes the advantages outweigh the drawbacks.

Finishing

Finishing is another area where considerable advances have been made. Today, 99% of manufacturers use spray-on cellulose finishes, applied to the furniture with air pressure through spray guns (and sometimes now with computer-programmed robots). If you have access to these facilities, use them, and if possible put a clear finish over the top of any colour used. It is a technique well known in the auto trade for giving a colour extra depth. But cellulose finishes are not as a rule sold in do-it-yourself stores and may only be available through auto-trade factors. If obtainable, they can be brushed on by hand, but they do dry *very* quickly. The process to follow is the same as for oil-based finishes (see TECHNIQUES p. 36 Finishing). Otherwise you will have to use traditional oil based finishes which, although they are slower to apply and take longer to dry, are more durable in day-to-day use as they are flexible and will move with the material beneath.

Joints

When jointing two pieces of wood together you will be employing the dowel joint most of the time. In industry this is the most commonly-used joint, basically because it is easier to drill a hole than to cut a tenon and in automatic plants a jig-borer can drill several at the same time. You will find that a small dowelling jig, bought at very little cost, will save a lot of time and make your joints more accurate (or you can make one yourself — see TECHNIQUES p.33).

During the course of the following group of projects you won't be required to make hand-cut dovetail joints; neither will you need to use beautiful woods. I'm sure you won't want to spend six months of your spare time making a chair that costs you much more than the chair is actually worth. And such precise techniques need much practice to perfect. Instead, you will learn how to make accessible, achievable and well-designed furniture quickly. For some of the projects you will be able to get up on a Saturday morning, buy the materials and be using the item by Sunday night. Others will take longer.

Following instructions

All the methods used are designed to be simple and fast; perfect results can be obtained if care is taken and the instructions are followed exactly. Always read through the instructions first, so that you know all that is involved and can prepare adequately for the projects. Please don't be tempted to compromise on any of the details. I have already simplified the methods as far as possible.

Bench and vice

For most of these projects you will need to use a bench and vice. You probably won't need a proper wood-worker's bench, but at least make sure you get a portable, folding workbench. Acquiring the proper tools and equipment will not prove a waste of money, particularly as I have designed the work to use the more basic of the DIY tools. These — if you haven't already got them — will always be on hand for future use and remain a lasting investment.

Cost and commitment

The earlier point about cost of materials has another relevance. That is, how much commitment in terms of time you want to make, when there is a possibility that you won't finish the project. No matter how I design a dining chair, for example, there will always be money to spend on materials and time spent in making it. Multiply that by six and you have a fairly large commitment. So decide on your project carefully. Choose one that will suit your present level of experience and ability first and then progress.

All the furniture designs are simple to make, but will produce items with style. The result will naturally depend on the care of the person making the furniture, but excellent results *are* obtainable if you have application, patience and determination. And, above all with this type of furniture, it is important to work crisply and cleanly. Keep your workshop like a clinic!

Suppliers

Sources of furniture materials fall into three categories:

- **Large multiple retailers mainly on out-of-town sites.**

These are useful for board and wood as they are kept in dry conditions. Many also have a good cutting service for customers. Everything else will probably be pre-packed.

- **Hardware stores and do-it-yourself shops.**

These will be useful sources for screws, glues and paints, but their supplies of wood will be limited, owing to lack of space.

- **Traditional yards.**

These are often the most useful of the three as they probably supply the local tradesmen. Most have their own machines and may do joinery work as a sideline. Their wood supplies may not be as good as those of the larger retailers, however, as they are often kept outside under cover and, being damp, will be susceptible to movement while drying out. Insist on the best quality material.

For most of these places, weekends are the busiest time of the week, bringing crowds of people eager to start their spare-time DIY tasks and placing extra demands on pressurized staff. You are not one of these people. Drop in a cutting list a few days in advance so they have time to get the material ready for you during one of their slacker periods. Always try and build up a friendly relationship with those who are serving you. Remember that it is only they who stand between you and the best quality materials. Put someone's back up and you will be palmed off with rubbish.

Out of stock

'If it's not on the shelf we haven't got it.' Yes, this attitude exists in DIY as well. I'm afraid that many shops do not keep the variety of merchandise they once did, and

you may well need to be patient in searching out material for some projects. But don't compromise. It is a fact of life when making furniture, even more so on a commercial scale, that materials may need some finding. Here I have restricted the requirements to very common raw materials and fittings. If you don't find what you are looking for the first time, then you have been most unlucky.

Checking Materials

All cutting lists for materials required give final cut sizes. You may decide to buy your materials over-size and cut them to final dimension yourself. But this will be time-consuming, and unless you feel able to cut materials better than your supplier, it is always preferable for them to cut the materials for you.

When buying solid hardwood or softwood, remember that you will only be able to cut it to length. Dimensioning to width and thickness is generally not possible for DIY work as you won't have the machinery to do it. So if you are considering using spare wood you may have at home, check the width and thickness. If it is not right for the job, get the supplier to cut it down for you or buy new.

Wherever possible, the designs for these projects use standard pre-machined sizes. Fortunately most suppliers will cut to size at no extra charge as there is, for them, little more work involved. You will need to insist on accuracy, however, and on selecting the best quality materials. This is where it is important to build a relationship with your supplier.

So before starting any of these projects, please check your sizes against the materials list and re-cut where necessary.

One important thing to remember is that in the wood trade it is standard practice to

define the direction of the wood grain with the first dimension, followed by the width, and lastly the thickness (or the smallest dimension).
For example

written as   375mm×210mm×22mm
(14¾"×8¼"×⅞")

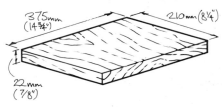

written as   210mm×375mm×22mm
(8¼"×14¾"×⅞")
It is a good idea to confirm this with your supplier when ordering the materials. On flat board piece parts there is only one project that is seriously affected, the table with red tube detailing. See the note with the cutting diagram, page 49).

Wood and board

The wood available from your local supplier falls mainly into two categories — hardwood and softwood.

Softwood is what the building trade uses as a constructional material, and because of this it is widely available. But, also for the same reason, the quality is very often not good enough for making furniture. Here are a few points that you need to check:

- PAR means planed all round. Check that this is indeed the case, and that there are no faces or edges with rough surfaces that have not been planed smooth.

● Check that the pieces of wood you select are straight. This is not always crucial as most suppliers store PAR section flat and it is therefore often held straight by weight. Also, a slight bend over a 3-metre (9 ft) length will not badly affect its suitability for our purposes. Do not, however, accept twists and bends that go up and down along the length — even the building trade would have difficulty in using this kind of wood.

● Bends and distortions across the width are more important and cannot easily be rectified; you should reject wood with these defects.

Most distortions occur because softwood is now grown very quickly and cut down young in order for forest owners to capitalize on their investment. It is also often kept in conditions far from ideal, and this causes the wood to warp and distort.

● Knots are a characteristic of softwood and cannot be selected out. But you can insist on there being no 'dead' knots. These are the loose ones which tend to drop out and leave you with gaping holes. (When applying paint to softwood over knots, it is important first to apply a liquid called 'knotting', otherwise resin from the knots will bleed through the paint.)

● Lastly you will need to make sure that the general condition of the wood is good and that there are no splints or cracks.

Hardwoods are very different and often not widely available from local suppliers, unless of course they are specialists. The most common hardwoods are mahogany, beech and oak, in that order. They are all more expensive than softwood, particularly oak, and it is even more important that, as you are paying a premium for this wood, you check it thoroughly before accepting it.

The checking list will be the same as for softwood, except that you are unlikely to encounter knots. You may well be asked to pay a cutting charge, however, and, unlike softwoods, you will need to insist on kiln-dried material.

Pre-veneered board is a sheet of chipboard which has been veneered on both sides — usually with a face or show veneer (oak, ash, *etc*) to one side, with an ordinary balance veneer (mahogany, sapele) to the reverse side.

For all the projects in this book we shall be using or showing the face side only; the reverse side must always be kept on the inside of the work.

PAR (Planed All Round) and standard sizes

All stock material sizes are graded in whole (unfinished) dimensions. When buying PAR stock the finished, machined size will be (as detailed in the material lists) slightly smaller — so, for example, 50mm × 25mm (2" × 1") will in fact probably measure 44mm × 22mm (1¾" × ⅞"). If your timber supplier is confused by a stock size of 44mm × 22mm (1¾" × ⅞") please draw his attention to this.

The Finished Furniture

From the moment the ideas for the first designs were formulated, it was clear that the best way of proving each design and perfecting the construction technique was to make careful and painstaking prototypes of every single piece of furniture included in this book.

In the following pages you will see photographs of each item in its finished state. Many were made not by an experienced furniture maker, but by somebody with limited woodworking experience and indeed with a minimum of tools and facilities — namely hand tools and a kitchen table!

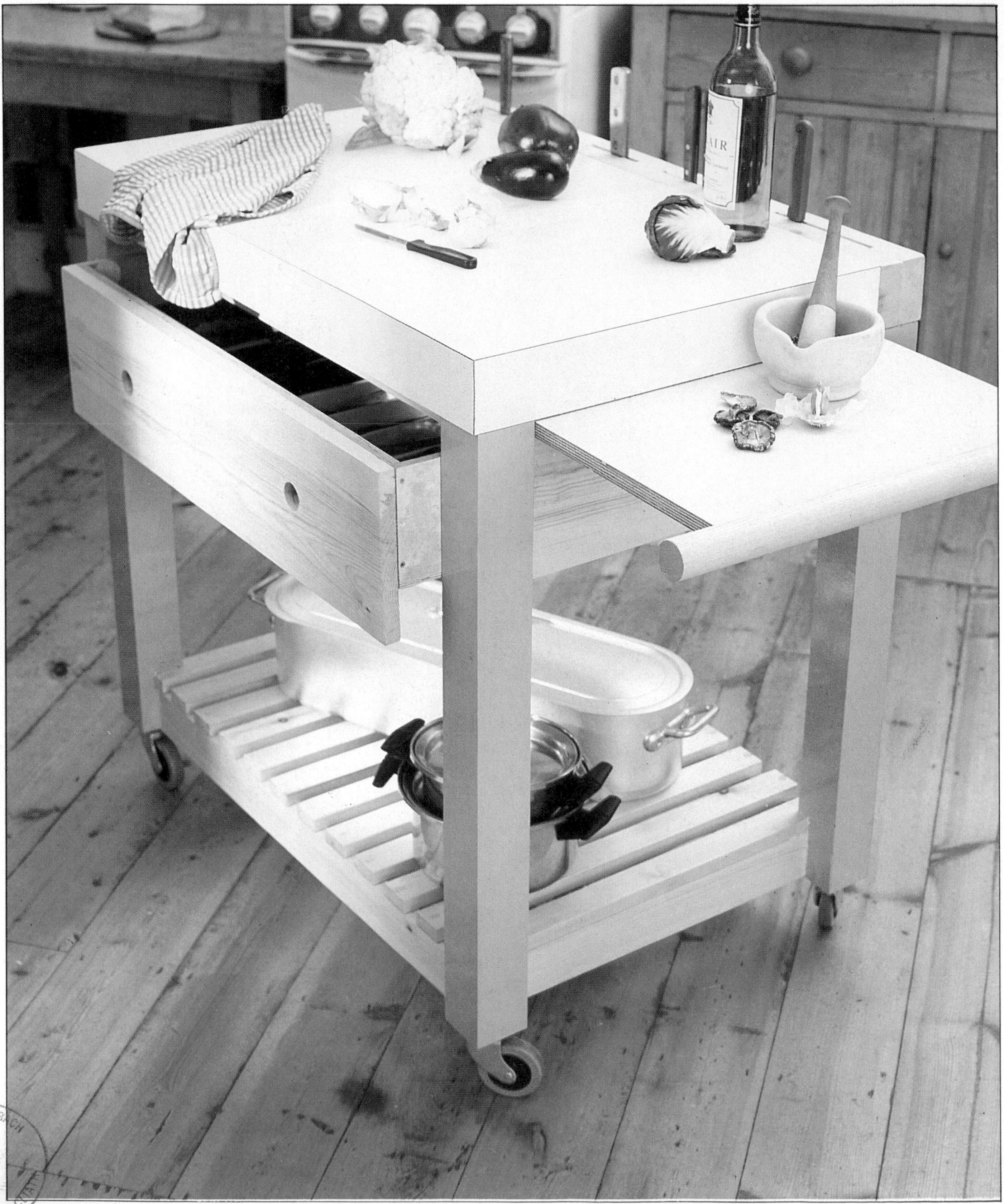

Efficiency, ease and style are brought to the kitchen with this trolley-style work station (left). Free-standing, mobile, or permanently placed against a wall, it provides the extra work space every kitchen needs. Similarly bright yet functional is the dining table above. Simple in construction, quick to make and honest in its use of modern materials, its matching chair echoes the red 'piping' effect, adding a simple upholstered pad for an up-to-the-minute look.

Kitchen work station finished with plastic laminate
See page 42 for materials and instructions

Dining table with red tube detail
See page 48 for materials and instructions

Chair with red dowel detail
See page 52 for materials and instructions

A matching of classic styles combines the trim, firm lines of this black-framed sofa with the practical adaptability of a nest of tables. Such smooth designs fit easily into rooms of any style or period. The tables — employing the same techniques and materials as for the laminate coffee table (page 70) — will mix with all kinds of existing upholstery and furnishings, however varied, and their dimensions can be altered to allow them to fulfil a variety of functions. The sofa's strong underframe forms a light-lined foundation for the fabric upholstery of your choice. Quick and simple to make, it is low in materials cost, and the zip fastened covers allow easy cleaning or a change of fabric to transform its appearance in a trice.

Black framed sofa
See page 56 for materials and instructions

Laminate coffee table
See page 70 for materials and instructions

Nest of tables finished in plastic laminate
See page 74 for materials and instructions

S prung with rubber webbing and covered in a soft quilt, this comfortable couch is among the more ambitious of the projects included here. The upholstery is made-to-measure separately, laid over the sturdy base frame and secured with ribbon ties.

Quilted sofa with wood-frame base
See page 62 for materials and instructions

Thus simple but practical coffee table is constructed by the same easy slot-together method as the bed on page 28-29. Well within anybody's capabilities, it requires few tools and little time to complete. When finished, it will prove an indispensable room-tidier, keeping your living room as uncluttered as its own straight lines.

Low tiered coffee table in fibreboard
See page 76 for materials and instructions

These three designs serve several functions. Above is a simple low table that can also be made in multiples for stacking as a storage unit. The square, glass-topped table (right) would suit an end-of-sofa position, to take a table lamp, while the console table (far right), elegant in a hall, could also double as a back-of-sofa table.

9

Low table/stacking unit of medium density fibreboard
See page 80 for materials and instructions

10

Criss-cross occasional table finished in plastic laminate
See page 84 for materials and instructions

11

Console table with angled legs
See page 88 for materials and instructions

 12

Cutout shaped table with speckle finish
See page 92 for materials and instructions

 13

Adjustable audio unit in steel tube and
laminate
See page 95 for materials and instructions

Here are two contrasting designs for solving basic storage problems. The wood and glass shelving system above is primarily for display, its traditional materials blending with most interior styles. The adjustable system (left) is intended for hi-fi equipment. In the foreground is an occasional table, with eye-catching cutout-shaped top.

 14

Display shelving unit in glass, wood and steel
See page 100 for materials and instructions

The fireplace shown above will blend into existing decorations and complement furniture of any period. Stylish, it is also very easy to make and incorporates a tiled area between it and the fire opening to conform to safety recommendations. Care, attention to detail and time willingly spent will repay dividends with this and with the tone-contrasting dining room suite (right). Relatively inexpensive to make, the matching table, six chairs and sideboard bring an individual flourish to a light and airy dining area. Spare and slim-lined, these larger pieces will add subtle character to a room.

15

Fireplace surround to fit variable dimensions
See page 104 for materials and instructions

Dining-room suite in hardwood

16

Dining table
See page 108 for materials and instructions

17

Dining chair
See page 112 for materials and instructions

18

Sideboard
See page 116 for materials and instructions

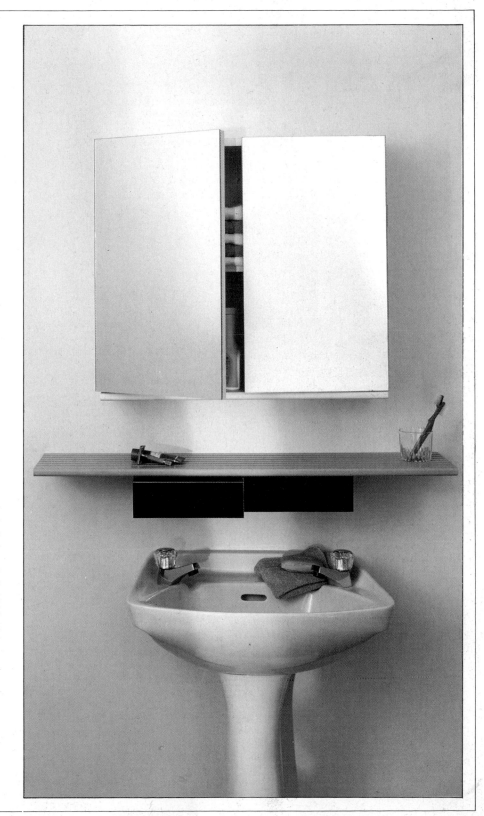

Most homes
need somewhere to keep files and store
stationery; the desk shown (left)
provides an ideal work-space for
writing letters, paying bills or even
working from home. It will fit unobtru-
sively into any living room and, with the
accent on practicality, incorporates the
option of a filing drawer if required.
Behind the desk is a matching shelf unit,
one of the easiest projects in the book.

Storage unit
See page 120 for materials and instructions

Work desk with optional filing
drawer
See page 124 for materials and instructions

Similarly, no mat-
ter what the décor or style of your bathroom, this cabinet and mirror will
complement its design and shade. An
ingenious feature is the right-hand door;
double-hinged and mirrored, it can
open to swing round and provide an
additional side-on view for all-round
grooming. A separate grooved shelf
provides handy drawer space for
additional storage of toilet requisites
and acts as a holder for toothmugs or
other accessories.

Bathroom cabinet and shelf
See page 129 for materials and instructions

 22

Bunk/twin beds in softwood
See page 134 for materials and instructions

Thearese adaptable
bunk beds for a children's or spare
room (above) are designed to be dis-
mantled and positioned separately as
twin beds when necessary. Should one
only be required, it can be made as an
individual unit and the twin added later.
Alternatively, the platform-style bed
(right) incorporates a wardrobe, multi-
adjustable desk, and activity/play area.

 23

Child's bunk bed and activities unit
See page 138 for materials and instructions

This simple bed, providing a firm, solid base for a mattress, is made from chipboard sheets cut and slotted together. An ideal project to start with, it is a *very* cheap way of adding that unique touch of style to your bedroom. The fabric-covered portable screen (extreme left) is free-standing and looks equally at home in the bedroom, as here, the living room, or wherever a temporary room divider is required.

Basic bed constructed from chipboard
See page 144 for materials and instructions

Free-standing fabric screen
See page 148 for materials and instructions

26

Dressing stand with mirror and shelves
See page 151 for materials and instructions

For bedrooms pre-ferred simple and uncluttered, consider the two designs above. The dressing stand and mirror (left) will hold all those odds and ends that normally clutter the dressing table, while the wooden-framed double bed features an optional circular side-table for alarm clock or bedside book.

27

Bed with integral table
See page 155 for materials and instructions

Techniques

Before beginning any of the projects, it is important to have some knowledge and mastery of the construction techniques required. A selection of those most often used in the designs is explained here in depth. And apart from their relevance here they will, of course, apply to any job of a similar nature that you may undertake in future.

It is important to follow the instructions closely, as the final result will always depend on the care taken. You will also find that the text often refers back to a specific technique mentioned here, so read this section thoroughly first. When you see the same technique again, you may not have to refer back for information.

Naturally, not all furniture-making techniques are included, but certainly some of the most important are described here. These tips will help you to achieve perfect results in the quickest and easiest way. None are particularly difficult and all would be performed in much the same way by skilled craftsmen. The hardest thing to learn will be patience.

Cutting Joints

To cut the basic joints known as a cross halving, mortise and tenon, *etc*, use the following procedure.

1 Square across one piece of wood, using the second piece to define the width of the section to be cut out.

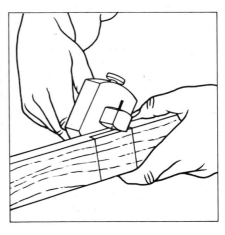

2 Take a marking gauge to mark the bottom edge of the cut.

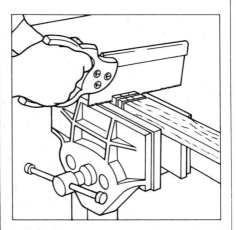

3 Hold the first piece of wood in a vice. Cut down to the line with a tenon saw at both ends of the joint. Cut in the middle also, at 10mm (³⁄₈″) intervals.

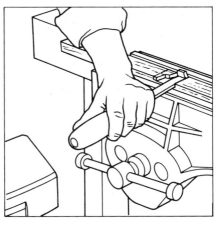

4 Knock out the waste wood with a sharp 12mm (½″) chisel and mallet. Finish down to the line with the chisel, using only its cutting capability to shave off the last few pieces.

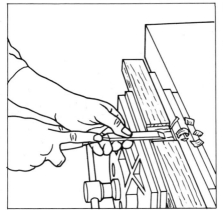

5 For extra neatness, and this is almost essential when working in hardwoods, use a piece of packing between each side of the wood and the vice. Line up the top edges of these spacers with the bottom line of the joint and use them as a guide for the final cutting. If your vice has good wooden linings, the face packing will not be needed.

For a halved angle joint or tenons, *etc*, use the following procedure.

1 Mark out the joint with a square and marking gauge as before.

2 Cut out as before with a tenon saw.

3 Hold the chisel against the end grain and hit the handle smartly with the mallet. Finish down to the line using the cutting action of the chisel only.

As you get more confident, you will find that when working with softwood you need only one saw cut at the shoulder of the tenon, and one sharp knock on a 25mm (1″) chisel to remove most of the waste. Note that this quick method is *not* advisable on hardwood.

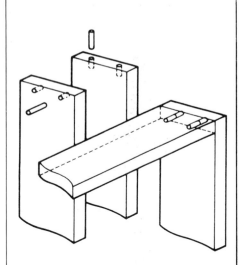

Constructing a Dowel Joint

It would be difficult to say exactly who first used the dowel joint, but it has really come into wide usage this century because of its ease of machining compared to the more traditional joints. The dowel joint uses hardwood pins that penetrate both parts to be joined, thereby effectively distributing the stress of an ordinary butt joint into a perfectly sound construction. The dowels have grooves running along their length, both to allow excess glue to escape and to distribute the glue over the full length of the dowel, maximizing the strength of the joint. The dowel is not as strong as a mortise and tenon joint but, if cut accurately, will be more than adequate for the projects in this book. In most cases, holes of equal length are drilled in the two pieces of wood to be brought together. These are then joined by the dowel, which is inserted into both holes across the joint, and the whole thing is glued under pressure (*ie*, cramped) until the glue has dried properly. Dowels can also be used as location points by which to ensure that two pieces of wood fit together in exactly the right position.

When constructing a dowel joint, it is crucial to align the holes in both parts perfectly, as any discrepancy in positioning will result in the joint not coming together. The purchase of a dowelling jig will solve the problem of alignment, but these tools can be expensive and an adequate template can be constructed for a single job by using the technique described below.

Making a dowel jig

A very useful dowelling jig can easily be made from beech wood. It must be beech, or oak, otherwise the wood will wear after repeated use and produce an enlarged, inaccurate drill hole. The illustration here shows a jig made to drill wood of 22mm ($\frac{7}{8}$″) thickness and 68mm ($2\frac{11}{16}$″) width. Obviously, all sizes can be accommodated by enlarging or reducing the 11mm ($\frac{7}{16}$″) dimension. When employing the dowel jig, use it on both parts to be joined and cramp it accurately to these parts with a C-clamp while you drill.

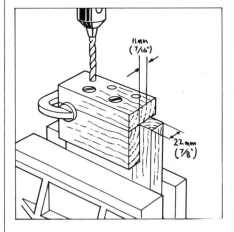

Jig Saw Cutting

For some of the designs a power electric jig saw will prove an invaluable tool. These are not expensive to buy but if you don't want to purchase one, at least borrow or hire one. It will save you much time and frustration.

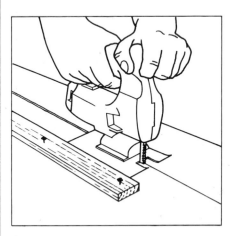

Sharp blades are obviously important for cutting a straight edge, but a good trick is to use a fence (a long piece of straight wood or board) as a guide to cut along. Clamp the fence at either end of the material to be cut with a C-clamp. Then run the jig saw along the edge, thus maintaining a perfectly straight line.

All electric jig saws cut on the upward stroke. This means that any 'break-out' of wood fibres will occur on the top surface. Some jig saws are supplied with a small plastic disc that can be inserted into the foot of the machine to help reduce this 'break-out'. Unfortunately, these wear away quickly and a useful tip is to apply masking tape to the board along the line of the proposed cut before you use the machine. Remove the tape afterwards to reveal a clean cut line.

Cutting interlocking slots

To cut a slot in a piece of board, first mark out the exact position of the slot on the surface. If the slot is to be square to the edge, then use a square when marking.

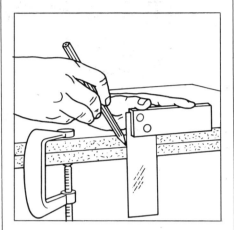

Carry the line down the edge of the board (again, use a square) as this will help anyone cutting by hand to saw at right angles. Cut the slot with your saw. If you use a tenon saw, start at an angle and if possible finish vertically. Knock out the waste with a chisel of the appropriate width and a mallet. It is useful to make a small cut on the reverse side first, so that when you knock out the waste you are left with a clean end to the slot.

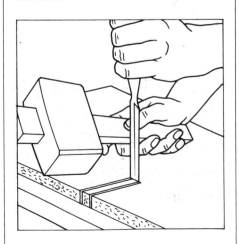

Filling Holes with Plastic Filler

There are many kinds of proprietary plastic fillers. Most consist of a tub of sticky grey paste and a separate tube of catalyst, a dark grey paste. As they are used mainly for metal bodywork repairs these fillers are always available from auto accessory shops if not from your DIY store.

We shall make use of plastic filler to fill holes for screw heads and in general preparation prior to painting. It is not suitable for use under clear finishes because of its colour.

● Always follow the maker's instructions when mixing in the catalyst. After a while you will be able to judge the amount yourself. Generally speaking, the more catalyst you add, the quicker the mixture will be ready, but the weaker the dried filler will be. Conversely, the less catalyst you use, the longer it takes to reach hardness but it will be much stronger.

● Wait until the filler is completely dry before you sand down. Start with 80 grit sandpaper and block, working in a circular motion.

Nailing

It may sound like teaching grandmothers to suck eggs, but there is a technique to successful nailing.

First of all it is very difficult to hammer a nail through one piece of hardwood and into another. Drill a clearance hole, slightly smaller than the nail itself, in the wood before you start.

● Generally speaking, hold the nail between the thumb and forefinger of the left hand and tap once with the hammer. Remove your vulnerable fingers from the area and hammer home. Always grip the hammer at the end of the handle and not by the head. This will give the stroke more inertia and also keep it at the right angle.

● If you are driving oval nails into softwoods, line up the flat sides with the grain in the wood to reduce the possibility of splitting. *Never* leave exposed nails in discarded pieces of wood — they are *very* dangerous.

Screwing into Wood

All screws need pilot holes (see the chart below for respective drill diameters). This not only makes it easier to screw them in, but also allows for maximum strength. A screw put in without a pilot hole may have been stressed to the point of fatigue (*ie,* be about to break). In most cases you will want the screw head to be countersunk (*ie,* flush with the surface of the wood). For countersunk screws you will need to countersink the material and in softwood you may well find it easier to do this before making the clearance hole. So here, in essence, is the procedure.

1 Drill your clearance hole and then countersink into the first piece of wood (a batten or similar).

2 Cramp the first piece of wood to the second with a C-clamp or sash cramp and drill through to the required depth with the pilot drill.

3 Take the screw and choose a screwdriver with an appropriately-sized head or bit. This should fit snugly into the slot of the screw head and not be too loose — don't attempt to use a small electrical screwdriver on a number 8 screw for example. If you are using a Philips head or Posidrive screw (which has a cross instead of a slot) ensure you have the correct screwdriver head. There are several different kinds.

Screw Size	Clearance Drill	Pilot Drill
No. 6	3.5mm ($\frac{5}{32}$")	2.0mm ($\frac{3}{32}$")
No. 8	4.5mm ($\frac{3}{16}$")	3.0mm ($\frac{1}{8}$")
No. 10	5.0mm ($\frac{7}{32}$")	3.5mm ($\frac{9}{64}$")

Glueing

A number of glues are commercially available. Each has its own advantages and disadvantages, making different types of glue more suitable for various tasks.

PVA This adhesive is sold under a variety of trade names and is usually white, or sometimes pale yellow. It has become the most widely used glue in both the trade and the home workshop, being generally faster to cure and more convenient to use as it comes in a plastic squeezy bottle. This also means less waste; what you don't use for one job you can use another time.

Squeeze the glue straight onto the wood and cramp or screw the pieces together. Wipe off excess with a hot damp cloth.

Powder glue (urea formaldehide) This adhesive is more difficult to use but has certain advantages. One is that it is a filler-glue and will fill gaps in bad or sloppy joints. It is also waterproof and so used in boat construction. The drawbacks are several, however. It is probably more expensive than other glues, you always have to mix up more than you need (so you don't run out) and it is definitely more messy! But having said that, all the traditionalists still use it and I for one have more faith in it for strength than other varieties.
You will need to save yoghurt or cream pots to mix the glue in. Add the water first and then the powder. Mix with a stick until the glue is the consistency of double cream.

Applying glue
It is important with all glueing processes to prepare properly for the operation and always have a 'dry run'. Once the glue is in the joints it is too late to find you have made a mistake.
As the glue spurts out of the joints,

clear it up with your glue stick. Always have a kettle full of hot water to clean off the excess — the hotter the better. If you get the wood wet, as opposed to damp, wipe it dry.
Glues set quicker in the summer than in the winter (even if your workshop is heated) but in all cases glue is best left overnight to dry, so it is a good idea to time your work accordingly.

Clamping (Cramping)
When using a sash clamp or a C-clamp , always adjust them to their settings before you start to glue. Then you have less to do when the glue has been applied. A 'dry run' will probably have forced you to do this anyway.
Clamps should never come in direct contact with the material as they will easily bruise the furniture. It is always useful to have lying around small pieces of soft wood to act as 'cushions' between cramp and material.

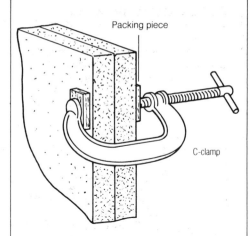

C-clamp (above), also known as G-cramp.

Sash clamp (below), also known as sash cramp.

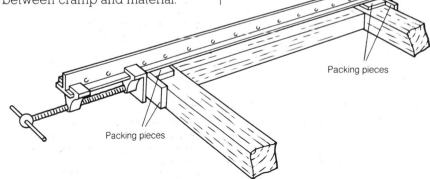

Sash clamp

Packing pieces

Packing pieces

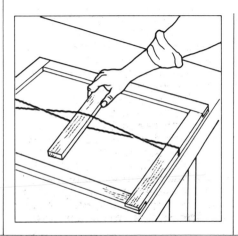

A method of holding glued-up frames together without clamps is to use some tough string and a piece of wood. Tie the string around the frame as illustrated, left, and then insert your piece of wood. Turn until tight, and then push the piece of wood through so that it rests against the side of the frame.

Planing

The only plane you will need is a small smoothing plane, or Bailey plane. It is obviously essential to keep the blade sharp, so you can 'let the tool do the work'.

Respect it too — take the plane apart and understand how it works. Keep it clean and rust-free and the moving parts lubricated. In terms of technique, you will learn most skill through practice. There is, however, one essential piece of advice to follow. Always plane with the grain and not against it. You will soon find out if you are going against the grain, as wood will chip out. But if you want to avoid this in the first place, have a look at the edge of the wood and see which way the grain is going.

Edge Profiling

Many of the projects in this book have an edge profile applied to a piece of solid wood. This should be done as follows.

1 Mark out the radius so that it touches the outside edge (use a coin, jam jar or anything round of the correct size).

2 Mark along the length.

3 Remove waste with a smoothing plane. Having removed as much as possible, finish the curve with a piece of 80 grit sandpaper *and block*, working first across the grain around the curve and then finally down the length. Finish sand with 120 grit sandpaper down the length.

Sanding

The only two grades of sandpaper you will need for these projects are 120 grit (fine) and 80 grit (rough). Glass paper is good, but Garnet paper is much better as it does not clog as quickly and therefore lasts longer. Unfortunately it is also more expensive.

There is a basic rule which is important to understand when sandpapering. The change from rough to smooth sandpaper is only necessary to remove sanding marks made by the coarser sandpaper. So do *all* the work with the coarse grade before you move on to using the finer paper.

● To make your sandpaper go further, split a sheet not into 4 but into 6: — 3 down the length and 2

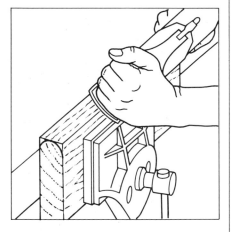

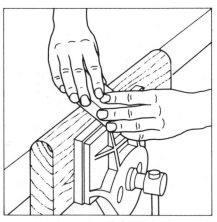

across the width. Even so, sandpaper does not last for ever, and is useless after it has lost its cut, so throw all worn bits away.

● Always use a block to sand with, wrapping the paper around it. A good cork block is best, but a piece of wood is better than nothing. Always sand in the direction of the wood grain; scratches across the grain are very difficult to remove afterwards.

● When the edge of your sandpaper looks likely to catch a splinter, turn the block so that it is at right angles to the direction in which you are sanding.

Painting and Finishing

Unless you have access to cellulose spraying facilities, paint and clear varnish finishing will be a fairly lengthy process. Cellulose finishes can be brushed on but you have to work very quickly. For those using oil-based finishes, keep the following points in mind.

1 Finish all parts as smoothly as possible with 120 grit sandpaper (glass paper or Garnet paper).

2 Apply primer/undercoat. Use a good-quality brush and leave to dry *thoroughly*.

3 When dry, cut back with fine sandpaper, removing all nibs and high spots.

4 Remove dust with a tack rag or damp cloth and proceed with the first application of top coat, making sure that the paint itself is not too thick (thin down with turpentine if necessary).

5 When thoroughly dry (leave overnight if possible) cut back with wet and dry silicone carbide paper — or similar. Use 220 grit if possible. Again, wipe off all dust with a cloth prior to the final application.
Parts to be finished must be coated and left to dry in a dust-

free atmosphere.
Again, leave undisturbed overnight if possible and then apply the final coat.

6 You can put a final coat of clear, semi-matt varnish over the top for extra depth if you wish, depending on how much time and effort you are prepared to give to achieve your finish.

When painting over knots on softwood, don't forget to cover them with knotting *prior* to applying the undercoat. This applies with opaque finishes only.

Thinners
When using oil-based paints and finishes, keep some white spirit or turpentine substitute handy in order to clean your brushes or thin down your paint. It is well worth buying a large container of thinners as it keeps indefinitely, is always useful and will save you money in the long run.
For cleaning brushes you will need a container of glass or metal. Plastic cream or yoghurt cartons are not suitable as the thinners will melt the plastic.
At this point it is worth mentioning the quality of paint brushes and to say that basically you get what you pay for. Always buy a good one. If you look after it well, a brush can be used again and again, but do clean it thoroughly. When you think you have finished, clean it once more in some fresh thinners just to be sure. Above all, don't leave brushes standing in jars as this will cause the bristles to curl.

Staining
The practice of staining wood is as old as the furniture craft itself. All kinds of preparations have been used to effect colour changes on wooden surfaces, and practically any coloured liquid will stain wood fibres. Today there is a varied range of proprietary stains available from your DIY store. These are the most effective

substances to use because they are light-proof and will not fade. Most commercial stains are dye solutions which penetrate the fibres of the wood and their effect relies on the porosity of the material used. I would recommend using a spirit-based stain; the water-based type tends to raise the grain on application. · It is very important to remove all traces of glue before applying the stain as any glue-covered areas will fail to take the colour. Should you find this happening as you wipe on the stain, stop. Sand off the glue and start again.
The stained article is best left for 12 hours to dry out completely before finishing. Prepare for this stage by rubbing over the surface very lightly with '00' grade wire wool.

Applying Plastic Laminates
For this job you will need a contact adhesive. This is the type used to coat both surfaces, which are then only brought together when the adhesive is tacky.
● Cut your laminate oversize. On large areas allow 5mm (¼″) all round or 10mm (½″) overall on each dimension. On small areas — when edge-lipping, for example — a smaller margin will do.
● Apply laminates in reverse order — the one to be applied last is that which will be seen most and receive most wear. In the case of a table top, the top laminate should be applied last in order to cover the vulnerable edge lippings.
● Remember the golden rule in panel work — 'what you do to one side, you must do to the other' — *ie*, keep a balance. This is because unequal stresses will cause the board to bow or buckle. So you must buy a 'balance' laminate to back the unseen face. The only exceptions to this would be carcases, such as kitchen cabinets, where the cabinet construction is strong enough to

brace the laminated panel and stop it from bowing.
You may well be asked to pay for a whole sheet of your facing laminate, in which case it would be more sensible not to buy a 'balance' laminate, but to use the face laminate on all surfaces.
● Having worked out the order in which to apply the laminate and pre-cut all your pieces, proceed with the first one. Spread the glue (most shops will give you a free applicator) evenly over the laminate and make sure the whole area is covered — particularly the edges, as these are the most vulnerable points. Repeat this on the other surface and leave until both are 'tack' dry, usually about 5-10 minutes, but check the manufacturer's instructions.
You will find that chipboard and MDF have a more absorbent surface than the non-porous laminate, so always coat the laminate first as this will remain workable for a longer period. The edges of board materials are even more absorbent so these may have to be coated twice.
● Bring the two surfaces together by lining up one long edge and slowly lowering the laminate until it is in contact — you may need help on large areas to line them up properly. Then press home. The excess material can be planed off and finish sanded, or trimmed by a power electric router with a laminate trimmer bit. Special hand-workable tools are also now available for trimming laminates. Keep edges square and apply the laminate to bevelled or softened edges last. Finish the softened edge with fine sandpaper to give it a professional feel, but always use a sanding block. This will stop you from scratching the surfaces.
To remove contact glue from your hands, *etc*, paraffin is the usual solvent, but *don't* use it to clean glue from the furniture itself as it could well dissolve the glue adhering the laminate.

Fitting Adjustable Hinges

The adjustable hinge has probably done more to help cabinet furniture design than any other recently introduced furniture fitting, particularly in the case of cheaper, mass produced carcases, and above all in knock down or quick-assembly furniture. An adjustable hinge affords the means to manoeuvre a door into perfect alignment, thus overcoming tolerances occurring through inaccurate manufacture or bad assembly.

It has also allowed designers the opportunity to plant doors on the front of cabinets, without exposing any part of the hinge mechanism. Cabinet furniture manufacturers are also now able to position several doors along a run of compartments with no more than 2mm (⅛") between them. This is because adjustable hinges have an essentially different movement from ordinary hinges, opening within their own width.

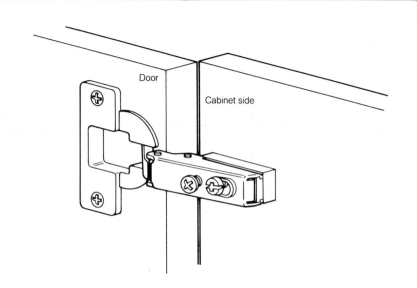

Adjustable hinges all consist of two parts: the spacer, which is a piece of cast metal that you screw into the cabinet side; and the hinge itself, which should be slid along it.

When using these hinges on a centre panel (and in the case of the sideboard on p.116) you will need to pack out the spacer with a small piece of wood and, using screws longer than usual, screw through into the sideboard.

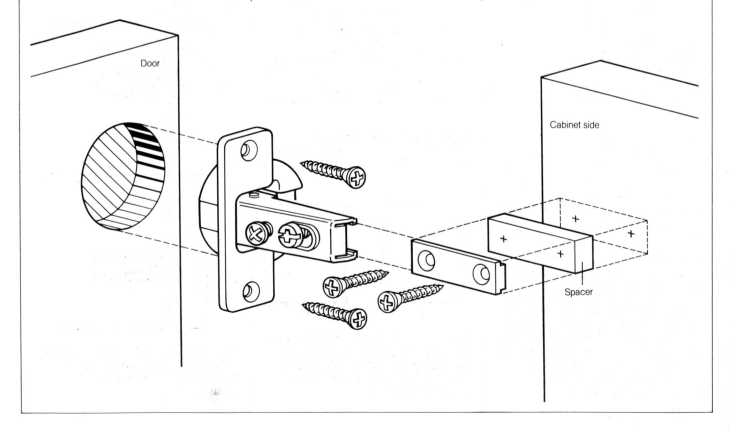

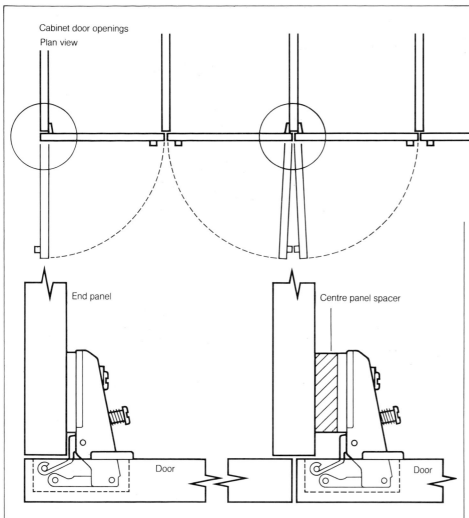

Cabinet door openings
Plan view

End panel

Centre panel spacer

Door

Door

To move the door as in diagram **B**, do the same but on the top hinge. Similarly, all the hinges allow doors to be adjusted in the other plane as well. To do this, just slacken off the rear retaining screw and pull the door forward at the top or bottom to the required distance.

Make sure that the door is not binding on the edges of the vertical panel. If it is, slacken off screw **Y** and pull forward, as drawn below.

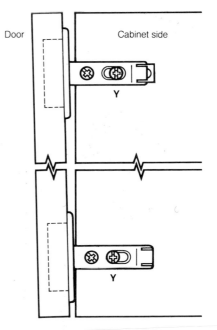

Door

Cabinet side

Y

Y

In order to determine the thickness of the spacer, get a scrap piece of 19mm (¾″) board — chipboard will do — and sink the hinge into it, using the appropriate diameter bit: 25mm or 35mm (1″ or 1⅜″).

If you then offer this experiment up to the vertical panel and line the edge of your (imaginary) door up to the centre line of the front edge, you will be able to measure the distance between the metal spacer and the vertical panel. This will be the effective thickness of your wooden packing piece. Use the metal spacer as a runplate to draw out a) the shape of the packing piece and b) the positions of the holes.

How to adjust the hinges
Sideways and vertical adjustment — do this first.

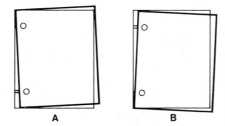

A

B

To move the door as in diagram **A**, turn the adjusting screw on the bottom hinge (depending on the make of hinge it will be clockwise or anti-clockwise).

Don't forget to retighten the screw securely so that the doors are kept firmly in the adjusted position.

Tricks of the Trade
Knowing a few of the ways to avoid pitfalls or rectify mistakes can prove invaluable. Here are a few tips learned by experience.

Screwing
Screwing into hardwood can be made easier by the application of wax or soap to the screw.
If you use brass (or chrome) screws, first insert a steel one of the same size, extract it and then put in the brass one. (Brass is a softer metal than steel and can break.) If you have several screws to put in — for a batten on a wall, for example — locate all the screws in their holes before you tighten up.
● Never use old screws.
● Buying screws is one area where you can make substantial savings in cost. Look in the back of woodwork magazines for mail order addresses and buy screws by the box.

Marking out
To mark a line along a piece of wood, hold the pencil as you would normally and use the fingers below the pencil as a guide touching the edge of the wood. Pull the pencil towards you, marking as you go.

Sharpening tools
One good tip in the trade is to 'let the tool do the work'. If your plane or chisel is sharp, it will cut very easily. A well cared for and sharp-ended plane should glide along an edge, cutting as it goes. On the other hand, a blunt tool will cause you to push too hard and damage the wood. So keep your tools very, very sharp. Make sure you have a sharpening stone, an essential piece of maintenance equipment for anyone with woodworking tools.

Quick repairs
I have often pondered on the thought that in making furniture, most operations involve removing material. At a rough guess, out of a sawn plank of wood with its bark still on, maybe only 20-30% of the wood actually ends up in the furniture it was intended for. The rest is used for other purposes or is wasted. In other words, furniture-making, particularly with wood, is a continual process of removing material in one operation or another. And sometimes you can take off a bit too much!
Although it's hard to explain what to do in all cases, I can say that I have never (touch wood!) made a mistake that cannot be rectified. However good or bad any repair is obviously depends on the individual, but after all it is only what antique repairers and restorers do every day of the week.

Dents
If a piece of wood has been dented, the wood fibres have become compressed. It is possible to expand these fibres back to their original state with the application of some clean water and a hot iron.
Take a few drops of clean water and rub it gently into the localized area. Leave for a few minutes and then with a hot iron, gently pass over the area in a slow, circular motion. If either the iron or wood is dirty, slip a piece of clean white paper over the wet area first.
If this doesn't work the first time, try it again. You can repeat the process until it stops having any effect.

Scratches
can be tackled in the same way to start with, as raising the grain will give you more chance of sanding it back down to a good surface.

Cracks and splits
If the edge of a piece of wood is cracked or split, here is a quick way to repair it.

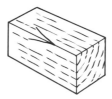

1 Rub some glue (PVA) into the split.

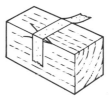

2 Press the area flat and secure with masking tape.

3 Take a hot iron and rub over the area for about 2 or 3 minutes. This will set the glue. Then the tape can be removed and the piece of wood reworked.

Plans and Instructions

On the following pages appear plans and instructions for making the items of furniture illustrated on pages 12–30. The original plans were designed using the metric system of measurements, but imperial dimensions are also given, usually in brackets. Being direct conversions of the originals, these are therefore rarely round figures (for conversion table, see page 160). Choose whichever system you are used to and work as accurately as you can.

The plans are not drawn to scale, so follow the dimensions rigidly. Comprehensive materials lists are given, together with a diagrammatical view of all piece parts. Your supplier should be able to cut them for you and it may be worth asking for a costings estimate of the materials before you buy. There are tools lists also, so that you can prepare totally for the job.

Some designs include cutting plans for the boards to be used. This will help you get the maximum amount of material out of one sheet. Show the plan to your supplier so that he may use it to cut the sheets economically.

Kitchen Work Station

Many people cannot consider a free-standing work station because of the size of their kitchen. This easy-to-build design will work well in the middle of the room, but equally well against a wall, its lower shelf providing ample storage for saucepans or vegetables. There is a very useful knife rack at the back and the generous drawer will accommodate the largest of kitchen implements.

To produce a trolley version you will need to locate and buy a set of industrial or catering trolley casters. Two out of the set should have brakes in order to keep the trolley immobile while you are working at it. But if you don't wish, or need, to push it around your kitchen, then merely lengthen the legs of the

work station so that it can be positioned anywhere, even against a wall. If you set it into a row of kitchen units, and you can do this as the heights are compatible, you will not need the pull-out shelves.

The design will be further enhanced by using one of the modern Italian-style plastic laminates. These new speckled and striped designs are sold by all the large manufacturers. Look at the latest pattern ranges in your local DIY stockist.

Plans and dimensions

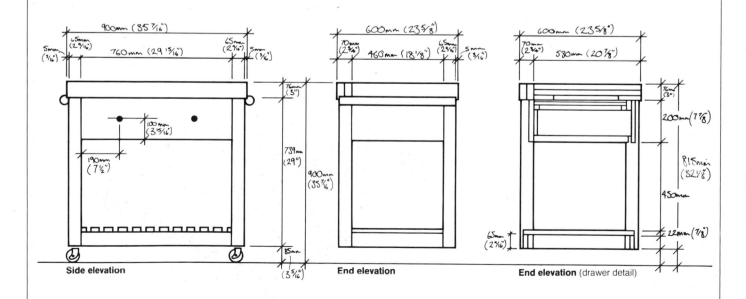

Side elevation

End elevation

End elevation (drawer detail)

You will need

Materials

Board

25mm (1″) chipboard

897mm × 597mm	(35⁵/₁₆″ × 23½″)	(1)	**A**
897mm × 100mm	(35⁵/₁₆″ × 3¹⁵/₁₆″)	(2)	**B**
697mm × 100mm	(27⁷/₁₆″ × 3¹⁵/₁₆″)	(2)	**C**
597mm × 100mm	(23½″ × 3¹⁵/₁₆″)	(2)	**D**
397mm × 100mm	(15⁵/₈″ × 3¹⁵/₁₆″)	(2)	**E**

15mm (⁵/₈″) birch plywood

458mm × 440mm	(18¹/₃₂″ × 17⁵/₁₆″)	(2)	**F**

12mm (½″) birch plywood

734mm × 128mm	(28⁷/₈″ × 5″)	(2)	**G**
470mm × 128mm	(18½″ × 5″)	(2)	**H**

6mm (¼″) birch plywood

758mm × 470mm	(29²⁷/₃₂″ × 18½″)	(1)	**J**

PAR softwood

65mm × 65mm	(2⁹/₁₆″ × 2⁹/₁₆″)	739mm	(29″)	(4) **K'**
200mm × 22mm	(7⁷/₈″ × ⁷/₈″)	760mm	(29¹⁵/₁₆″)	(1) **L**
198mm × 22mm	(7²⁵/₃₂″ × ⁷/₈″)	756mm	(29¾″)	(1) **M**
182mm × 22mm	(7⁵/₃₂″ × ⁷/₈″)	460mm	(18¹/₈″)	(2) **N**
65mm × 22mm	(2⁹/₁₆″ × ⁷/₈″)	760mm	(29¹⁵/₁₆″)	(2) **O**
65mm × 22mm	(2⁹/₁₆″ × ⁷/₈″)	460mm	(18¹/₈″)	(2) **P**
44mm × 22mm	(1¾″ × ⁷/₈″)	760mm	(29¹⁵/₁₆″)	(1) **Q**
44mm × 22mm	(1¾″ × ⁷/₈″)	555mm	(21⁷/₈″)	(12) **R**
22mm × 22mm	(⁷/₈″ × ⁷/₈″)	760mm	(29¹⁵/₁₆″)	(1) **S**
		470mm	(18½″)	(2) **T**
		415mm	(16¹¹/₃₂″)	(2) **U**
76mm × 35mm	(3″ × 1³/₈″)	900mm	(35⁷/₁₆″)	(2) **V**

*Increase length to 824mm (32⁷/₁₆″) if casters are not used

Plastic Laminate

Choose a 1.5mm (¹/₃₂″) plastic laminate with a new special finish

905mm × 605mm	(35⁵/₈″ × 23¹³/₁₆″)	(1)	**W**
905mm × 80mm	(35⁵/₈″ × 3⁵/₃₂″)	(1)	**X**
605mm × 80mm	(23¹³/₁₆″ × 3⁵/₃₂″)	(2)	**Y**

Dowel

Ramin, obeche or birch dowel

35mm (1³/₈″) diameter	590mm	(23⁷/₃₂″)	(2)

Hardwood Dowels

50mm (2″)   (60)
10mm (³/₈″) diameter

Glue

Tin contact adhesive
Bottle PVA wood glue

Filler

Small tin cream wood stopping

Screws

No. 8 × 25mm (1″) countersunk steel	(5)
No. 6 × 25mm (1″) roundhead steel	(4)

Nails

Oval wire nails 32mm (1¼″)	(250)
Oval wire nails 50mm (2″)	(5)
Panel pins 25mm (1″)	(60)

Tape

19mm (¾″) masking tape, 1 roll

Paint

Tin silver grey undercoat
Tin flake grey gloss

Varnish

Tin clear satin finish polyurethane varnish

Casters

4 industrial/catering trolley casters (2 incorporating brakes)

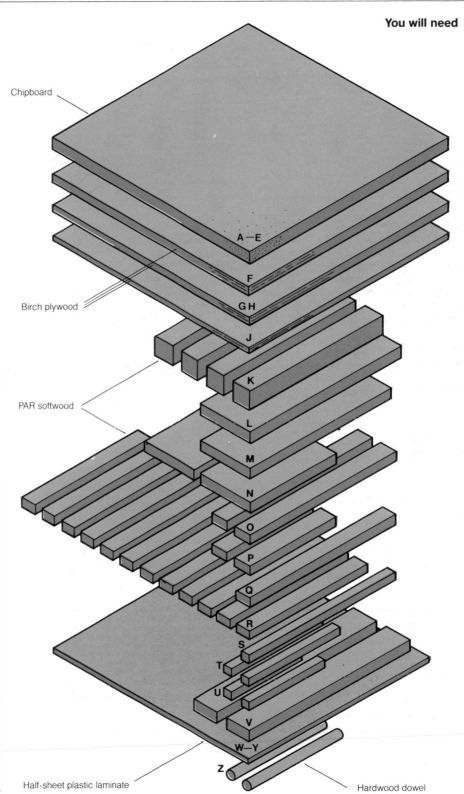

Chipboard

A–E

F

G H

J

Birch plywood

PAR softwood

K

L

M

N

O

P

Q

R

S

T

U

V

W–Y

Z

Half-sheet plastic laminate

Hardwood dowel

Tools

Bench and vice
Dowelling jig
Drill and countersink
Drill bits   10mm (⅜″)
                   4.5mm (³⁄₁₆″)
                   3mm (⅛″)
100mm (4″) C-clamps   (3)
Screwdriver
1220mm (48″) sash clamps   (2)
Plastic glue spreader
Square
Hammer
Nail punch
Sandpaper   80 grit (3 sheets)
            120 grit (3 sheets)
Sanding block
Brace and 35mm (1⅜″) diameter centre bit

Cutting plans

Chipboard

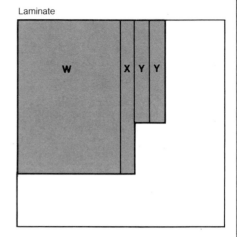

Laminate

Instructions

Making the top

The work-station top is made from a single sheet of 25mm (1″) chipboard, with 25mm (1″) chipboard linings to build up the thickness. These underlinings overlap to increase stability. Check all sizes of **A, B, C, D, E** against the materials list before you start.

1 Take the sheet of chipboard **A** and apply the underlinings **D** and **C** dry to check the fit. Then glue and pin down with 32mm (1¼″) oval nails.

2 Repeat the process with **B** and **E**, this time sinking the nail heads beneath the surface.

3 Sand flush with 80 grit paper and plane off any high spots.

4 Apply the two end facings **Y** to the top assembly with contact adhesive (see TECHNIQUES p. 37 Applying Plastic Laminates).

5 Plane and sand flush and then apply the single front facing **X**.

6 Plane and sand flush and apply the top facing **W**. Make sure all areas are covered with adhesive and that the laminate overhangs all edges.

7 Plane and sand flush and apply a final touch by sanding the corners with 120 grit sandpaper and sanding block. Be careful not to scratch the surface.

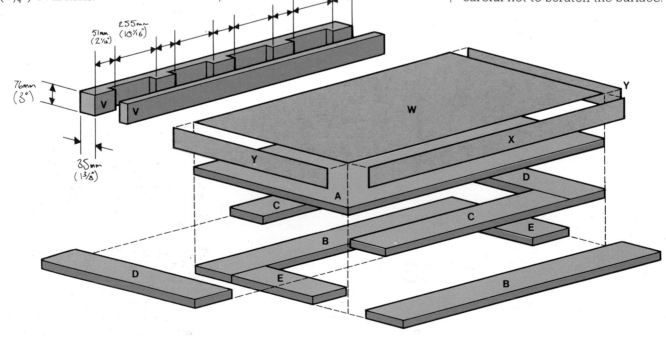

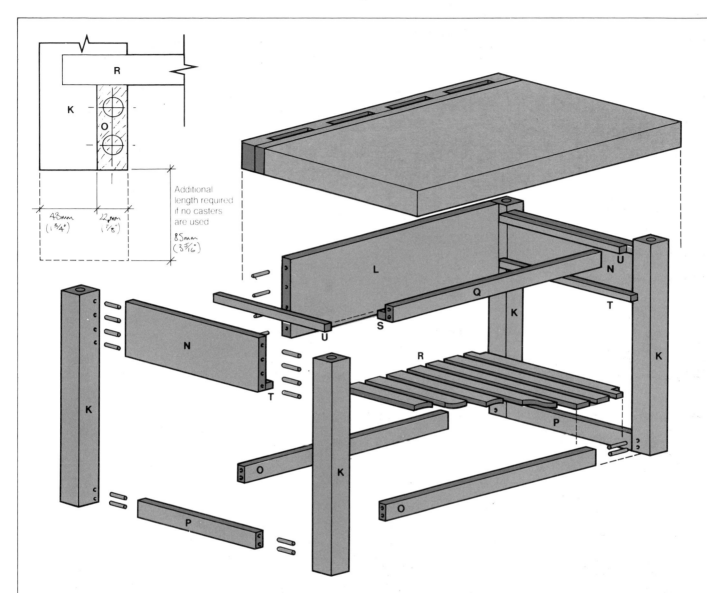

Additional length required if no casters are used

85mm (3⁵/₁₆")

43mm (1³/₄")   22mm (⁷/₈")

8 Take parts **V** and on one of them mark out the slots to be cut (see TECHNIQUES p. 32 Cutting Joints).

9 Cut out these slots and finish the insides well, as the knives will need to pass smoothly through them.

10 Coat the inside slot surfaces with 3 coats of clear lacquer, but leave dry all the high spots (*ie*, the glueing areas).

11 Put a spot of PVA glue on all the high areas and cramp the two parts **V** together. Make sure edges are all flush.

12 Nail through from the inside (that is the **V** without the cutouts) to secure with 5 × 50mm (2") oval wire nails.

13 When dry, sand all surfaces flush and smooth. Coat all areas with clear lacquer. (See TECHNIQUES p. 36 Finishing.) Leave the inside face dry for glueing.

14 When dry, glue the knife rack assembly to the top with ample quantities of glue and 2 sash clamps. Don't forget to use packing pieces at both ends. Wipe off the glue. When dry the top is now complete, so put to one side.

Making the two end frames
15 On the legs **K**, mark out the positions of **N** and **P** at the top and bottom respectively. They are flush with the inside faces of **K**, but **N** must be dropped down from the top by 18mm (¹¹/₁₆").

16 Mark out the holes for the dowel joints and, using your dowelling jig, drill all the holes.

17 Glue the two frames together. Do them separately and make sure that the joints are square and that you wipe off excess glue with a hot damp rag.

18 When these frames are dry, they can be assembled into the complete underframe with the remaining parts. Take parts **O, O, L, Q** and mark out their respective positions on the legs **K**. The lower rails **O** are flush with the leg bottoms (unless no casters are used — see diagram) and are in both cases set central across the leg width. The back panel **L** is positioned so as to be flush with the outside of **K** to conceal the knives and the front rail **Q** is set flush with the inside edge of **K** (*ie*, where it meets panel **N**, 495mm (19½") being the final distance between **L** and **Q**). Both **L** and **Q** should be positioned level with the top of the legs **K**.

19 Drill all the dowel joints with drill and dowelling jig and assemble the complete frame to check the fit.

20 Glue the complete frame together, clamping across the joints with sash clamps and packing pieces.

21 When dry, apply the drawer runners **T** by glueing and pinning them flush with the bottom of **N**. Next the tablet runner **S** should be glued, applied, lined up flush with the top edge of **N** and pinned to secure with 32mm (1¼") nails to rail **Q**. Finally, add in the kickers **U** (these prevent the drawer from tipping) in the same way, making sure that they are flush with the top edge of **N**.

22 Using white undercoat, paint the legs only and, if you have a shaky hand or want to make the job easier, mask off all the horizontal parts where they meet the legs.

23 Take 2 of the piece parts **R**, one for each end of the frame. Mark the cutouts to be removed from both ends (see TECHNIQUES p. 32 Cutting Joints) 48mm × 23mm (1⅞" × $^{29}/_{32}$"). This ensures that these end slats hang neatly over the horizontal rail **P**.

24 Pin and glue (just a spot will do) these 2 end slats in position over **P** and **P**. Then equally space the remaining slats along rails **O**. Glue and pin down, making sure that with their small overhang they all line up. The spacing will be approximately 25mm (1") depending on the exact width of the slats.

25 Finish the entire frame (including the painted parts) with 3 coats of clear matt varnish.

The tablets

26 Mark out the long edge (458mm/18$^{1}/_{32}$") on **F** for 3 hole centres to form the dowel joints with **Z**.

27 Mark out their respective position on **Z** so that the dowel (**Z**) is central and there is a 132mm (5³⁄₁₆") overhang on both sides.

28 Drill these holes, taking care not to wander. Hold the parts *firmly* in the vice while drilling.

29 Glue up and clamp Remove excess glue.

Constructing the tablets

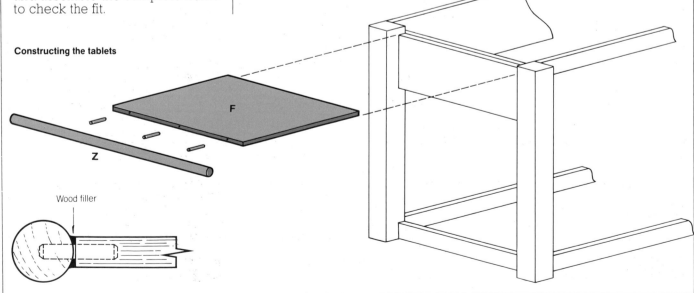

Wood filler

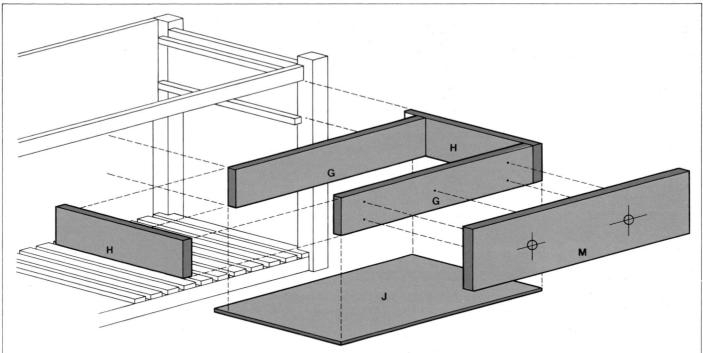

30 When dry, fill the cracks between the dowel and the board with wood filler. Leave to dry. Fit to frame to check the size.

31 Sand down with 120 grit. Clean up and coat with clear varnish.

The drawer

32 Drill 5 clearance holes (4.5mm/³⁄₁₆″ diameter) in the front panel **G**.

33 Hold **G** end up in the vice. Hold **H** against it end-to-end and flush and, having applied glue between them, pin through to secure.

34 Hold this assembly together with the second part **G** in the vice. Glue and pin through. Don't forget to remove excess glue with a hot damp rag.

35 Turn the assembly round and attach the second drawer side **H**.

36 Now glue and pin the bottom panel **J** in position.

37 Leave to dry and sand and plane flush and smooth.

38 Put the drawer into the drawer cavity.

39 Take the drawer front **M** and C-clamp it in position onto the drawer and the underframe.

40 Check that there is a 2mm (¹⁄₁₆″) gap at either end of the drawer and also at the top. When this has been done, screw to secure from the inside of the drawer through the part **G** with No. 8 screws. It helps to pilot drill (3mm/¹⁄₈″ diameter) first.

41 Take out the completed drawer and hold it front upwards in the vice. Mark out the hole centres as indicated in the diagram above. C-clamp a spare piece of board to the back of the drawer front (this will prevent breaking out) and bore through a 35mm (1³⁄₈″) hole with a brace and bit.
Repeat the process for the second hole.

Final assembly

42 Lay the top down on a carpet and place the underframe upside down on it.

43 Manoeuvre the frame until it is central and mark position of the legs **K** on the top.

44 Remove the frame and drill a 10mm (³⁄₈″) hole in the centre of the leg tops and in their reciprocal positions on the underside of the top — these are location dowels.

45 Stand the frame upright and run glue all along the top 2 edges, legs included. Put the dowels in the holes and bring down the top in position. Check that the knife rack is at the back and weight the top while the glue dries. Wipe off excess glue.

46 Slide in the two tablets and stop them from falling out by inserting 2 No. 6 roundhead screws 10mm (³⁄₈″) in from the inside end of **F**.

47 Apply the casters.

Dining Table with Red Tube Detail

This design is among the projects which I have tried to keep as simple as possible. It is a much easier table to make than the one on page 108 and, like the chipboard bed (page 144), is about simple and honest use of material. You should be able to go to the supplier, buy the board, come home and put it together. While the job may not be quite as simple as this in practice, that essentially is what you are going to do.

The design incorporates a tube under-frame that literally holds the table together, but at the same time adds to its visual appeal. There is also a set of accompanying chairs

(page 52). The colour of the dowels need not be the red specified, but obviously the shade chosen for the chairs and the table under-frame ought to be the same.

Several designer craftsmen are now using plywoods for their furniture,

making a feature of the striped edge detail. That is what we intend to do here, but be careful. There is plywood and plywood. Birch-faced plywood is generally accepted to be the most attractive, but there are different grades. Most are pine or softwood core laminates, which means that only the outside faces are of birch. While this is fine to use, more care has to be taken in cutting the edges, and getting a good sanded edge will be more difficult. If you can afford it, buy the plywood which has birch plies throughout. Try and select a board that is white throughout, and watch your hands when sanding down the edges.

Plans and dimensions

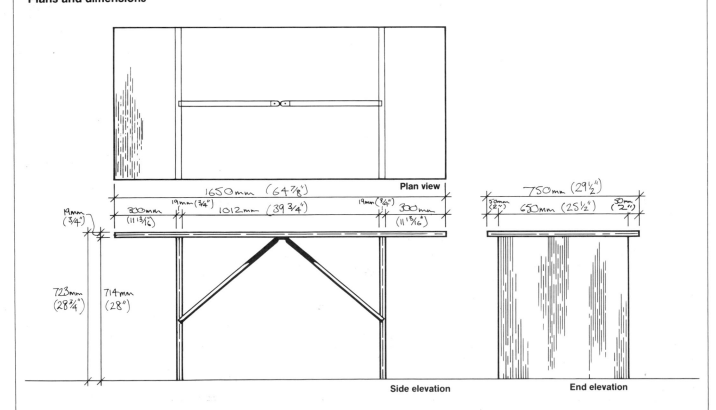

1650mm (64⅞")

19mm (¾") 300mm (11¹³⁄₁₆") 19mm (¾") 1012mm (39¾") 19mm (¾") 300mm (11¹³⁄₁₆")

19mm (¾")

723mm (28¾") 714mm (28")

Plan view

750mm (29½")

50mm (2") 650mm (25½") 50mm (2")

Side elevation

End elevation

You will need

Birch faced plywood

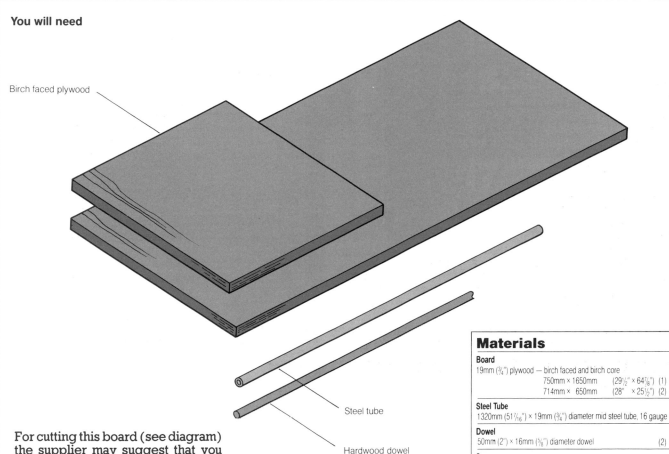

Steel tube

Hardwood dowel

For cutting this board (see diagram) the supplier may suggest that you reduce the width of 650mm (25½″) down to 600mm (23½″) in order to get all 3 parts out of one sheet. You can do this, but be warned. The specified cutting sheet is designed to place the edges, which are most vulnerable to chipping out when cut, at the top and bottom. Working the other way will mean that these edges are on the sides (*ie*, the most visible edges). If your supplier guarantees no chipped edges, however, you may well save yourself some money.

Materials

Board
19mm (¾″) plywood — birch faced and birch core

750mm × 1650mm	(29½″ × 64⅞″)	(1)	**A**
714mm × 650mm	(28″ × 25½″)	(2)	**B**

Steel Tube
1320mm (51⁷⁄₁₆″) × 19mm (¾″) diameter mid steel tube, 16 gauge

Dowel
50mm (2″) × 16mm (⅝″) diameter dowel   (2)

Screws
No. 6 × 16mm (⅝″) roundhead steel   (22)

Brackets
Table shrinkage plates   (4)

Glue
Small bottle PVA wood glue

Varnish
Medium tin clear satin finish polyurethane varnish

Paint
Small tin metal primer. Small tin red paint

Tools

Drill
Drill bits 3.5mm (⁵⁄₃₂″) 2mm (³⁄₃₂″) 16mm (⅝″)
Metal worker's vice
Hack saw
Protractor or set square
Bevel gauge
File
Screwdriver
Sandpaper   80 grit (2 sheets)
                    120 grit (2 sheets)
Sanding block
Hammer
Centre punch
25mm (1″) paint brush
65mm (2½″) paint brush
Pencil
Rule

Cutting plan

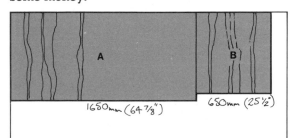

A

B

1650mm (64⅞″)   650mm (25½″)

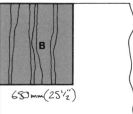

B

650mm (25½″)

Instructions

1 Take the top panel **A** and choose the best face. This will be the outer surface. Mark out the position of the 2 leg panels 1012mm (39¾") apart on the underside (see diagram).

2 Degrease the steel tube with paraffin or degreasing agent. Wipe clean and mark the centre point.

3 Hold the tube vertically in the metal vice so that the centre line of the tube is positioned halfway up the flat of the vice.

4 Crush the tube flat by screwing up the vice.

5 Pull the tube towards you until you have bent it over a full 40°. To measure this, set a bevel gauge with a protractor or a set square (see diagram).

6 Turn the tube over in the vice and bend the opposite end to the same angle.

7 Lie the tube on the upturned top with the crush bend lying on the long edge centrally between the 2 marked positions of the leg panels. Position the tube so that the arms splay out at identical angles.

Marking out the metal tube

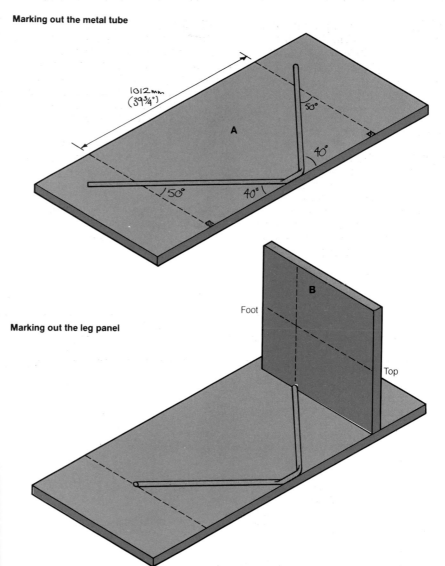

Marking out the leg panel

8 At the point where the tube crosses over the first leg panel line, mark on the tube the 50° angle to be cut.

9 Cut both ends of the tube off at the prescribed length and angle with a hack saw. File off the sharp ends.

10 Lie the tube back on the top panel and offer up the leg panels on their side, in order to mark across the height of the tube joint.

11 Mark the centre point of the tube on to part **B**. Transfer the measurement of the height, approximately 305mm (12"), marking it onto the centre of the leg panel.

12 With the leg panels thus marked, drill the blind holes for the dowels. Start from vertical and penetrate the surface by about 5mm (¼"). Then start to swing the drill over until you have achieved the 50° angle. Set the bevel gauge and get somebody else to check it as you drill.

13 Take the dowels and check that they fit into the tube. Stick the 2 pieces of dowel into their respective holes with ample quantities of glue. Wipe off the excess glue with a hot damp rag and leave to dry. Check the angle with a protractor.

14 Drill the tube with 2 × 3.5mm (⁵⁄₃₂") diameter holes in the crushed flat section and 2 more of the same at both ends (see diagram). Centre punch the positions before you drill (select a slower speed than normal) and always hold the tube in the vice.

15 Paint the tube red after applying the metal primer.

16 Screw the 2 table shrinkage plates to the top of each leg panel. Use the No. 6 roundhead screws and pilot drill with a 2mm (³⁄₃₂") diameter bit.

17 Screw the centre section of the bent tube exactly in the middle of the top (underneath, of course).

18 Now offer the 2 leg panels to the top, locating each protruding dowel into the tube ends and the tops of each leg panel to the pre-drawn pencil line.

19 Prepare the plywood for finishing by sanding. Then cover all surfaces (including the tube) with clear semi-matt varnish (see TECHNIQUES p. 36 Finishing).

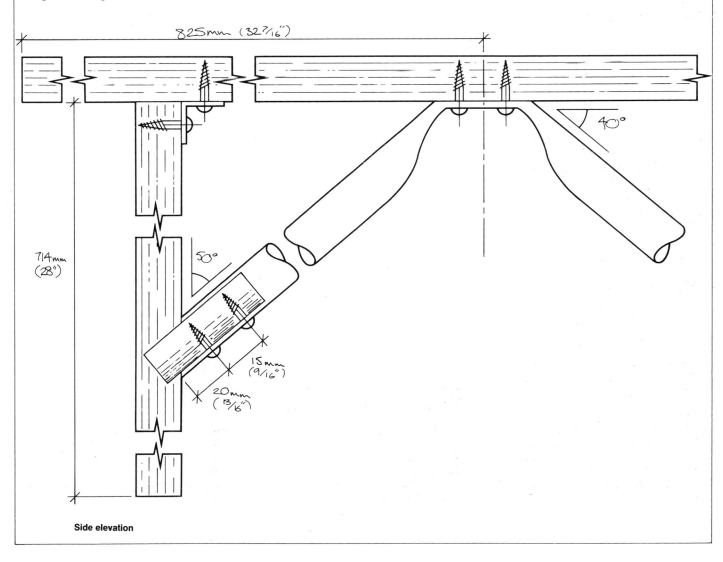

825mm (32⁷⁄₁₆")

714mm (28")

40°

50°

15mm (⁹⁄₁₆")

20mm (¹³⁄₁₆")

Side elevation

51

Chair with Red Dowel Detail

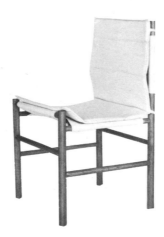

This chair matches the tube and plywood dining table on page 48. Literally several lengths of dowel that are drilled and glued together, it is very easy to make.

Comfort relies on the seat material being stretched over the frame, and the chair itself is completed by the application of a loose cover, which is just tied in position. Although the cover is not reversible, it can easily be removed for cleaning if any accidents should occur.

The dimensions of the chair are defined by the depth of the drilled holes and the length of the dowel, so try to maintain your accuracy. It is not difficult to bore the dowel holes. The important thing is to keep the brace vertical — particularly when drilling in at right angles to those holes already drilled. The best way of doing this is to enlist the help of a friend.

Plans and dimensions

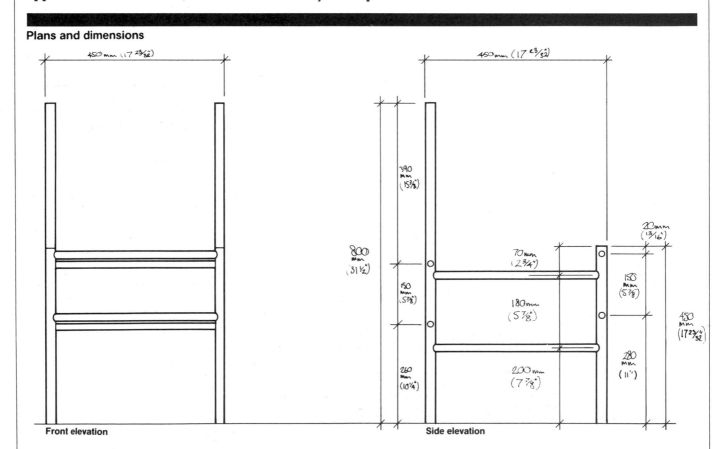

Front elevation

Side elevation

You will need

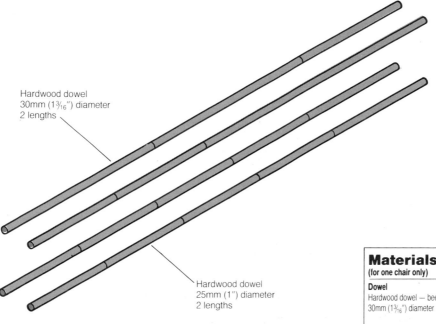

Hardwood dowel
30mm (1³/₁₆″) diameter
2 lengths

Hardwood dowel
25mm (1″) diameter
2 lengths

Upholstery
Cutting pattern

Shown below is the minimum area of material you
will need to buy. Adjust the pattern to fit the width of
material used and to accommodate any pattern or
weave in the fabric.

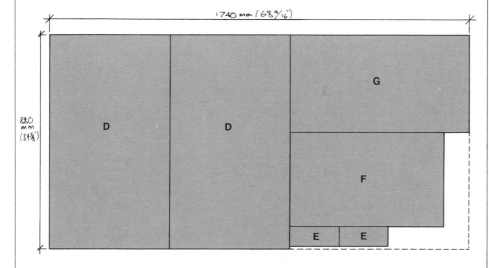

1740 mm (68⁹/₁₆″)

880 mm (84⅝″)

D   D   G

F

E   E

Materials
(for one chair only)

Dowel
Hardwood dowel — beech, birch or ramin

30mm (1³/₁₆″) diameter	800mm	(31½″)	(2)	**A**
	450mm	(17²³/₃₂″)	(2)	**B**
25mm (1″) diameter	424mm	(16¹¹/₁₆″)	(8)	**C**

Glue
Bottle PVA wood glue

Stain
Tin red stain

Varnish
Tin clear polyurethane satin finish varnish

Upholstery materials

Fabric
Stone coloured canvas type material, or fabric to choice

880mm (34⅝″) × 490mm (19⁹/₁₆″)	(2)	**D**
200mm (7⅞″) × 75mm (3″)	(2)	**E**
640mm (25³/₁₆″) × 380mm (14¹⁵/₁₆″)	(1)	**F**
760mm (29¹⁵/₁₆″) × 380mm (14¹⁵/₁₆″)	(1)	**G**

Fire Retardant Foam
12mm (½″) foam

840mm (33¹/₁₆″) × 450mm (17³/₄″)	(1)	**H**

Ribbon
0.5m (1ft 6″) cream coloured material

Tools
Bench and vice
Brace
Centre bit 18mm (0.7″) diameter (check diameter of parts **C** and
match to it)
1220mm (48″) sash clamps   (2)
Hammer
Sandpaper   80 grit (1 sheet)
            120 grit (1 sheet)
Sanding block
Pincers
Drill
Drill bit 3mm (⅛″)
Wire wool '00' grade
25mm (1″) paint brush

Instructions

1 Each leg has 4 holes — 2 in one direction and 2 more at right angles. Hold each leg in turn in the vice and, starting from the bottom, mark up the leg the first 2 hole centres. Drill these holes first with a 3mm (⅛″) drill. They will guide your brace and bit, which should be used to bore out a flat-bottomed hole exactly 12mm (½″) deep. Be careful at all times not to break through with the point of the bit.

2 Now drill the other 2 holes, following the same procedure. To check you are drilling square, insert a length of dowel into the first hole and use this to check that you are drilling at right angles to it; *ie*, it should be horizontal in line with the bench top and you should be drilling vertically — get a friend to check that you do not tilt over. It is possible to make a guide for drilling. Take a hardwood block 70mm × 70mm × 70mm (2¾″ × 2¾″ × 2¾″). Drill through a hole of diameter to suit the larger dowel. Now slide it along some 30mm (1³⁄₁₆″) dowel and drill through with the 25mm (1″) bit. This block can then be used again and again (see illustration below).

Constructing your own drill block

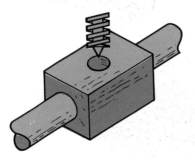

3 Repeat the process on all 4 legs, but do check the marking out positions in pairs before you drill, so that you don't have holes (which are difficult to fill) in the wrong place.

Chair assembly

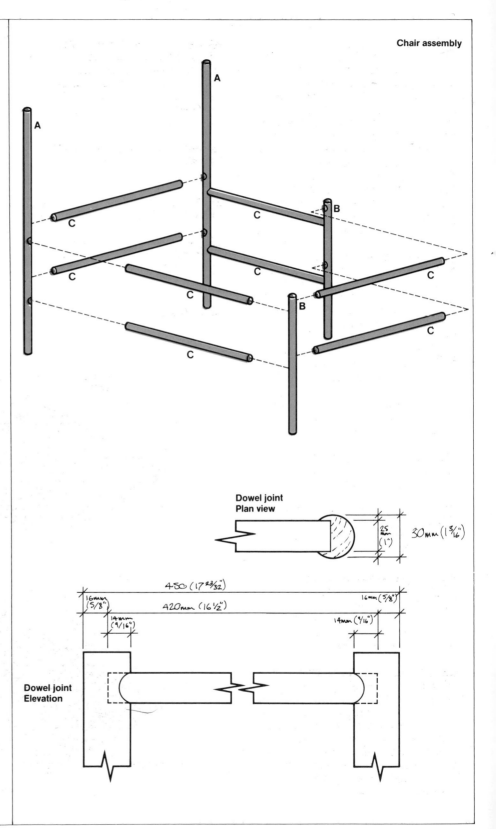

Dowel joint Plan view

25 mm (1″)

30mm (1³⁄₁₆″)

Dowel joint Elevation

450 (17²³⁄₃₂″)

420mm (16½″)

16mm (5/8″)

16mm (5/8″)

14mm (9/16″)

14mm (9/16″)

4 Glue up in two stages — taking parts **A**, **C**, **C**, **B**. Apply glue to both the ends of the dowels **C** and inside the holes in the legs **A** and **B**. Lay each frame in a pair of sash clamps and clamp up. The second frame can go in at the same time if you wish, but be sure to separate them with some newspaper and wipe off all excess glue with a hot damp rag. Always use packing pieces. (You can clamp this frame using string — see TECHNIQUES p. 35 Tricks of the Trade: Clamping)

5 When these 2 frames are dry, assemble the complete chair frame by cramping the frame in the other direction. Always make sure you have thoroughly wiped clean all the excess glue.

6 When dry, sand down the frame. Smooth off the sharp edge and pay particular attention around all the joints. Be methodical here and take your time so that you don't miss any rough bits or glue.

7 With a soft rag, apply red stain all over the frame (see TECHNIQUES p. 37 Staining).

8 Cut back by gently rubbing with wire wool before applying the clear lacquer (see TECHNIQUES p. 36 Finishing).

Making the seat covers
9 Take the 2 covers **D** and, putting the face sides together, pin and sew a 15mm (⁹⁄₁₆″) hem around 3 edges, leaving one end open.

10 Form the pockets by taking the 2 pieces of material **E**. Fold back all ends and make a hem. Then fold each one in half so that the face sides are together. Sew in the 2 hems, leaving a distance of 60mm (2³⁄₈″) between the lines of stitching. Turn inside out and press both pieces.

11 Turn the cover inside out and pin the pockets to the top covers. Stitch all round, securing the pockets in place and leaving the bottom of the cover open. Trap the ribbon in place as you go.

12 Insert the foam pad **H**, tuck in the material and pin. Stitch across.

13 Sew in the stitched feature as drawn. Put to one side.

14 On both parts **F** and **G**, sew a hem down the length on both edges.

15 Take part **F** and sew it onto the seat frame around the front and back rails.

16 Take the piece of material **G** and repeat this process on one side only. Pull it tight over the piece **F** around the side dowel and secure with tacks, at the same time pulling it as taut as you can.

17 Fix the seat and back pad in position by slipping the pockets over the back dowels and then secure it down at the seat by tying the ribbon around the dowel leg.

Sewing the seat covers

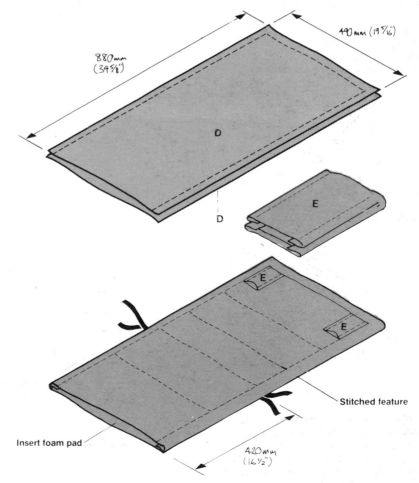

880mm (34⁵⁄₈″)

490mm (19⁵⁄₁₆″)

D

D

E

E

E

420mm (16½″)

Stitched feature

Insert foam pad

Black Framed Sofa

This, a classic sofa, will look equally at home in a contemporarily furnished room as in an interior decorated, say, in Art Deco style. The hard lines of the under-frame and the use of hard panels instead of full upholstery direct it in feeling away from the softer-looking range of chairs and sofas.

Easier and quicker to make than the quilted couch on page 62, it should also be less expensive in material costs. Both sofa designs can be adapted to make a chair, but it would be unwise to enlarge either to make a 3-seater version without increasing the strength of the seat base frame. Make sure on the under-frame that the edges are as crisp and flat as possible, even if this means filling and sanding prior to finishing.

The upholstery for both sofas will need the availability of a sewing machine, and this part of the job is best left to someone with experience in its use. **Putting zippers in the loose cushions will enable you to have the covers dry cleaned.**

Plans and dimensions

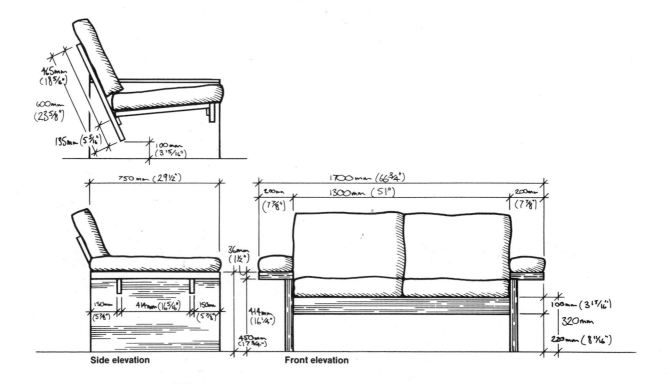

Side elevation   Front elevation

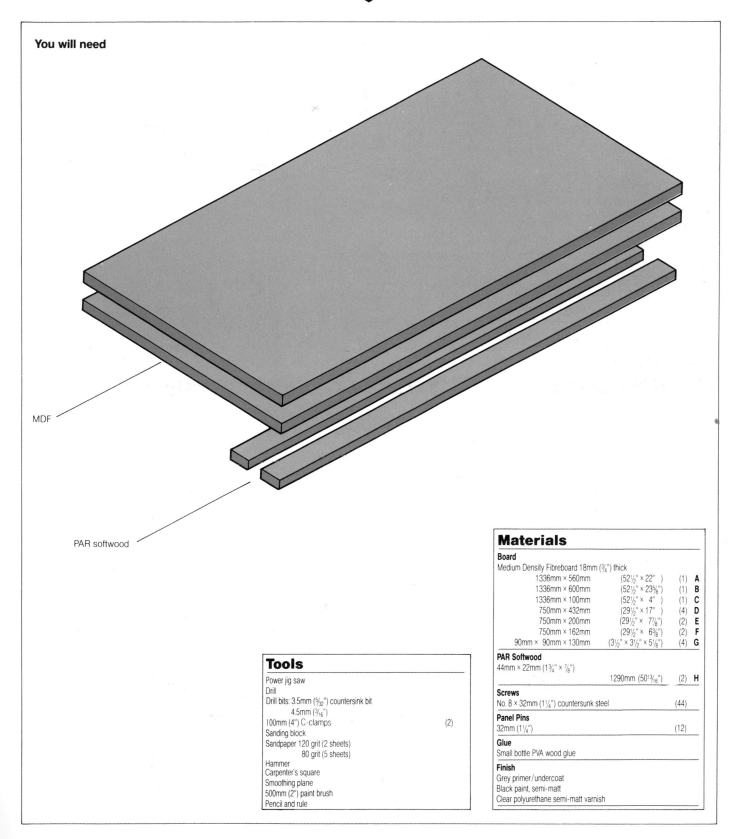

You will need

MDF

PAR softwood

Tools

Power jig saw
Drill
Drill bits: 3.5mm ($\frac{5}{32}$") countersink bit
4.5mm ($\frac{3}{16}$")
100mm (4") C-clamps   (2)
Sanding block
Sandpaper 120 grit (2 sheets)
80 grit (5 sheets)
Hammer
Carpenter's square
Smoothing plane
500mm (2") paint brush
Pencil and rule

Materials

Board
Medium Density Fibreboard 18mm ($\frac{3}{4}$") thick

1336mm × 560mm	(52$\frac{1}{2}$" × 22")	(1)	**A**
1336mm × 600mm	(52$\frac{1}{2}$" × 23$\frac{5}{8}$")	(1)	**B**
1336mm × 100mm	(52$\frac{1}{2}$" × 4")	(1)	**C**
750mm × 432mm	(29$\frac{1}{2}$" × 17")	(4)	**D**
750mm × 200mm	(29$\frac{1}{2}$" × 7$\frac{7}{8}$")	(2)	**E**
750mm × 162mm	(29$\frac{1}{2}$" × 6$\frac{3}{8}$")	(2)	**F**
90mm × 90mm × 130mm	(3$\frac{1}{2}$" × 3$\frac{1}{2}$" × 5$\frac{1}{8}$")	(4)	**G**

PAR Softwood
44mm × 22mm (1$\frac{3}{4}$" × $\frac{7}{8}$")

	1290mm (50$\frac{13}{16}$")	(2)	**H**

Screws
No. 8 × 32mm (1$\frac{1}{4}$") countersunk steel   (44)

Panel Pins
32mm (1$\frac{1}{4}$")   (12)

Glue
Small bottle PVA wood glue

Finish
Grey primer/undercoat
Black paint, semi-matt
Clear polyurethane semi-matt varnish

Cutting plan

Medium density fibreboard

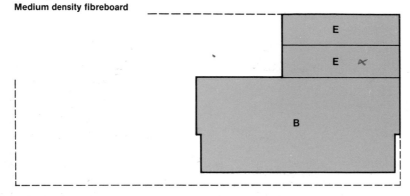

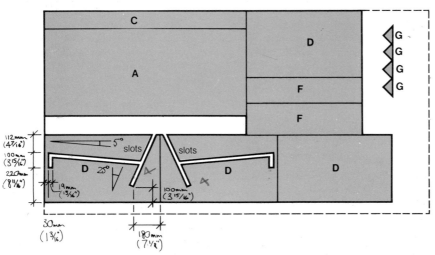

4 Panels **D** should now be specified left and right. Drill and countersink 4.5mm (³/₁₆″) diameter holes along all the edges of both cut-out panels **D**. When screwed together these ensure that the panels are secured firmly at their most vulnerable points.

5 Take one of the other 2 side panels **D** and apply some glue sparingly but evenly over one face. Glue also the concealed face of one of the cut-out panels **D**. Bring the 2 surfaces together and clamp in position with 2 × 100mm (4″) C-clamps.

6 Check that all the edges of the 2 panels line up. Pilot drill through the clearance holes with a 3.5mm (⁵/₃₂″) drill and secure with No. 8 × 32mm (1¼″) screws.

7 Take an arm panel **E** and glue and pin it in position on the top of the side panel so that it is flush on the 3 sides as drawn. Repeat steps 6 and 7 with the second arm-to-side panel assembly.

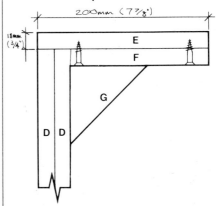

Instructions

1 Check all the MDF board pieces for size against the cutting layout.

2 Take 2 of the 4 side panels **D** and mark out the slots which will take the seat and back panels (see diagram).

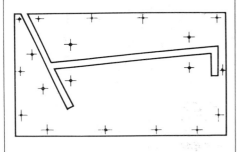

3 Saw along the lines with a power jig saw, being careful not to wander. Do this with one piece at a time, as a jig saw blade will bend over if you try and cut through a double thickness. Check the cut width with a panel offcut.

When you have cut out the slots you may find that the part is liable to break. Try and keep the panel in one piece, but if it breaks, don't worry. Once it is applied to the other side panel and glued in position, any imperfections will not be visible. You will improve the camouflage by glueing the break and then sanding down when it is dry.

8 Place the arms upside down on the floor. Take the arm panels **F** and glue and screw them down to the underside of the arm panels **E** through pre-drilled clearance holes (see steps 5 and 6). Make sure that the inside edge of **F** is pushed well into the side panel **D** and that the outside edges are flush. The inside edge of panel **F** should also be glued.

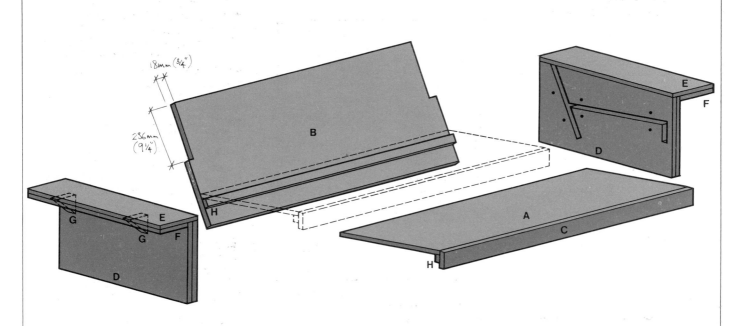

18mm (¾")

236mm (9¼")

9 Take the 4 support braces **G** and, glueing the 2 short square edges, rub them into position, spacing them equally to support the arm panel and secure with two panel pins. Remove all the excess glue with a hot wet cloth and leave to dry.
Repeat steps 8 and 9 with the other side panels.

10 Now clean up the edges. This is *very* important. If your alignment is generally poor you will need to use a smoothing plane to clean up these edges first. Keep the blade sharp and continually check that all is square.
When you finish with sandpaper, be sure to use a sanding block, gripping it with both hands. Apply a softness to the sharp edges only with 120 grit sandpaper.
Clean up both side panels in this way.

11 Take the back panel **B** and trim back the 2 ends as drawn. Keep your lines crisp and clean up neatly.

12 Pre-drill 6 equally-spaced clearance holes in each of the support battens **H**. Glue and screw one into position on back panel **B** with 6 × 32mm (1¼") No. 8 wood screws. Wipe off the excess glue and leave to dry.

13 Take the front horizontal rail **C** and apply the second of the 2 support battens **H** in position, just as in step 12, positioning it one panel thickness from one long edge (*ie*, stepped down from the top edge).

14 Now try a 'dry' assembly of the entire structure. This is done on its side (see diagram). Begin by fitting **A**, **B** and **C** into one arm panel laid on the floor and capping them with the second. It helps to use some packing to keep the arm panel horizontal.

15 If everything fits, apply liberal quantities of glue to the slots in the side panel and assemble the whole sofa.
Hold in position either with long sash clamps, or by pinning through from the outside of the arm panels.

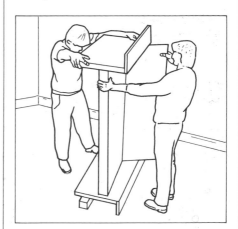

16 Add an undercoat and top coat of black paint. A clear varnish over the top will give you a superior finish.

Upholstery

Foam Seat Cushion
Fire Retardant Foam 27 density

650mm × 600mm × 100mm	(25⅝″ × 23⅝″ × 4″)	(2) **A**
25 density		
650mm × 450mm × 100mm	(25⅝″ × 17¾″ × 4″)	(2) **B**
750mm × 200mm × 75mm	(29½″ × 7⅞″ × 3″)	(2) **C**

Fibre Wrap (10mm/⅜″ thick)

5m × 600mm	(16ft × 23⅝″)

Zippers

650mm (25⅝″), to match material	(4)

Material
Approximately 6m (19ft 6″) upholstery, quality and fabric to your choice. The amount required will depend on the pattern repeat and the width of the material.

Velcro strip to match material 3m (9ft 9″)

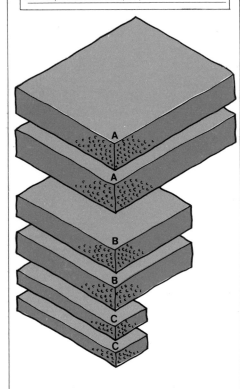

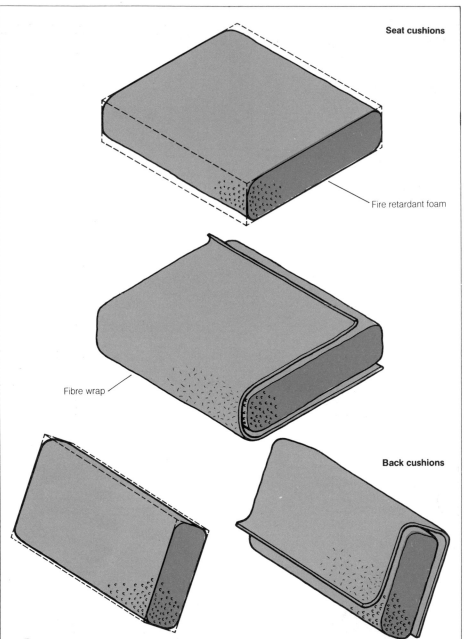

Seat cushions

Fire retardant foam

Fibre wrap

Back cushions

Instructions

1 For the cushion pads, take the foam slabs and cut the 25mm (1″) nosings along all the long edges (650mm/25⅝″ dimensions). This is done with a large pair of scissors (shears).

2 Cut the fibre wrap to length and wrap it round all the cushions, leaving the back edge free to avoid the fibre catching the zip when inserting the cover.

3 For the cushion covers, mark out the cover parts on the inside surface of your material. Remember that with a patterned material you may have to add a little extra so that the centre of the pattern appears on the centre of the cushion.

4 For each cushion, cut out the pieces and cut notches as drawn. Label the parts.

5 Bringing the inside faces of the material together, line up the notches of the three parts, pin in position and sew the side panels to the facing, leaving a 10mm/⅜″ seam all round.
Start sewing at the notch on the front edge of the cushion. Sew back along the marked line to the zipper and repeat underneath. Do the same for all cushions.

6 Trim back the excess material to leave enough to form a hem on either side.

7 Apply zipper to the two hems, stitching through and making sure that the front of the zipper is on the inside.

8 Turn the cover inside out and insert cushion.

Making the arm pads

9 The covers for each arm pad are made in a similar way to those of the seat and back cushions, so measure, mark out and cut the material.

10 Sew along the hem as drawn, but see how zipper must end on the bottom flat surface of the arm pad. Again, be sure to mark the inferior side and sew up the cover inside out.

11 Zipper is applied again in the same way, but after you have turned the cover inside out you will need to sew the velcro strip onto the bottom surface

12 Apply the opposite strip of velcro to the tops of the arms with contact adhesive. These should effectively hold the arm cushion in position.

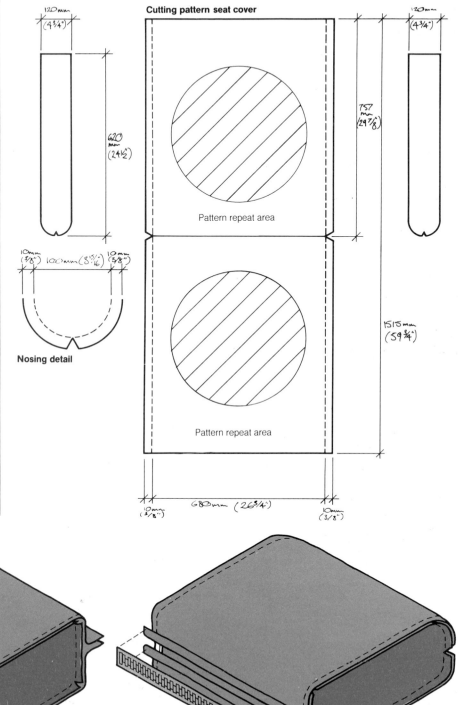

Cutting pattern seat cover

Pattern repeat area

Pattern repeat area

120mm (4¾")

620mm (24½")

757mm (29⅞")

1515mm (59¾")

10mm (⅜") 100mm (3¹⁵⁄₁₆") 10mm (⅜")

Nosing detail

680mm (26¾")

10mm (⅜")

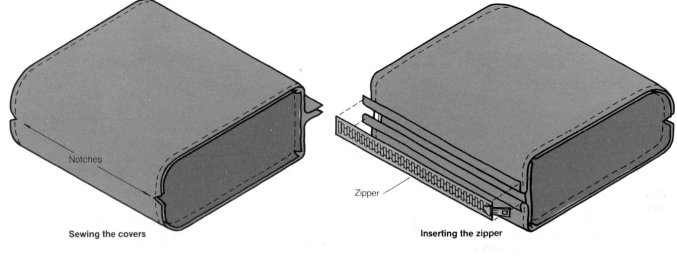

Notches

Sewing the covers

Zipper

Inserting the zipper

Quilted Sofa

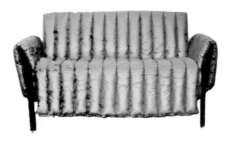

The sofa has been created as a simple, light piece of upholstered furniture, requiring no special skills and no previous upholstery experience. It reflects a style and approach similar to other projects, but do remember that the finished result will not be quite the same as interior sprung upholstery. Pleasantly comfortable, nevertheless, its visual appeal will make a strong impact on your sitting room. And if you later decide to replace this sofa with another, the design is well suited to adapt as occasional furniture for a bedroom or hall.

The design, complete with quilted cover, uses a light but strong underframe to bring a fresher look to a

two seater couch. Its quilted detail allows the additional advantage of achieving interest on cheap and plain materials. For best results choose a strong, pure, bright colour. Go for primary shades rather than muddy browns, although a cool grey will also look smart. Use the show material on both sides or, if you prefer, pick

another colour for the reverse side to create a contrast.

Making upholstered furniture on a do-it-yourself basis can be difficult, particularly for an inexperienced person tackling heavy upholstery. The outlay in foam and cover material on top of the cost of frame construction could easily prove to be as expensive as buying the item from a furniture store. Add to that the time involved in completing a project of this sort, and it is clear that the prospective maker should be aware of the commitment required when, as a first attempt, there is a possibility of the work being abandoned or postponed through lack of time.

Plans and dimensions

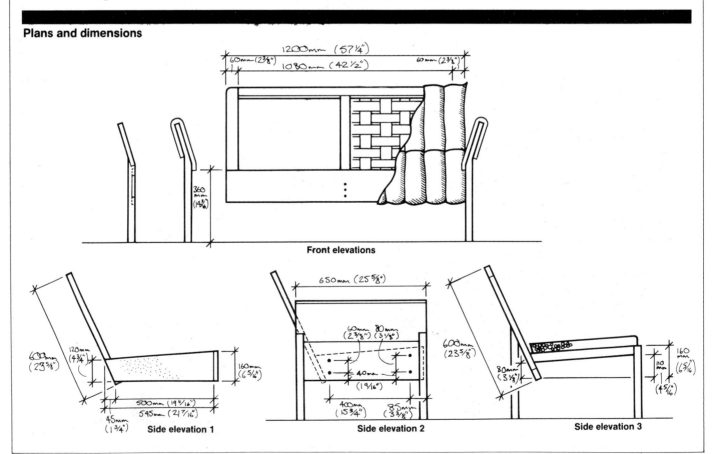

Front elevations

Side elevation 1

Side elevation 2

Side elevation 3

You will need

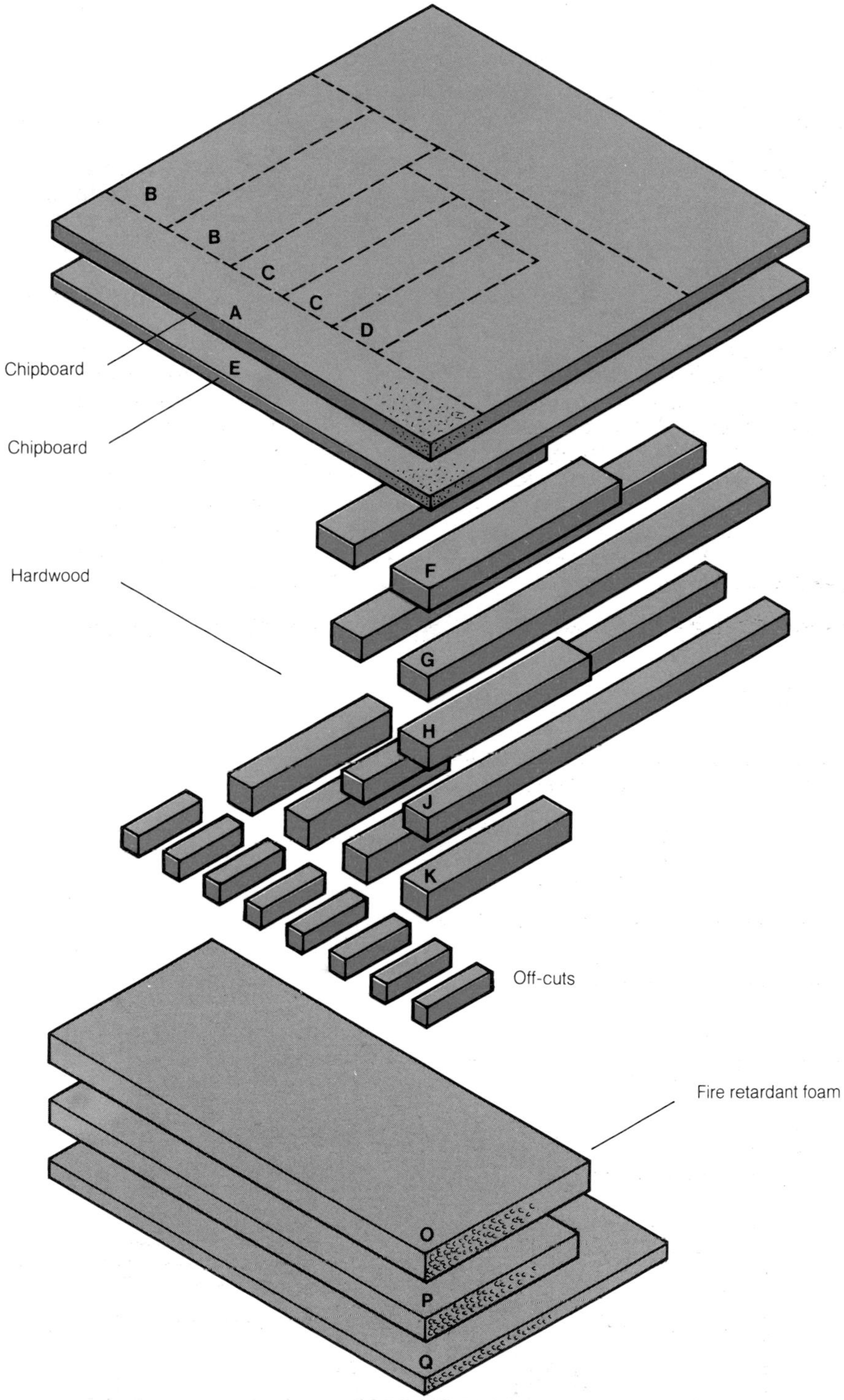

Chipboard

Chipboard

Hardwood

Off-cuts

Fire retardant foam

Materials

Board
18mm (¾") chipboard

1200mm × 160mm	(47¼" × 6⁵/₁₆")	(1)	**A**
650mm × 200mm	(25⅝" × 7⅞")	(2)	**B**
545mm × 160mm	(21½" × 6⁵/₁₆")	(2)	**C**
520mm × 135mm	(20½" × 5⁵/₁₆")	(1)	**D**

16mm (⅝") chipboard

650mm × 190mm	(25⅝" × 7½")	(2)	**E**

Hardwood
Beech or mahogany (no splits)

60mm × 25mm	(2⅜" × 1")	600mm	(23⅝")	(2)	**F**
44mm × 25mm	(1¾" × 1")	1080mm	(42½")	(2)	**G**
		512mm	(20")	(1)	**H**
35mm × 25mm	(1⅜" × 1")	1150mm	(45¼")	(2)	**J**
35mm × 35mm	(1⅜" × 1⅜")	445mm	(17½")	(4)	**K**

offcuts

22mm × 22mm	(⅞" × ⅞")	50mm	(2")	(8)	

Dowels
(hardwood)

50mm × 10mm (2" × ⅜") diameter	(12)

Screws

No. 8 × 50mm (2")	(22)
No. 8 × 32mm (1¼")	(30)

Bolts

M.8 × 50mm (2") bolt	(8)
washers (2) and a nut	

Tacks

Covered tack or stud	(300)

Glue
Small bottle PVA wood glue
Medium tin resilient foam adhesive

Paint
Small tin black satin finish paint

Fire Retardant Foam
Back 25mm (1") density 25

120mm × 480mm	(4¾" × 18⅞")	(1)

Seat 50mm (2") density 35

1200mm × 510mm	(47¼" × 20")	(1)

12mm (½") density 25

1200mm × 510mm	(47¼" × 20")	(1)

Arms 12mm (½") density 25

630mm × 420mm	(24¹³/₁₆" × 16½")	(1)

Rubber Webbing 50mm (2") — 26m (85ft)

Tacks (for webbing) 1 box

Tools

Dowelling jig
Hammer
Pincers
Screwdriver
Drill
Drill bits. 4.5mm (³/₁₆") 8mm (⁵/₁₆") 3.5mm (⁵/₃₂") countersink bit
Power jig saw or panel saw
100mm (4") C-clamp

1220mm (48") sash clamps	(2)

Set square or protractor
Combination square

Sandpaper	80 grit (2 sheets)
	120 grit (2 sheets)

12mm (½") paint brush
Electric sewing machine and sewing equipment

Instructions

Making the seat frame

1 Take the two side panels **C** and cut them to shape (see diagram right) to make the seat angle of 5°.

2 To define the back angle of 65°, take the horizontal long edge of **C** and mark a point 45mm (1¾") in from the narrow end. Draw a line up from this point to the corner (see diagram). Cut along this line. Drill 4 equally-spaced clearance holes 4.5mm (³⁄₁₆") diameter and countersink. Hole centres are to be 12mm (½") in from the back edge (see diagram). Take care not to allow the drill to wander.

3 Take the centre brace **D** and cut to shape as shown, following the same procedures as in 1 and 2. Use part **C** as a template for the angle. With part **D** laid over part **C**, the angled end should show a 25mm (1") step.

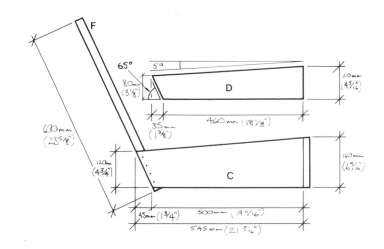

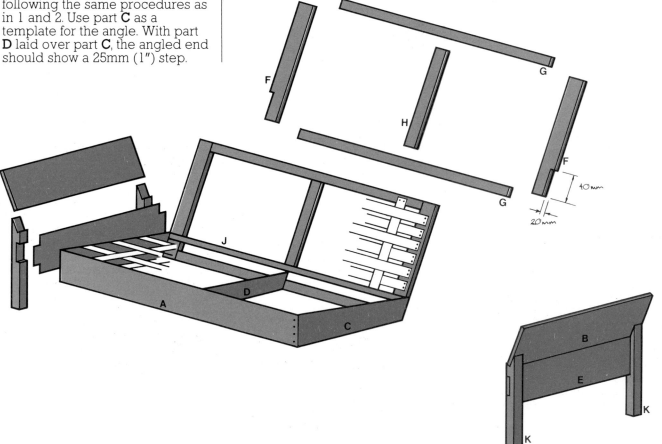

Making the back frame

4 The back frame is made from solid beech, and should be dowel-jointed with your dowelling jig. Use 2 dowels to each joint (see TECHNIQUES p. 33) and make sure you drill a full 26mm (1") into each member. You will find it easier to cut out the notches in the upright **F** before you glue the frame together. Also apply the top radii to round off the corners (see diagram). Have a 'dry' trial run first to check for square and then apply glue to *all* surfaces to be joined. Leave to dry in clamps and wipe off all excess glue with a hot damp rag.

5 You are now ready to assemble the frame. Stand the completed back frame end up, gripping it in the vice so that the notch in **F** is horizontal. Place the respective part **C** in position on the back frame, if necessary supporting its other end with something suitable, such as a paint tin. Pilot drill 3.5mm ($^5/_{32}$") diameter clearance holes into the back frame.

6 Apply glue to both **F** and **C** and secure with 4 No. 8 × 50mm (2") wood screws. Repeat step 5 at the opposite end. Gripping this joint with a 100mm (4") C-clamp as you drill and screw will help to keep it lined up at all times.

7 In the front panel **A**, drill all the clearance holes (4.5mm/$^3/_{16}$" diameter and countersink) 9mm ($^3/_8$") from either end and 3 in the centre.

8 Now also drill 3 clearance holes in the back frame to screw into **D** from the back. These are positioned centrally along the length and the first hole should be 20mm ($^3/_4$") up from the bottom of the frame, with the other 2 spaced upwards at 20mm ($^3/_4$") intervals.

9 Lie the frame on its back with the side panels **C** sticking up. Lie the front panel **A** on the side panels **C** and, holding the joint flush, drill through with a 3.5mm ($^5/_{32}$") pilot drill at both ends. Apply the glue before screwing to secure with No. 8 × 50mm (2") screws.

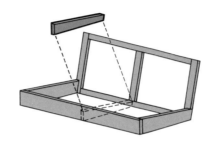

10 Drop centre panel **D** in position and check fit. Remove and apply glue to both ends. Screw to secure with No. 8 × 50mm (2") screws. Wipe off excess glue and leave to dry.

11 Take the 8 hardwood offcuts and, after applying glue to 2 faces, rub these pieces of wood into every corner and leave them to dry. These will add much strength to the frame.

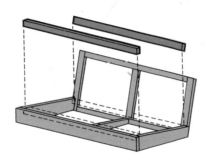

12 To screw and glue the horizontal bars **J** to the inside of the frame, drill the front panel **A** with clearance holes 20mm ($^3/_4$") from the top edges. After applying glue, clamp in position 5mm ($^3/_{16}$") below the top edge. Make sure the bar is parallel to the top edge, then pilot drill (3.5mm/$^5/_{32}$" diameter) and secure with No. 8 × 32mm (1$^1/_4$") wood screws. The rear rail should be fitted in the same way, lining the rail up 5mm ($^3/_{16}$") below the side panel tops and screwing through the back frame members **F, H, F**.

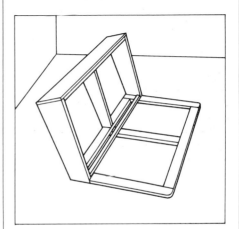

Arm and leg assemblies

13 All the leg sections **K** must now be notched out at the top to take the arm panel **B** and further down for the side panel **E** (see diagram overleaf). It is essential to use a set square for marking out the angle. Hold the parts in the vice with each notch in turn being positioned horizontally prior to cutting. Cut out joints with a tenon saw (see TECHNIQUES p. 32 Cutting Joints).

14 Mark out and cut the notches on the side panels **E** to take the legs.

Leg section elevation

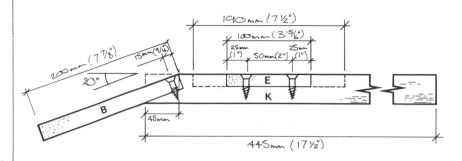

190mm (7½")
100mm (3¹⁵⁄₁₆")
25mm (1") 50mm(2") 25mm(1")
200mm (7⅞") 15mm(9⁄16")
20°
B
E
K
45mm
445mm (17½")

15 Apply glue to these notches and clamp legs in position with a 100mm (4") C-clamp. Pilot drill through with a 3.5mm (⁵⁄₃₂") drill and screw to secure with No. 8 × 32mm (1¼") wood screw. Check that the legs are square and parallel before you leave the frame to dry. If not, gently tap them square with a mallet, using a block of wood as a cushion to prevent the leg from being bruised.

16 Drill and countersink clearance holes in the arm panels **B** as drawn. Glue all surfaces to be joined together. Hold the arm panels in position on the leg frames, pilot drill through (3.5mm/⁵⁄₃₂" diameter drill bit) and secure with a No. 8 × 32mm (1¼") wood screw.

17 Sand off all sharp edges on all frames.

18 Stand the sofa frame on its end and lay on the respective arm/leg assembly. Cramp the two together so that the front leg protrudes by 20mm (¾") beyond the front panel **A**, and the bottom edges are flush. Mark out the bolt positions in **E** and drill through both frames with an 8mm (⁵⁄₁₆") drill. Dismantle, repeat the procedure at the other end and dismantle again.

19 Apply black paint to the arm/leg assemblies, all faces of every leg and the edges of the arm panels.

20 Take each piece of rubber webbing in turn. Start at the same side and tack one end in position with 3-4 tacks. Take the loose end of the strip over to the other horizontal rail **J** and mark the position of the rail on the strip. Then stretch the rubber strip so that it extends 50mm (2") beyond the marked line. Tack to secure and trim off the spare material. Space each strip by its own width and work down the frame. Finally, interweave 3 rubber strips transversely down the complete length. Stretch as before and secure on the outside of the side panels with tacks.

21 Apply the webbing to the back frame with more of the same tacks.

22 Check the size of the 25mm (1") foam **P** on the back frame and, applying some foam glue around the frame and on the foam edges, glue it down in position against the frame.

23 Do the same for the 50mm (2") foam **O** on the seat.

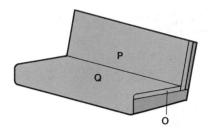

24 Now apply glue all over the foam seat and the front panel **A** and wrap over the 19mm (¾") foam skin **Q**.

25 Take the piece of calico and, stretching it along its length, lead it into the crevice at the back of the seat and pull taut. Tack to secure at both ends with a couple of tacks into the side panels **C**. Run your hand from the back of the seat to the front, over and down the front panel **A**. Hold the calico round the bottom edge of **A** and secure with a tack from the back. Tack along, working alternately in both directions from the centre of **A**, stretching the material gently as you go by drawing your hand across the surface. Trim off the excess material 25mm (1") from the tacks.

26 Follow the same procedure with calico on the back, but tack around the *edge* of the back frame.

27 Cover the back side of the back panel with black ticking, again tacking round the edge frame.

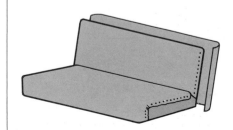

28 Take the arm assembly and, starting with the inside face at a height of 360mm (14″), glue the foam to the arm panels **B**. Leave a 10mm (⅜″) step at either end.

29 Screw the arm/leg assemblies to the seat frame.

30 Check the frame to ensure all exposed wood is painted black.
The sofa is now ready for the quilt.

Upholstery

You will need

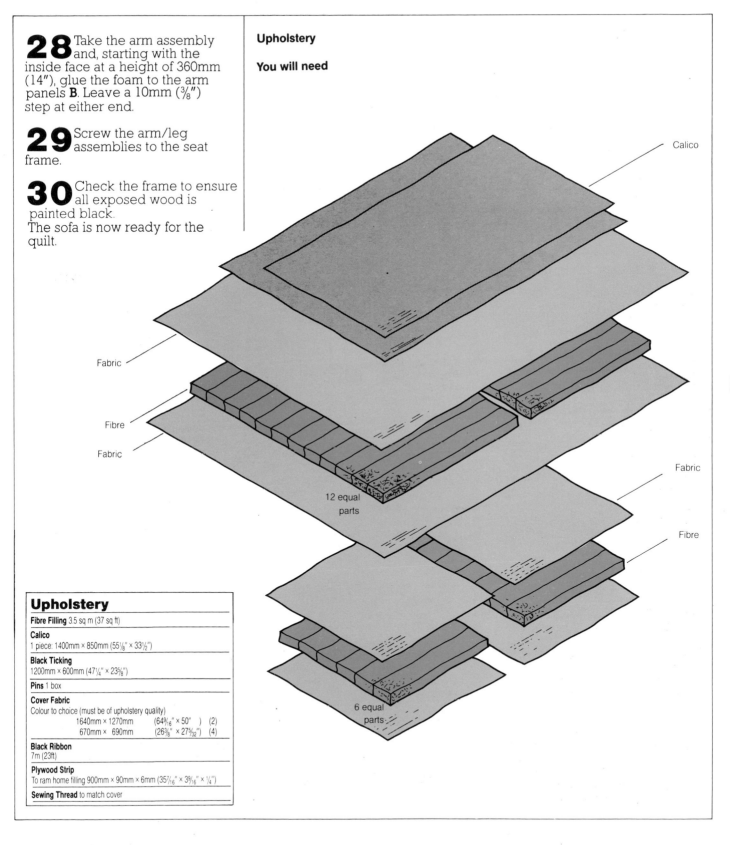

Calico

Fabric

Fibre

Fabric

12 equal parts

Fabric

Fibre

6 equal parts

67

Upholstery

Fibre Filling 3.5 sq m (37 sq ft)	
Calico 1 piece: 1400mm × 850mm (55⅛″ × 33½″)	
Black Ticking 1200mm × 600mm (47¼″ × 23⅝″)	
Pins 1 box	
Cover Fabric Colour to choice (must be of upholstery quality) 1640mm × 1270mm (64⁹/₁₆″ × 50″) (2) 670mm × 690mm (26⅜″ × 27⁵/₃₂″) (4)	
Black Ribbon 7m (23ft)	
Plywood Strip To ram home filling 900mm × 90mm × 6mm (35⁷/₁₆″ × 3⁹/₁₆″ × ¼″)	
Sewing Thread to match cover	

Seat and back covers

31 Take the 2 largest pieces of material. Turn over the ends by 10mm (³⁄₈″) and stitch a seam.

32 Bring the two faces together and sew a seam along both sides, 10mm (³⁄₈″) in from each edge. Sew in the black tapes as you go, leaving 250mm (9⁷⁄₈″) outside the cover.

33 Turn the cover inside out and sew the seams to define the pockets, equally spaced at 104mm (4³⁄₃₂″) apart.

34 Take the 20mm (³⁄₄″) dowel and wrap the cover around it, as drawn, in the appropriate position. Mark the seam. Remove the dowel and stitch down the line.

35 Take the fibre filling and cut it into 100mm (3¹⁵⁄₁₆″) wide strips of the appropriate length. Stuff into each pocket with your plywood strip.

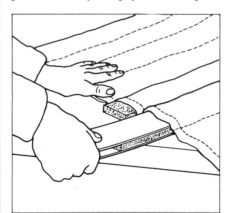

36 When all the pockets are filled, trim the ends inside and close each end with a seam 3–4mm (¹⁄₈″) in from the end.

Side covers

37 These are made in exactly the same way, but with different dimensions. There is no centre dowel.

Seat quilt

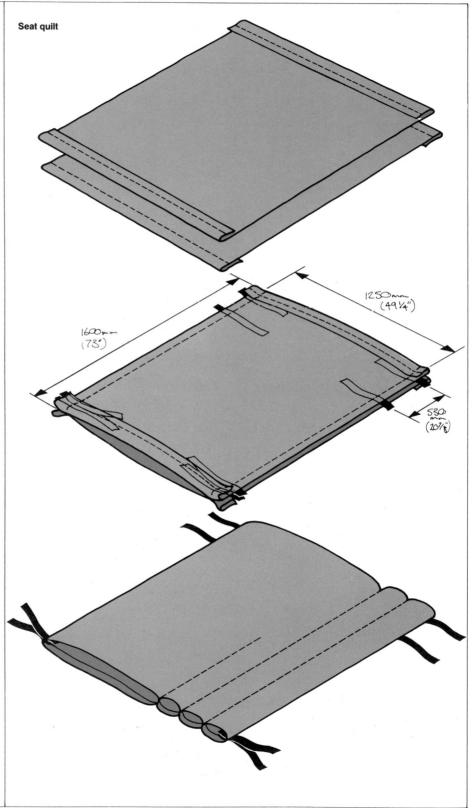

1250mm (49¼″)

1600mm (73″)

530mm (20⁷⁄₈″)

68

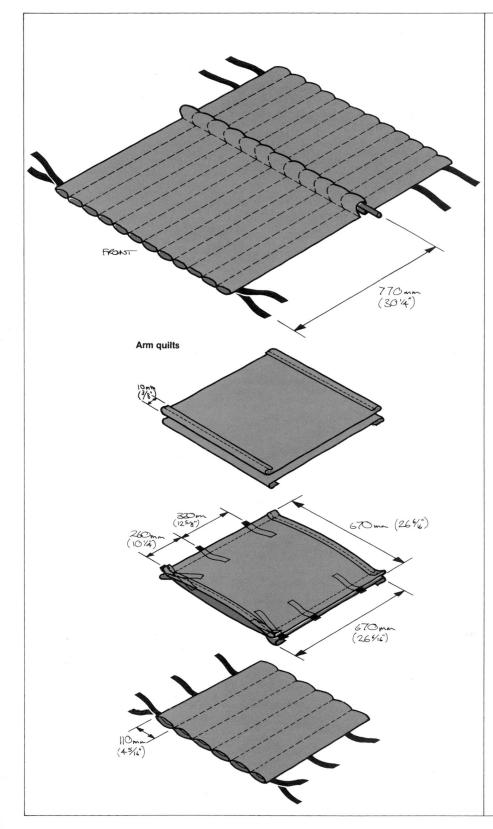

FRONT

770mm
(30¼")

Arm quilts

10mm
(3/8")

320mm
(12⅝")

260mm
(10¼")

670mm (26⁵⁄₁₆")

670mm
(26⁵⁄₁₆")

110mm
(4⁵⁄₁₆")

Attaching the quilt to the frame

38 Take the seat and back quilt and push the dowel into position down the crack at the back of the seat.

39 Stroke the quilt forward over the seat, bring it down over the front edge and secure it at each side by tying the ribbons around each leg in a bow.

40 Now run your hands up the back, taking the quilt over the top and down the outside back. Secure it in place by tying the ribbons together around each end of the back.

41 The arm quilts are positioned in a similar way. Tie the two central ribbons together and slip over the arm panel so that the end with ribbons is on the outside. Tuck in the free end and trap it between the seat and the arm panel. Secure the outside by tying the free ribbons to each leg.

Laminate Coffee Table

This design is classic, elegant and simple. Its style will not date and looks equally at home with furniture of the 1930s, 1960s or the 1980s. The dimensions are also adaptable, so should you wish to make a lamp table (*ie*, a square version at the end of a sofa), a console or back-of-sofa table, just amend the dimensions to suit your need. Even transforming the design into a dining table is possible, but remember you wouldn't be able to sit anyone at either end. Treat this project as a good exercise in the use of plastic laminate. Prepare your work-space well and work clinically. You can get a superb finish with these materials if you take care. A sharp plane is *essential*, and smooth-sanding the edges will also help to give a really crisp look.

To a beginner, low tables might seem an easy project to design, but in reality they are among the more difficult pieces I am asked to produce. The problem is not in construction, as the pure scale of the thing requires less bracing and support than a full-sized table. No, it is more the need to get the style right. Furniture store buyers always need to keep in mind the variety of upholstery that a low table will be required to co-ordinate with, and commercially the most successful tables are the plainer and more classic shapes. That is not to say that a low table should be uninteresting; much is achieved with shape, proportion, use of material and detailing. But it is not a good idea to create something so startling that the eye is drawn away from everything else in the room.

Plans and dimensions

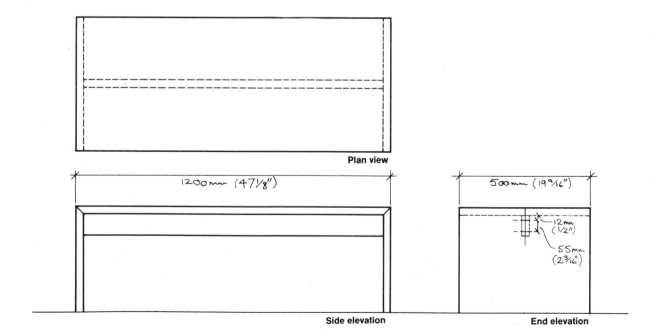

Plan view

1200mm (47⅛")

Side elevation

500mm (19⁹⁄₁₆")

12mm (½")

55mm (2³⁄₁₆")

End elevation

You will need

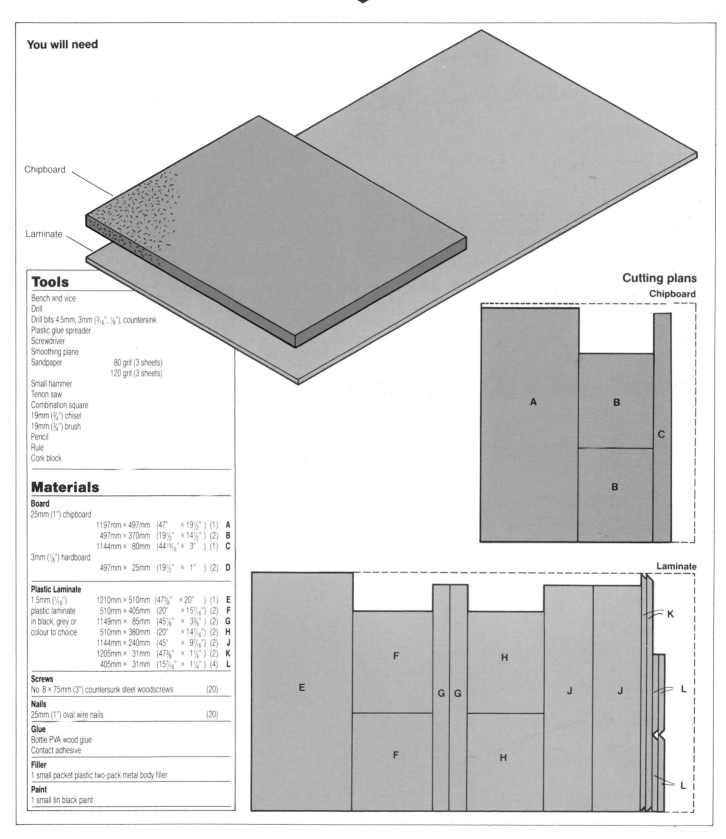

Chipboard

Laminate

Tools

Bench and vice
Drill
Drill bits 4.5mm, 3mm (³⁄₁₆", ¹⁄₈"), countersink
Plastic glue spreader
Screwdriver
Smoothing plane
Sandpaper   80 grit (3 sheets)
                              120 grit (3 sheets)

Small hammer
Tenon saw
Combination square
19mm (³⁄₄") chisel
19mm (³⁄₄") brush
Pencil
Rule
Cork block

Materials

Board
25mm (1") chipboard

1197mm × 497mm	(47"	× 19½")	(1) **A**
497mm × 370mm	(19½"	× 14½")	(2) **B**
1144mm × 80mm	(44¹⁵⁄₁₆" × 3")		(1) **C**

3mm (¹⁄₈") hardboard

497mm × 25mm	(19½"	× 1")	(2) **D**

Plastic Laminate

1.5mm (¹⁄₁₆")	1210mm × 510mm	(47⅝"	× 20")	(1) **E**
plastic laminate	510mm × 405mm	(20"	× 15⁷⁄₁₆")	(2) **F**
in black, grey or	1149mm × 85mm	(45⅛"	× 3⅜")	(2) **G**
colour to choice	510mm × 380mm	(20"	× 14⁷⁄₁₆")	(2) **H**
	1144mm × 240mm	(45"	× 9⁷⁄₁₆")	(2) **J**
	1205mm × 31mm	(47⅞"	× 1¼")	(2) **K**
	405mm × 31mm	(15⁷⁄₁₆"	× 1¼")	(4) **L**

Screws
No. 8 × 75mm (3") countersunk steel woodscrews   (20)

Nails
25mm (1") oval wire nails   (20)

Glue
Bottle PVA wood glue
Contact adhesive

Filler
1 small packet plastic two-pack metal body filler

Paint
1 small tin black paint

Cutting plans

Chipboard

A B C B

Laminate

E F G G H J J K L F H L

Instructions

1 Take the top panel **A** and mark out the 6 clearance holes at both ends, 12mm (½″) in from the edge.

2 Drill through and countersink (4.5mm/³⁄₁₆″ diameter).

3 Drill and countersink 2 holes (4.5mm/³⁄₁₆″ diameter) in both panels **B** for screwing through into the ends of **C**.

4 Hold a panel **B** in the vice with the top uppermost and flush with the bench top. Offer up the top panel **A** and pilot drill your screw positions (3mm/⅛″ diameter). Apply glue to the joint and screw down to secure while holding the panels exactly flush.

5 Put in all 6 screws and repeat step 4 at the opposite end. Leave to dry. Wipe off all excess glue with a hot damp rag.

6 Plane and sand down all protruding edges and any high spots.

Applying the plastic laminate
(see TECHNIQUES page 37)

7 The first laminates to apply are the inner end facings **H**. When laying them down, push the long edge up into the corner first. Bring it down onto the chipboard and press flat.

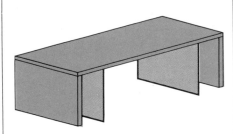

8 Trim off the excess with a smoothing plane and sand flat all 3 exposed sides with 80 grit sandpaper and block.

9 Repeat the process at the opposite end.

10 Now take the brace **C** and apply to it the facings **G**. Trim flush and square.

11 Underneath the top, mark out centrally the position of the brace.

12 Apply some PVA glue to one long edge and, holding in position, screw in one screw through from the top. Next screw in from both ends and then put in all the remaining screws along the centre line of the top.

13 Now that all the screws are in place, fill all the holes with plastic filler. (See TECHNIQUES p. 34).

14 Next fit the under facings **J** for the top. You will need to trim to the exact size and practise with a 'dry run' before glueing down. When you have fixed them in position, trim off the edges square.

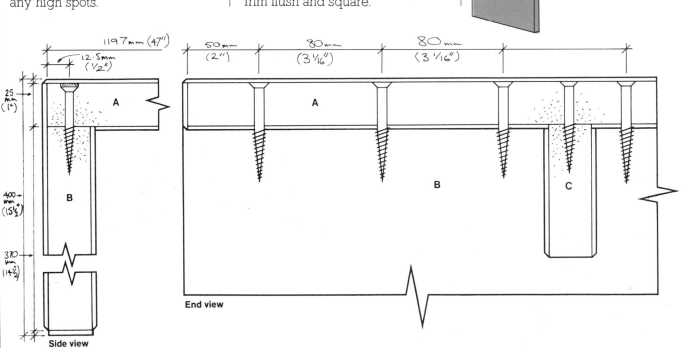

Side view

End view

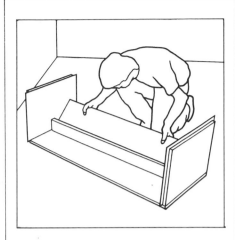

15 Now comes the tricky bit. We are going to apply the edge facings, and these have to be mitred. Take one of the short facings **L** and then with your combination square, draw a line at 45° across one end. Cut off the small triangle with a tenon saw, 2mm (¹⁄₁₆″) outside the drawn line. Hold in the vice and plane back to the line with a smoothing plane.

16 This facing can now be applied to the edge of the table. Be very careful here. It is essential that the 45° angle you have just cut lines up perfectly with both the internal and external corners of the chipboard corner joint.

17 Work round the next side of the table – first the long facing **K** and finally the second facing **L**. Be sure to check the length of **K**, which has 2 opposing mitres. You will be able to raise or lower **K** by a fraction, giving you a little tolerance to get a good fit.

18 When all the edgings have been applied, plane off the excess laminate. On the outside surfaces, plane and sand the edges flush with the chipboard surfaces. On the internal edges, plane along as far as you can and finish the run with a sharp 19mm (¾″) chisel.

19 Now apply the 2 end panel facings **F**, finishing flush and smooth. The top edge must be kept flush and flat in line with the top chipboard surface.

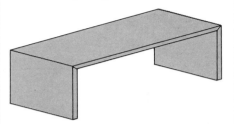

20 Apply the top facing **E** and trim.

21 Sand off all the sharp edges with 80 grit sandpaper and block. Finish to a regular and smooth level with 120 grit sandpaper and block.

22 Tack and glue on the hardboard strips **D** to the bases of the leg panels – smooth side outwards. Finally, paint them black, together with the underside of the brace **C**.

73

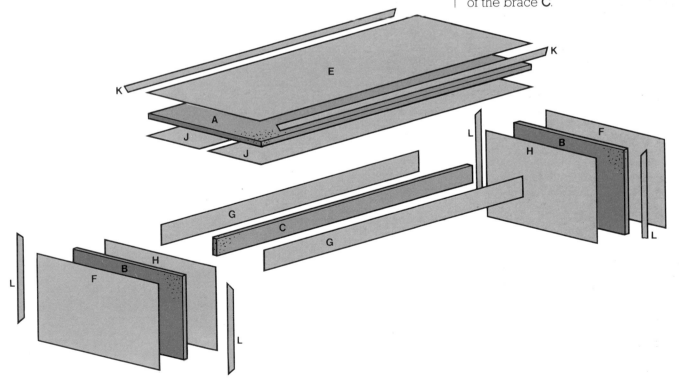

Nest of Tables

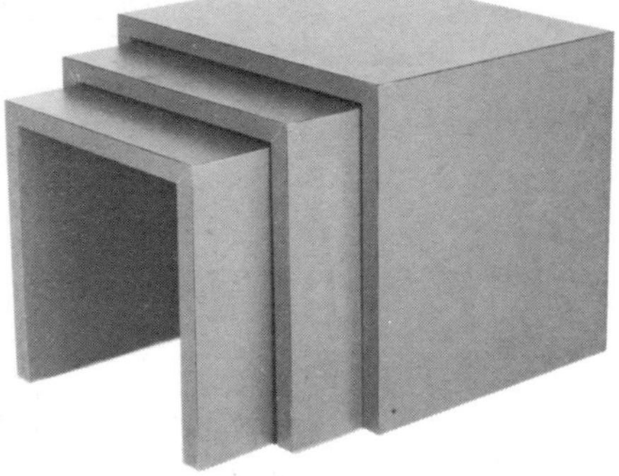

You may have space and requirement for more than one occasional table. If so, you might consider making a nest of the low tables featured on page 70. The construction techniques remain the same, but you must bear in mind that the job will take you nearly three times as long as the single piece. I remember that when making low tables and nests of tables for department stores, we were, in effect, supplying three products as opposed to one. A nest does not command three times the price of one table or anything like it, but it did take us three times as long to make.

The method for constructing this nest of tables is similar to that of the single low table on page 70, except that their small size negates the need for a brace under each top. So, follow the same instructions and techniques as for the previous design, taking your dimensions from the plans below.

Plans and dimensions

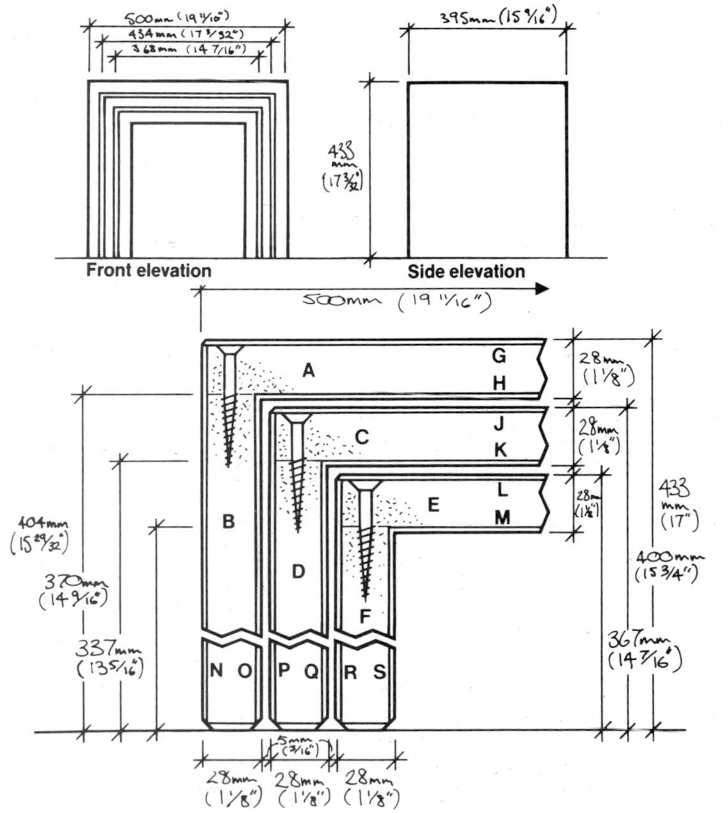
500mm (19 11/16")
434mm (17 3/32")
368mm (14 7/16")
395mm (15 9/16")
433 mm (17 3/32")
Front elevation
Side elevation
500mm (19 11/16")
A
B
C
D
E
F
G
H
J
K
L
M
N O
P Q
R S
28mm (1 1/8")
28mm (1 1/8")
28mm (1 1/8")
433 mm (17")
400mm (15 3/4")
367mm (14 7/16")
404mm (15 29/32")
370mm (14 9/16")
337mm (13 5/16")
5mm (3/16")
28mm (1 1/8")
28mm (1 1/8")
28mm (1 1/8")

Materials

Board

25mm (1") chipboard

Table 1				
	497mm × 392mm	(19 9/16" × 15 7/16")	(1)	**A**
	404mm × 392mm	(15 29/32" × 15 7/16")	(2)	**B**
Table 2				
	431mm × 392mm	(16 31/32" × 15 7/16")	(1)	**C**
	371mm × 392mm	(14 5/8" × 15 7/16")	(2)	**D**
Table 3				
	365mm × 392mm	(14 3/8" × 15 7/16")	(1)	**E**
	338mm × 392mm	(13 5/16" × 15 7/16")	(2)	**F**

Plastic Laminate

1.5mm (1/16")

Table 1				
	505mm × 400mm	(19 7/8" × 15 3/4")	(1)	**G**
	445mm × 400mm	(17 1/2" × 15 3/4")	(1)	**H**
Table 2				
	436mm × 400mm	(17 5/32" × 15 3/4")	(1)	**J**
	379mm × 400mm	(14 15/16" × 15 3/4")	(1)	**K**
Table 3				
	370mm × 400mm	(14 9/16" × 15 3/4")	(1)	**L**
	339mm × 400mm	(13 11/32" × 15 3/4")	(1)	**M**
Table 1				
	434mm × 400mm	(17 3/32" × 15 3/4")	(2)	**N**
	404mm × 400mm	(15 29/32" × 15 3/4")	(2)	**O**
Table 2				
	401mm × 400mm	(15 25/32" × 15 3/4")	(2)	**P**
	371mm × 400mm	(14 19/32" × 15 3/4")	(2)	**Q**
Table 3				
	368mm × 400mm	(14 1/2" × 15 3/4")	(2)	**R**
	338mm × 400mm	(13 5/16" × 15 3/4")	(2)	**S**
Table 1				
	505mm × 30mm	(19 7/8" × 1 3/16")	(2)	**T**
Table 2				
	439mm × 30mm	(17 9/32" × 1 3/16")	(2)	**U**
Table 3				
	383mm × 30mm	(15" × 1 3/16")	(2)	**V**
Table 1				
	434mm × 400mm	(17" × 15 3/4")	(4)	**W**
Table 2				
	401mm × 400mm	(15 3/4" × 15 3/4")	(4)	**X**
Table 3				
	368mm × 400mm	(14 1/2" × 15 3/4")	(4)	**Y**

Hardboard

3mm (1/8")

	392mm × 25mm	(15 7/16" × 1")	(6)	**Z**

Spacers

	350mm × 20mm	(13 3/4" × 25/32")	(4)

Contact Adhesive

Medium tin

Screws

No 8 × 63mm (2 1/2") countersunk steel (30)

Nails

Oval wire nails

19mm (3/4") (50)

You will need

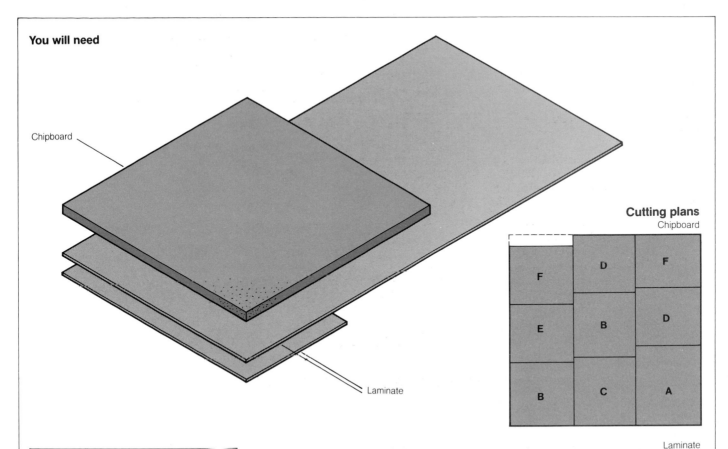

Chipboard

Laminate

Cutting plans
Chipboard

	F	F
F	D	
E	B	D
B	C	A

Laminate

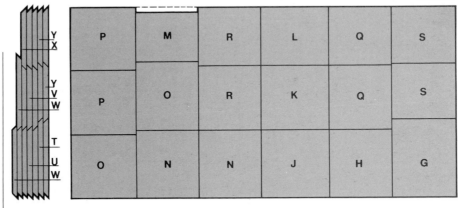

Y X	P	M	R	L	Q	S
Y V W	P	O	R	K	Q	S
T U W	O	N	N	J	H	G

Tools

These are as for the laminate coffee table on page 70.

Instructions

1 Screw and glue all three top panels **A, C** and **E** down on to their respective leg panels **B, D** and **F** through pre-drilled clearance holes.

2 Make sure that these are square (check with a combination square) and leave to dry overnight. A good way of keeping them square as the glue dries is to nest them together, and with some square pieces of 44 × 22mm (1¾″ × ⅞″) softwood, nail through into each leg panel, thereby stopping any movement.

3 When dry, take each table at a time and plane and sand flush any high spots or protruding edges. The tables are now ready to have plastic laminate applied.

4 Following the same procedure and order as for the design on page 70, glue and apply the plastic laminates (see TECHNIQUES p. 37 Applying Plastic Laminates).

5 Work methodically through the order of applying the laminate, but work only on one table at a time so that you don't mix up the laminate pieces.

6 Apply the feet exactly as for the long table (page 70) and also cut some spacers to go at the top of the inside face of each leg panel on the two largest tables. This will do three things: stop the tables from rubbing together and marking the surfaces; keep all the tables apart in the nest so that they look better; and guide them into position.

Low Tiered Coffee Table

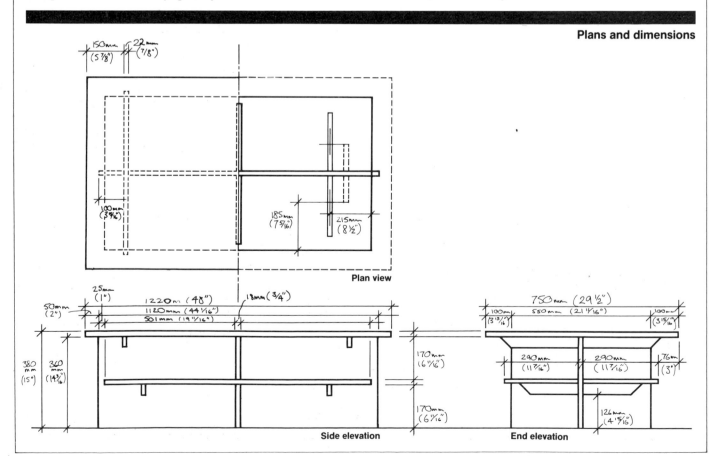

This coffee table is designed to be placed in front of a sofa, where its lower shelf will prove useful for storage of newspapers and magazines, or for additional space, when playing board games, for example. Its construction is related to that of the simple chipboard bed on page 144 — both use a basically slot-together method, enabling you to complete the work fairly quickly.

The table's simple form has not been complicated with special finishes or laminates; a number of neatly cut boards are just fitted together after being painted, either to blend in with your own interior decoration or decorated in the stronger colours as shown in the photograph on page 17.
It is inadvisable to veer away from

the specified dimensions for this project, as the table will then become unstable. Do try to get the supplier to cut the MDF for you, particularly the top panel, as the effect of this design will be totally spoilt if the edges are rough. For the same reason it would certainly be worth planing out any saw marks on the edges before you finish sanding.

Plans and dimensions

Plan view

Side elevation

End elevation

You will need

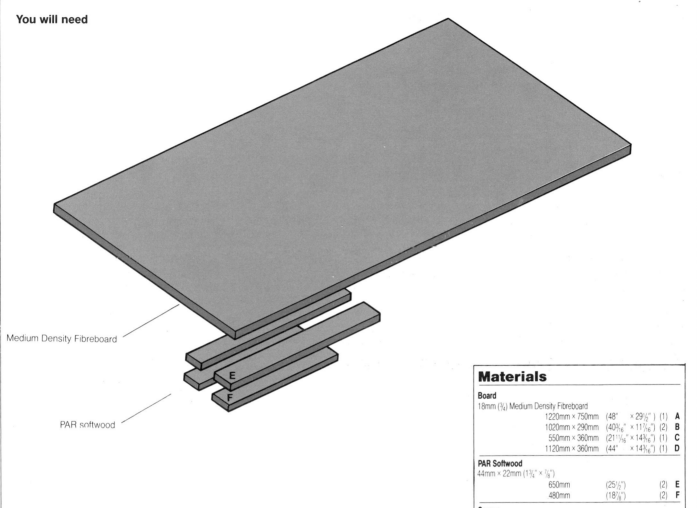

Medium Density Fibreboard

PAR softwood

E

F

Materials

Board
18mm (¾) Medium Density Fibreboard

1220mm × 750mm	(48" × 29½")	(1)	**A**
1020mm × 290mm	(40³/₁₆" × 11⁷/₁₆")	(2)	**B**
550mm × 360mm	(21¹¹/₁₆" × 14³/₁₆")	(1)	**C**
1120mm × 360mm	(44" × 14³/₁₆")	(1)	**D**

PAR Softwood
44mm × 22mm (1¾" × ⅞")

650mm	(25½")	(2)	**E**
480mm	(18⅞")	(2)	**F**

Screws

No. 6 × 16mm (⅝") roundhead steel	(16)
No. 8 × 50mm (2") countersunk steel	(4)
No. 8 × 32mm (1¼") countersunk steel	(4)

Table Shrinkage Plates

Steel (see illustration overleaf)	(4)

Glue
Small bottle PVA wood glue

Paint
Tin green paint
Tin grey paint
Tin mauve paint

Tools

Power jig saw
Rule and pencil
Square
Screwdriver
Drill and 4.5mm (³/₁₆") bit + countersink
Sanding block
Sandpaper   80 grit (3 sheets)
                      120 grit (3 sheets)
Tenon saw
50mm (2") paint brush

Cutting plan

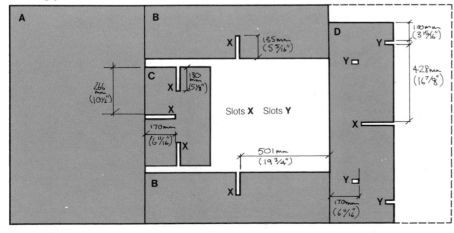

A

B

C

D

266 mm (10½")

135mm (5⁵/₁₆")

130 mm (5⅛")

170mm (6¹¹/₁₆")

X

X

X

X

Slots **X**   Slots **Y**

Y

Y

X

Y

Y

100mm (3¹⁵/₁₆")

428mm (16⁷/₈")

501mm (19¾")

170mm (6¹¹/₁₆")

B

Instructions

1 Take all the MDF piece parts **A**, **B**, **C**, and **D** and mark them accordingly. Check that all the dimensions are accurate and then mark out all the slots X as shown in the diagram.

2 Cut out the slots with a power jig saw, working accurately to the line. Note that the 18.5mm ($\frac{3}{4}$″) slots (X) are for the MDF and the 22mm ($\frac{7}{8}$″) slots (Y) are for the softwood battens. The slots on the long edge of **D** define the top edge and are to accept the battens **E**, which are merely slid into place. The holes in this panel **D** are to accept battens **F** and should fit accordingly. Begin the holes with a drill to create enough depth to accept the jig saw blade (see TECHNIQUES p. 33 Jig Saw Cutting).

3 Check that all the slots are wide enough by sliding another piece of waste MDF into each one.

4 Clean up with sandpaper and block, taking care to keep the edges crisp.

5 Take the battens **E** and **F** and cut a 45° angle off all the ends as drawn.

6 Mark the position of the battens **E** on the underside of the top by offering up the long vertical panel **D** into position. Drill and countersink 2 × 4.5mm ($\frac{3}{16}$″) diameter holes into both battens **E** and then glue and screw them into position.
Put to one side ready for painting.

7 Assemble panel **C** onto **D** and place the two battens **F** centrally in position. Mark the points where they support the mid-shelves **B**. Then take apart and on both panels **B** mark and drill a clearance hole for No. 8 wood screw (4.5mm/$\frac{3}{16}$″), including countersink, to locate over the centre line of the batten.

8 Check over all panels finally and apply the paint, cutting back between coats (see TECHNIQUES p. 36 Finishing). Leave overnight before applying a second coat. A superior finish can be obtained by adding a coat of clear satin varnish.

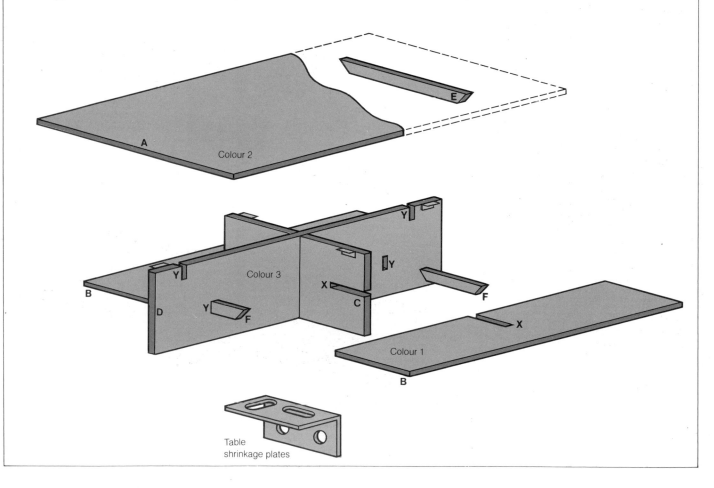

Colour 2

A

E

Y

Y

Colour 3

B

Y

D

Y

F

X

Y

C

F

X

Colour 1

B

Table shrinkage plates

Assembly

9 Slot **C** into **D**.

10 Position the 2 battens **F**.

11 Slide in shelves **B** and secure with 32mm (1¼") screws through clearance holes.

12 Lay the assembled structure onto the upturned top **A** and secure with 4 table shrinkage plates.

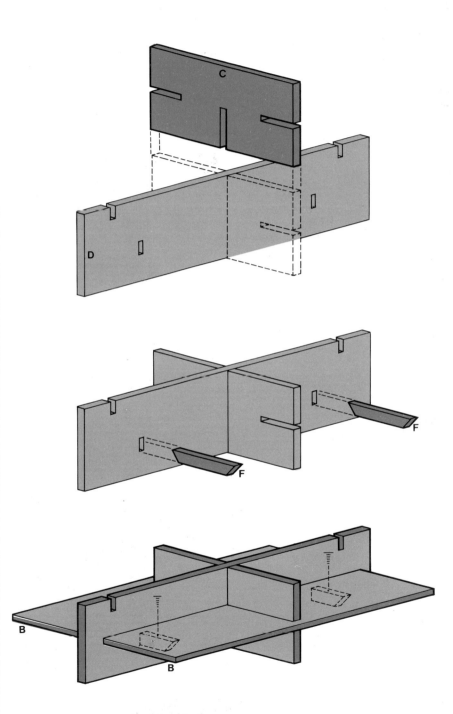

Stacking Units

This item has a place in every room and an endless variety of uses. As a low table, it can fit between sofas, or against a wall, while the design is such that several stacked together can become a storage unit. In unit form the piece can also take up a position in the middle of the room, as the back is exactly the same as the front. The design is so simple to make that you could probably put it together over a weekend.

The colour of finish you choose will depend on what else you have in the room. A light colour may blend with the walls, whereas the cool grey as illustrated on page 18 will effect a stylish contrast.

Try and get the wood suppliers to cut the piece parts for you. As the widths of all the panels are exactly the same, they will set their saw once and put through all the parts on the same setting. This will ensure the correct alignments of vertical and horizontal panels — a very important consider-ation, as the quality of the piece will depend on the flatness and crispness of the edges.

Plans and dimensions

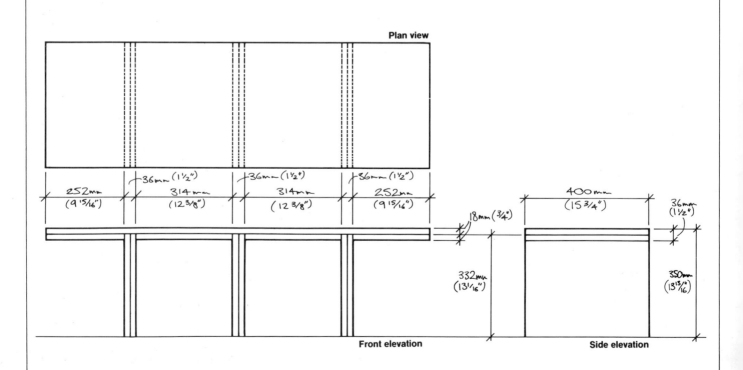

Plan view

252mm (9 ⁵/₁₆″)   36mm (1½″)   314mm (12 ³/₈″)   36mm (1½″)   314mm (12 ³/₈″)   36mm (1½″)   252mm (9 ¹⁵/₁₆″)

400mm (15 ¾″)   36mm (1½″)

18mm (¾″)

332mm (13 ¹/₁₆″)

350mm (13 ¹⁵/₁₆″)

Front elevation   Side elevation

You will need

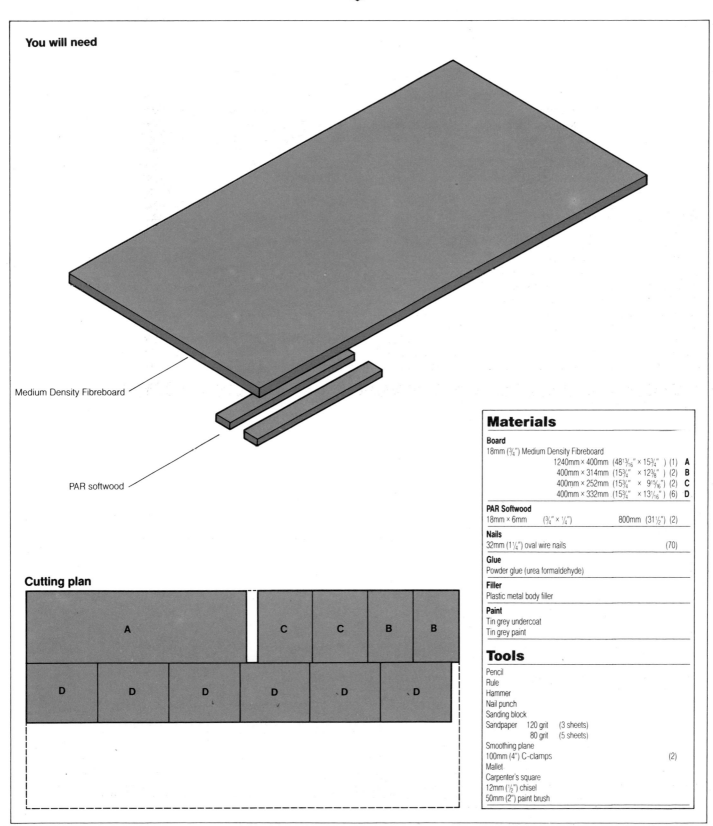

Medium Density Fibreboard

PAR softwood

Cutting plan

A		C	C	B	B
D	D	D	D	D	D

Materials

Board
18mm (¾") Medium Density Fibreboard

1240mm × 400mm	(48¹³⁄₁₆" × 15¾")	(1)	**A**
400mm × 314mm	(15¾" × 12⅜")	(2)	**B**
400mm × 252mm	(15¾" × 9¹⁵⁄₁₆")	(2)	**C**
400mm × 332mm	(15¾" × 13¹⁄₁₆")	(6)	**D**

PAR Softwood

18mm × 6mm	(¾" × ¼")	800mm (31½")	(2)

Nails
32mm (1¼") oval wire nails   (70)

Glue
Powder glue (urea formaldehyde)

Filler
Plastic metal body filler

Paint
Tin grey undercoat
Tin grey paint

Tools

Pencil
Rule
Hammer
Nail punch
Sanding block
Sandpaper   120 grit   (3 sheets)
                  80 grit   (5 sheets)
Smoothing plane
100mm (4") C-clamps   (2)
Mallet
Carpenter's square
12mm (½") chisel
50mm (2") paint brush

Instructions

1 Check dimensions of all the MDF parts against the cutting sheet. Also check the diagonals. Measure from corner to corner twice on each panel. If the difference is above 3mm–4mm ($\frac{1}{8}$″), then that panel is out of square and needs to be cut again. (This may sound drastic, but will be less work in the long run, as you will have less cleaning up to do.)

2 Prepare all the panels for glueing together by very quickly rough sanding the panel faces.

3 Mix up enough glue to join the three leg assemblies together — about 40 cl (14 fl oz) or a beer-can full. Mix to the consistency of single cream (see TECHNIQUES   p. 35 Glueing).

4 Using a flat piece of wood or stiff card, spread the glue on 2 panels **D**. Make sure all the outside edges are well covered.

5 Bring the 2 panels **D** together, and, using 2 C-clamps , gently secure in position. Check that all edges are flush.

6 Following the C-clamp around the assembled panel, drive in with a hammer and nails to secure at 150mm (6″) intervals (see TECHNIQUES p. 34 Nailing). Wipe off excess glue with a hot damp rag and sink the nail head below the surface with a nail punch. Leave to dry.

7 Repeat this operation with the other 2 leg panel assemblies.

8 Lay panel **A** on the floor or a sturdy surface and place a panel **C** flush on one end. Mark across with a sharp pencil and remove panel **C**.

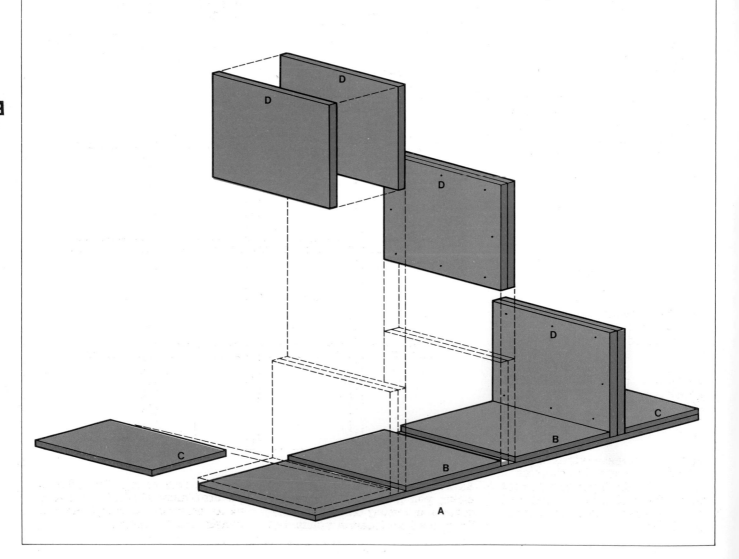

9 Mix a similar amount of glue as before and apply some to the small end area of **A** just marked.

10 Apply glue also to one face of a panel **C** and bring it down onto the end of panel **A** (see diagram). This should be manoeuvred until the 3 outside edges are flush (particularly the 2 side edges) and then secured as before in step 6.

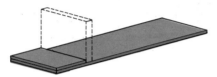

11 Working along the panel from that end, apply the remaining panels **B**, **B**, **C** in that order. Use the leg assemblies to gauge the distance between the panels, not forgetting to keep the outside edges flush and to wipe off the glue while it is wet. Take particular care in cleaning out the grooves.
Leave to dry overnight.

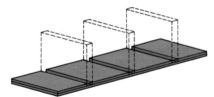

12 Check that the leg panels fit in the grooves and clean out any dried glue with a sharp chisel.

13 Mix up about a teacup full of powder glue and apply it to the 3 surfaces of each groove and to one long edge of each leg panel.

14 Insert these edges into their respective grooves one by one. Tap them home every time with a mallet, being prepared for glue to shoot out of the ends of the groove.

15 Check with a square that the legs are at right angles to the top. Then tack the two strips of pine in position to secure the legs in their proper upright position while the glue sets (see illustration below). Wipe off all excess glue and leave to dry overnight.

16 Clean up all the edges by first of all, and only if necessary, using a smoothing plane. Use a square continually to check all angles.

17 Then, using a sanding block, clean up the edges with, first, 80 grit and then 120 grit sandpaper. Hold the block with both hands and face the direction in which you are sanding.

18 Apply a small radius to the top, no more than 2mm ($\frac{1}{16}$") with 120 grit sandpaper (and block — of course!)

19 Fill all nail holes with plastic filler. Leave to dry and sand flush. The table is now ready for painting (see TECHNIQUES p. 36. Finishing).

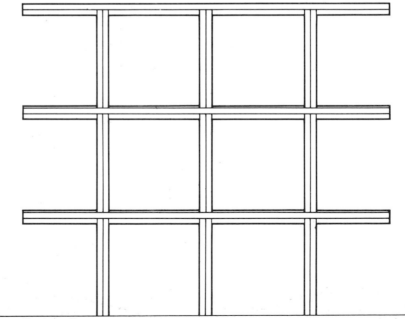

Front elevation

As these tables are so simple to make, you may consider making several and using them in a stack. They need no location points, but merely sit one on top of the other. If you are planning to do this, it is even more essential to keep the leg panels exactly square.

Criss Cross Occasional Table

Here is an occasional table with a little extra sophistication. Although the design requires more skill than other occasional tables presented here, it is not difficult to make. If, as with some of the other projects, you decide to make more than one table, it is best to buy all the materials together and to do all the operations at the same time.

Designed primarily as a lamp table, it would not be suitable for use in front of, or between, sofas. An ideal position would be at the end of a sofa, by a chair, in a corner, or just on its own. The materials will suit a

more sober type of interior and the tinted glass top in particular adds distinction to the design. It has the additional advantages of a very durable surface and of being inexpensive. Finish the underframe before you have the glass cut and polished, and take it with you to the glass supplier so that he cuts the glass as accurately as possible.

Plans and dimensions

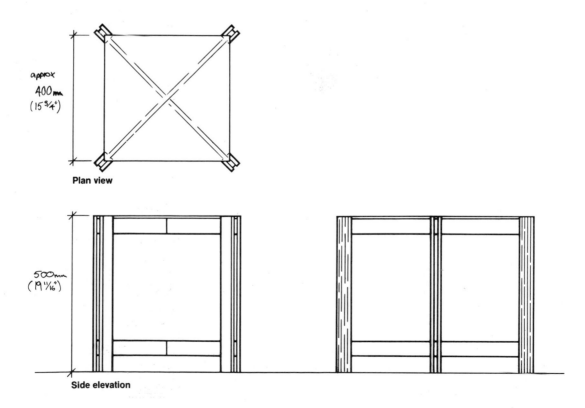

approx 400mm (15¾")

Plan view

500mm (19¹¹/₁₆")

Side elevation

You will need

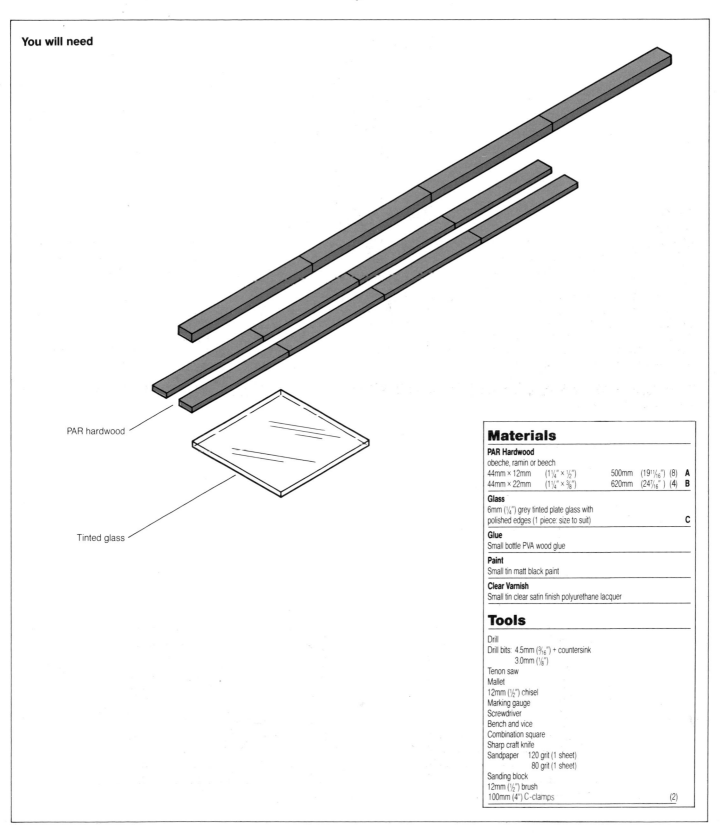

PAR hardwood

Tinted glass

Materials

PAR Hardwood
obeche, ramin or beech

44mm × 12mm	(1¼″ × ½″)	500mm	(19¹¹⁄₁₆″)	(8)	**A**
44mm × 22mm	(1¼″ × ⅜″)	620mm	(24⁷⁄₁₆″)	(4)	**B**

Glass
6mm (¼″) grey tinted plate glass with
polished edges (1 piece: size to suit)   **C**

Glue
Small bottle PVA wood glue

Paint
Small tin matt black paint

Clear Varnish
Small tin clear satin finish polyurethane lacquer

Tools

Drill
Drill bits: 4.5mm (³⁄₁₆″) + countersink
           3.0mm (⅛″)
Tenon saw
Mallet
12mm (½″) chisel
Marking gauge
Screwdriver
Bench and vice
Combination square
Sharp craft knife
Sandpaper   120 grit (1 sheet)
            80 grit (1 sheet)
Sanding block
12mm (½″) brush
100mm (4″) C-clamps   (2)

Instructions

1 Take the leg sections **A** and with a square mark out the positions of the tenon joints on the inside faces, top and bottom (see diagram).

2 Take the horizontals **B** and mark out the shoulders of the tenon joints and the half laps (centre joints). All parts **B** are identical.

3 Mark along the top of the tenon with a marking gauge.

4 Score along the shoulder line of the tenon joints with a sharp craft knife, cutting as deep as you can. Then with a tenon saw, cut a line 1mm (¹⁄₃₂″) to the waste side of this line.

5 Holding **B** horizontally in the vice, knock out the waste with a *sharp* chisel and mallet. Take out a little at a time and trim down to the gauged line exactly. (See TECHNIQUES p. 32.)

6 Trim back to the shoulder line, holding the chisel on the scored line and tapping it with the mallet. Repeat these stages on all 4 parts **B**.

Leg construction, detail

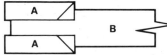

Plan (note 45° notches for glass)

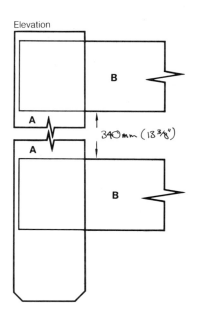

Elevation

340mm (13³⁄₈″)

7 Check that you have marked out the half lap joint centrally on each part **B** and cut with a tenon saw. Finish by knocking out waste down to the halfway line with a sharp chisel. Repeat on all 4 parts **B**.

Assembly

8 With a combination square, mark out the 45° notches at the top of leg parts **A** (7mm/¹⁄₄″ deep, see diagram). Cut with a tenon saw and trim neatly down to the lines with a chisel. These should be designated left and right in four pairs.

9 Take all the leg frame members and prepare them for finishing. Final sand with 120 grit sandpaper and block.

10 Take parts **B** and paint them black (see TECHNIQUES p. 36. Finishing); but leave bare areas to be glued.

11 Take parts **A** and coat them with clear varnish, leaving free those areas to be glued.

Cruciform components B
Order of work

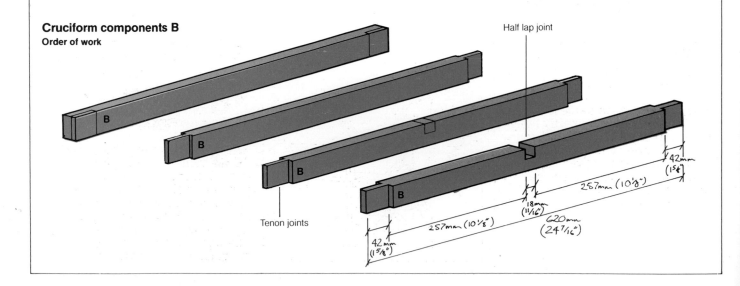

Half lap joint

Tenon joints

42mm (1⁵⁄₈″)

257mm (10¹⁄₈″)

18mm (¹¹⁄₁₆″)

620mm (24⁷⁄₁₆″)

257mm (10¹⁄₈″)

42mm (1⁵⁄₈″)

12 The underframe can now be assembled by taking one set of parts (2 × **B**s + 4 × **A**s) and glueing them up while laid flat on the bench. Place them in position dry to make sure that your cutting is correct and that the 45° notches at the top of legs **A** are handed properly (*ie*, to receive the right-angled corner of the glass top.

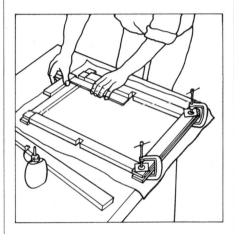

13 Apply glue to the surfaces left free of paint and varnish. Be sparing with the glue and then proceed to bring the respective parts together.

14 Secure each corner as you go round with a 100mm (4″) C-clamp and check that all is square before moving on to the next corner.

15 When the frame is complete, wipe off all excess glue with a hot damp rag. Leave for 6 hours.

16 The second frame is assembled in exactly the same way except that your first frame will need to be interlocked inside it (see diagram) just before you close up the frame with the final horizontal rail **B**.

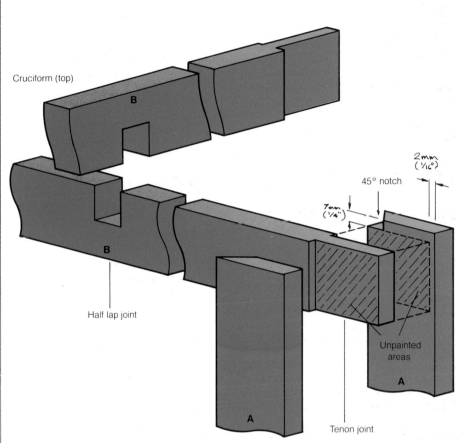

Cruciform (top)

B

B

Half lap joint

A

A

Tenon joint

2mm ('¹⁄₁₆″)

45° notch

7mm (¹⁄₄″)

Unpainted areas

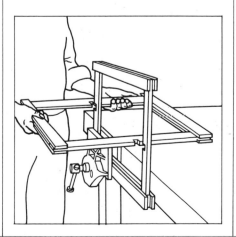

17 Again, make sure all the glue is removed with a hot damp rag and leave to dry.

18 Give the wood a quick rub over with wire wool and a final coat of clear lacquer.

19 Now take the completed frame to a glass supplier and ask them to fit the glass to your frame. Don't allow a greater tolerance than 3mm (¹⁄₈″). *Note*. A second shelf can, if desired be slipped over the lower frame — although not having the notches, the glass will be a smaller size.

Console Table with Angled Legs

This design will look equally good in a hall or at the back of a sofa. It is intended for use as an occasional table, but the dimensions could easily be adapted to make a dining table instead. Here is a project where care and patience will produce a result as fine as anything you could buy, as all the exposed materials are of a quality as good or better than the manufactured equivalent.

Use of plastic laminates has become more widespread in recent years, and while they were originally confined mainly to kitchens and table tops, the material is now used in the most expensive and sophisticated pieces of furniture. Continued advances in laminate technology stimulate designers' interest in the material, and increased usage obviously helps in the acceptance of what was once considered to be a cold material.

Plastic laminate sold in sheet form is 1.5mm ($\frac{1}{16}$") thick. The uppermost skin is 0.5mm ($\frac{1}{64}$") thick, and this is the colour or finish that you see on the completed article. It is bonded onto a backing skin that is 1.0mm ($\frac{1}{32}$") thick. Although this combination is necessary when used for a work surface or table top, on shelves or on pieces of furniture such as this, the thickness is more than adequate. In production the manufacturer would be able to use a foil, which is just the top 0.5mm ($\frac{1}{64}$") skin. Unfortunately, foils are not practical for our use, as you need a press to apply them properly, and they are too brittle to be easily transported or delivered. So we have to buy the full 1.5mm ($\frac{1}{16}$") thick laminate, which is more expensive and, on a job such as this, will be the larger part of the material cost. So treat your laminates with care.

Plans and dimensions

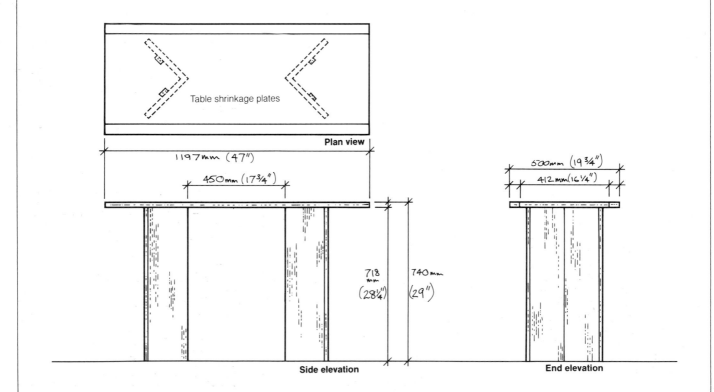

Table shrinkage plates

Plan view

1197mm (47")

450mm (17¾")

718 mm (28¼")

740 mm (29")

Side elevation

500mm (19¾")

412 mm (16¼")

End elevation

You will need

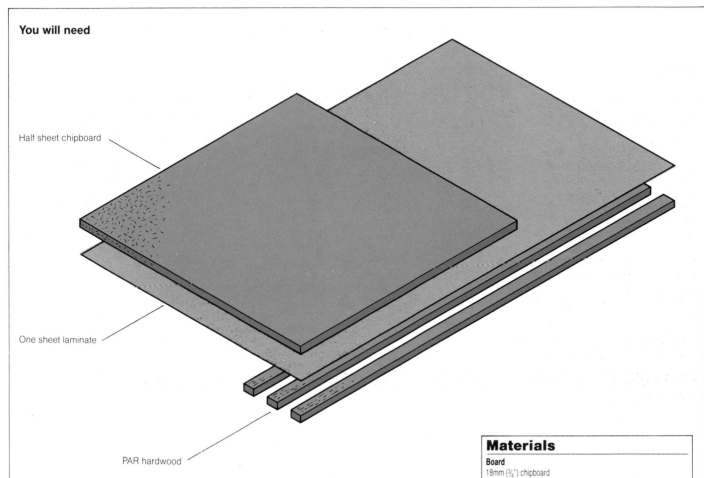

Half sheet chipboard

One sheet laminate

PAR hardwood

The semi-matt black plastic laminate chosen for the table contrasts with its ramin or obeche lip, and it is important to take care over applying the radius to the lip. Don't spoil the job by trying to hurry shaping and working the wood. It helps to cut out a radius template from a piece of card. Running this along the wood will help you find the high spots, which can then be removed. Lastly, try and buy laminate which is protected by a clear plastic film over the face surface. This prevents marking, and it is important not to remove it until the job is finished.

Tools

Rule and pencil
Dowel jig
Drill
Drill bits: 10mm (³/₈″) countersink
4.5mm (³/₁₆″)
3mm (¹/₈″) 2mm (³/₃₂″)
100mm (4″) C-clamps (2)
Plastic glue spreader
1220mm (48″) sash clamps (3)
Smoothing plane
Bench and vice
Sandpaper 120 grit (2 sheets)
80 grit (2 sheets)
Sanding block
25mm (1″) paint brush

Materials

Board
18mm (³/₄″) chipboard

1197mm × 412mm (47″ × 16¼″) (1)		**A**
718mm × 206mm (28¼″ × 8⅛″) (2)		**B**
718mm × 185mm (28¼″ × 7⁵/₁₆″) (2)		**C**

Plastic Laminate

1.5mm (¹/₁₆″) 1205mm × 417mm (47¹/₁₆″ × 16⁷/₁₆″) (2)		**D**
semi-matt 721mm × 193mm (28³/₈″ × 7¹⁹/₃₂″) (4)		**E**
black finish 721mm × 211mm (28³/₈″ × 8⁵/₁₆″) (4)		**F**

*Some laminates have a protective plastic coating. Leave this on until the table is completely finished.

PAR Hardwood

21mm (⁷/₈″) ramin, 1200mm × 44mm (47¼″ × 1¾″) (2)		**H**
obeche, beech 718mm × 44mm (28¼″ × 1¾″) (4)		**J**

*NB These are finished sizes of the lips and should not have damaged ends.

Contact Adhesive
Medium tin

Dowels
50mm (2″) × 10mm (³/₈″) diameter hardwood dowels (40)

Screws
No. 8 × 52mm (2″) countersunk steel (14)

Chipboard Screws
No. 6 × 19mm (³/₄″) roundhead steel (24)

Table Shrinkage Plates
Steel angle plates (6)

Varnish
Small tin clear satin finish polyurethane varnish

Cutting plans
Chipboard

Laminate

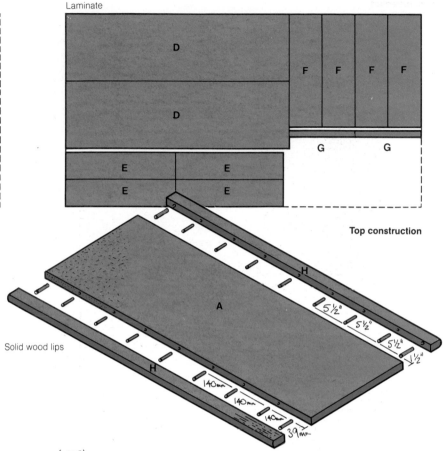

Top construction

Solid wood lips

Instructions

1 The first thing to do is drill for the dowels which join the long edge lips to the table top. So begin by holding the top panel **A** in the vice and mark out all the dowel hole centres as shown in the diagram. It will help also at this stage to clamp the side lips **H** to the board and mark across the respective dowel hole positions. Label these matching surfaces identically.

2 Mark and label the opposite edge of the top panel in the same way. Also mark out one edge on each of the leg panels **B** and **C**, together with their respective solid wood lips.

3 Using the dowel jig, drill all these holes to a depth of 26mm (1″). Remember, all the dowel holes must be centrally positioned along all edges in order to line up the lips perfectly.

4 To add a bevelled edge to the solid wood lips, mark out the edge profiles on all the sides that have not been drilled. On both ends of the lips, scribe a radius that touches the outside edge. Run along the length of the lip from end to end with your finger and a pencil, marking along the top face to join the 2 radii marked out on the ends. (See TECHNIQUES p. 40.)

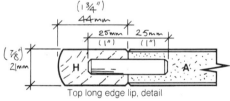

Top long edge lip, detail

5 One by one, place the lips in the vice and with a smoothing plane, plane down to the line. Start by planing a 45° bevel down to the radius and then remove each sharp edge, one by one, until you have a pure radius. Finish smooth with 80 grit sandpaper and finally sand with 120 grit, but only after the edge profile has been properly bevelled.(See TECHNIQUES p. 36.) Start finishing these parts with clear lacquer, but do not cover the areas (ie, dowelled edges) that are to be glued.

6 Take the leg panels **B** and mark out along the face at one side (ie, the edge that has not been drilled for dowels) a centre line for the screw clearance holes (9mm/³⁄₈″).

7 Drill out these holes with a 4.5mm (³⁄₁₆″) bit. Countersink.

8 Hold part **C** in the vice, with the untouched long edge face up and flush with the bench top. Apply some glue along this edge and bring part **B** down on to it, screwing into the glued edge through the clearance holes with 52mm (2″) No. 8 screws. Pilot drill first with a 3mm (¹⁄₈″) bit. Repeat this process (6–8) on the remaining leg assembly. Leave to dry after cleaning off all excess glue with a hot damp rag.

Leg construction

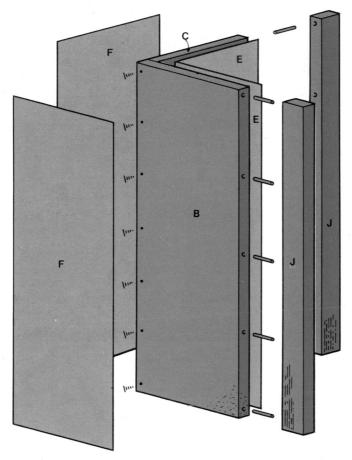

Leg corner detail

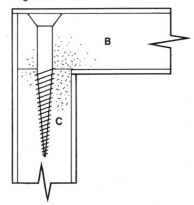

9 When dry, finish flush and smooth the joint at these corners with a keen plane and sandpaper.

10 Now it is time to apply the plastic laminate. (See TECHNIQUES p. 37.) Apply **E** to **C**; push good edge into corner. Repeat on the second leg assembly.

11 Apply **E** to **B**; push good edge into corner. Repeat on the second leg assembly.

12 Apply **F** to **C**. Repeat on the second leg assembly.

13 Plane all edges flush and square with a sharp smoothing plane.

14 Apply **F** to **B**, overlapping the **F** laminate already applied. Repeat on the second leg assembly.

15 Finish flush and square.

16 Apply a 2mm ($\frac{1}{16}$″) 45° bevel to all edges. Finish smooth with 120 grit sandpaper. It is essential to use a sand block otherwise you will scratch the laminate.

17 Apply both pieces **G** to the short edges of the top panel **A**.

18 Finish flush and square.

19 Apply both pieces **D** to face side and to reverse side of **A**.

20 Finish flush and square. Then apply the 2mm ($\frac{1}{16}$″) 45° bevels to the edges.

21 Take the lacquered lips and glue them to the laminated panels, taking care to apply glue inside the holes. Insert all the dowels for location and cramp together, *using packing pieces* to protect the laminate.

22 Wipe off excess glue and put to one side. Use a stick to remove glue from grooves.

23 Place the top panel **A**, best side down, on a carpet or blanket to protect the surface.

24 Pilot drill to 2mm ($\frac{3}{32}$″) and secure with No. 6 screws the table shrinkage plates — 3 per leg assembly (see plans and dimensions).

25 Place the leg assemblies on the reverse side of the top and screw down. Pilot drill to 2mm ($\frac{3}{32}$″) and use No. 6 screws.

26 Now that the table is complete, any protective wrapping to the laminate can be removed.

Cutout Shaped Table

This is probably the easiest project of all. It requires only basic skills, such as being handy with a screwdriver and having the ability to flick paint with a brush. The board, which is first painted with a light coloured base coat, is flicked over with colours of your choice to build up a splatter of speckle-finish. You can of course make the table any size or regular geometric shape you wish, and will be able to adjust the dimensions depending on where you want to use it. Just remember one golden rule – its stability will be wholly dependent on treating the shape as a triangle described by the positions of the three legs. Don't make a square and cut the corner off; it will fall over. Legs or sets of legs are widely available in woodworking shops. They need only to be screwed into the top.

Plans and dimensions

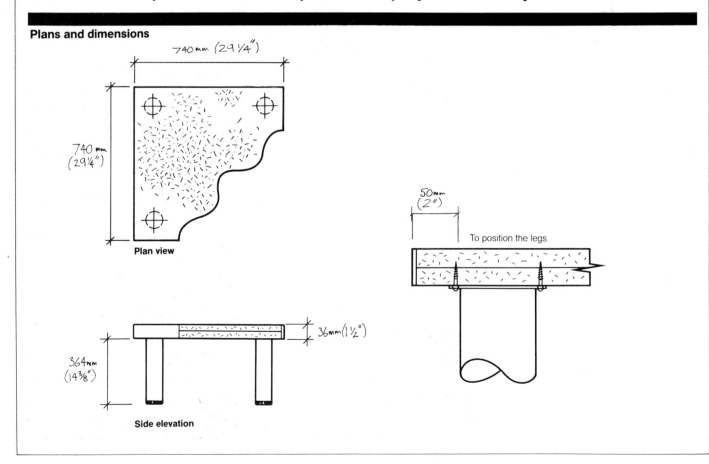

740mm (29¼")

740 mm (29¼")

Plan view

50mm (2")

To position the legs

36mm (1½")

364mm (14⅜")

Side elevation

You will need

Chipboard

PAR Hardwood

Materials

Board
18mm (¾") chipboard
730mm × 730mm   (28¾" × 28¾")   (2) **A**

PAR Hardwood
Obeche, ramin
755mm × 40mm × 5mm   (29¾" × 1⁹⁄₁₆" × ⁷⁄₃₂") (4) **B**

Legs
Widely available in sets for coffee tables
Buy 3 (if possible) at a height of approximately
364mm (14³⁄₈") (3)

Screws
As supplied with legs
No. 8 × 32mm (1¼") countersunk steel| (14)

Nails
19mm (¾") panel pins   (50)

Glue
Small bottle PVA wood glue

Filler
Plastic two-pack metal body filler

Paint
Small tin white undercoat
Small tin light blue paint
Medium tin red paint
Medium tin white paint
Medium tin grey paint

Tape
1 roll 19mm (¾") masking tape

Lacquer
Small tin clear satin finish polyurethane lacquer

Tools

Screwdriver
Hammer
Nail punch
Smoothing plane
Sandpaper   120 grit (1 sheet)
              80 grit (3 sheets)
Power jig saw
12mm (½") paint brush

Instructions

1 Take one of the boards. Drill and countersink four holes along each side and one in the middle (4.5mm/³⁄₁₆″ diameter bit + countersink).

2 Apply glue evenly and sparingly to both surfaces and bring them together exactly, holding with 2 C-clamps as you secure with No. 8 × 32mm (1¼″) screws. Wipe off all excess glue with a hot damp rag.

3 When dry, check that all edges are flush and square. Plane if necessary and sand all edges with 80 grit sandpaper, using a sanding block. Check at intervals as you plane that you are square at all times.

4 Now the wooden edge lippings can be applied. Simply glue both board and edging and apply the lippings, pinning through with 19mm (¾″) panel pins. Start with the opposite edges first and sand the ends flush before you apply the last two. Make sure that the lips overlap the chipboard in every case.

5 When the glue has set, finish all edges flush. Use a smoothing plane on the top and bottom surface only and sandpaper only at the ends. See TECHNIQUES (p. 36 Planing).

6 Using the hammer and nail punch, sink all the pin heads below the surface.

7 Following the instructions on the packet, take the plastic filler and fill all holes, pits and cracks. Leave to dry and then sand down with 80 grit sandpaper and block. Check for any gaps that may have been missed and repeat the process.

8 Form a small bevel of 2mm (¹⁄₁₆″) at 45° to all edges. Do this with 120 grit sandpaper and block, holding the paper tightly against the block as you work.

9 Now apply the primer/ undercoat and, when dry, apply the light blue base coat. See TECHNIQUES (p. 36 Finishing).

10 When all surfaces are completely dry, the remaining 3 colours can be flicked on. This job is *very messy*. If you have to do it in the house, protect the surrounding areas with dust sheets or polythene and raise the board off the floor with objects such as bricks. Flick the colours in rotation 2 or 3 times until you have built up an even texture all over.

11 Leave to dry for at least 24 hours.

Cutting the shape

12 Apply masking tape to the underside and on it draw a freehand curvy line where you want to make your cut. Working from beneath will prevent 'breaking out' when you make the cut.

13 Cut along this line with a power jig saw and a sharp new blade, leaving your finished triangular shape.

14 Remove the masking tape with extreme care.

15 Soften the edges with fine sandpaper and coat every surface with clear lacquer. See TECHNIQUES (p. 36 Finishing).

Drilling boards

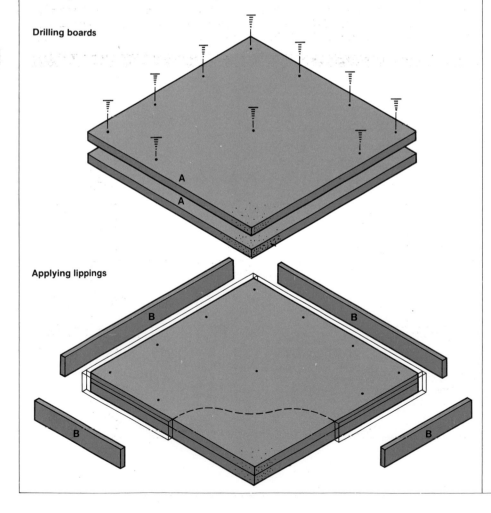

Applying lippings

Adjustable Audio Unit

Basically a hi-fi and video storage unit, this shelving will also double as a desk, because the middle shelf is at working or writing height. The television, video and hi-fi components fit on the middle shelf, while cassettes and records can be stored in the cabinets beneath. The unit can either stand against a wall, or work as a free-standing piece (this, as all other designs in the book, is finished to the same standard on both sides). Although no handles are detailed, you may wish either to plant one on the door fronts, or bevel (45°) the inside top of each door to provide a finger pull.

You can give the unit a hi-tech look by using one of the commercially available hammer finish paints. Contrast this with a patterned coloured laminate on the middle shelf and perhaps use a differently-patterned, but similar-coloured, edge.

Plans and dimensions

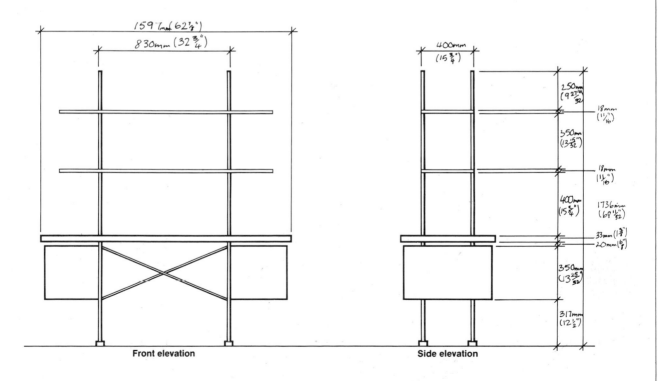

Front elevation

Side elevation

Materials

Board

16mm (⅝") chipboard

1597mm × 597mm	(62⅞" × 23½")	(1)	**A**
1437mm × 80mm	(56⁹⁄₁₆" × 3⁵⁄₃₂")	(2)	**B**
597mm × 80mm	(23½" × 3⁵⁄₃₂")	(2)	**C**

16mm (⅝") Medium Density Fibreboard

526mm × 350mm	(20¹¹⁄₁₆" × 13²⁵⁄₃₂")	(4)	**D**
526mm × 318mm	(20¹¹⁄₁₆" × 12½")	(4)	**E**
350mm × 350mm	(13²⁵⁄₃₂" × 13²⁵⁄₃₂")	(2)	**F**

18mm (¾") Medium Density Fibreboard

350mm × 350mm	(13²⁵⁄₃₂" × 13²⁵⁄₃₂")	(2)	**G**
1370mm × 356mm	(53¹⁵⁄₁₆" × 14")	(2)	**H**

PAR Softwood

44mm × 22mm (1¾" × ⅞")	435mm (17⅛")	(4)	**J**

PAR Hardwood Triangles

22mm (⅞") thick

40mm × 40mm × 55mm (1⁹⁄₁₆" × 1⁹⁄₁₆" × 2⁵⁄₃₂")	(8)	**K**

Dowel

19mm (¾") diameter

45mm (1¾")	(4)

Steel Tube

12mm (½") 16 gauge mild steel tube

1000mm	(39⅜")	(2)	**L**

22mm (⅞") 16 gauge mild steel tube

1736mm	(68¹¹⁄₃₂")	(4)	**M**

Plastic Laminate

Light blue or pattern to choice

1605mm × 605mm	(63³⁄₁₆" × 23¹³⁄₁₆")	(1)	**N**
1605mm × 37mm	(63³⁄₁₆" × 1¹⁵⁄₃₂")	(2)	**O**
605mm × 37mm	(23¹³⁄₁₆" × 1¹⁵⁄₃₂")	(2)	**P**

Screws

No. 8 × 32mm (1¼") countersunk steel wood screw	(52)
No. 8 × 50mm (2") countersunk steel wood screw	(32)
No. 8 × 19mm (¾") roundhead steel wood screw	(4)
No. 8 × 19mm (¾") countersunk chipboard screw	(8)

Glue

Tin contact adhesive
Bottle PVA wood glue
Small two-pack epoxy glue and fixer adhesive

Nails

Oval wire nails 25mm (1")	(100)

Plastic Filler

Small pack

Hinges

Automatic adjustable concealed hinge with integral catch	(4)

Paint

Tin deep pink undercoat
Tin poppy red
Tin mild grey undercoat
Tin flint grey gloss
Tin grey metal primer
Tin hammer finish dark grey paint

Paraffin

or degreasing agent

You will need

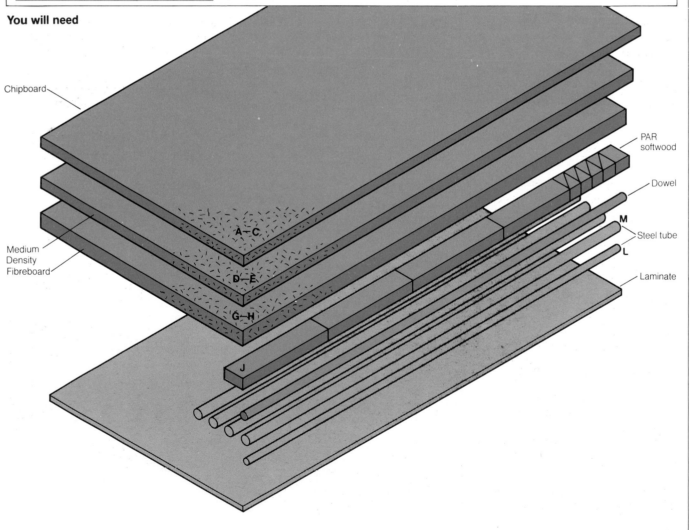

Chipboard

Medium Density Fibreboard

PAR softwood

Dowel

M

Steel tube

L

Laminate

A–C

D–E

G–H

J

Tools

Bench and vice
Drill
Drill bits 3mm (⅛") 9mm (⅜") countersink 4.5mm (³/₁₆")
Screwdriver
1220mm (48") sash clamps   (2)
Smoothing plane
Sandpaper   80 grit (2 sheets)
                   120 grit (2 sheets)
Sanding block
Plastic glue spreader
Brace and centre bit to cut in hinge
25mm (1") or 35mm (1³/₈")   (2)
100mm (4") C-clamps
Hammer
Centre punch
Nail punch
Set square or protractor
50mm (2") paint brush
19mm (¾") paint brush
Metal-working vice

Cutting plans

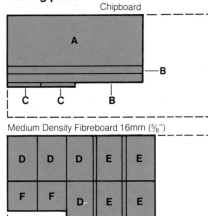

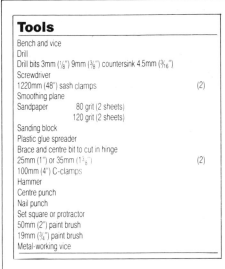

Instructions

1 Take the top panel **A** and place on it the underlinings **B** and **C** to check that they fit.

2 Apply some PVA glue down the complete length of **C** and apply it to the long edge of **A**. Line up the edges flush with **A** and C-clamp in position as you secure with pins.

3 Apply the other underlinings in the order **C**, **B**, **B**, **C**, making sure you line them up properly. Wipe off the excess glue with a hot damp rag.

4 When dry, sand edges with 80 grit sandpaper and block.

5 Screw and glue the spacers **J** to the top **A** with 50mm (2") wood screws. The outside spacer is positioned hard up against the **C** underlining. Distance between the spacers is 188mm (7¹³/₃₂").

6 Take the plastic laminate short facings **P** and apply them to the short edges with contact adhesive (see TECHNIQUES p. 37 Applying plastic laminate). Trim and plane flush.

7 Repeat the process with the long facings **O** and then the top face **N**.

8 Plane the top edges of the laminate flush — being careful not to take off too much — and apply a final bevel with 120 grit sandpaper and block.

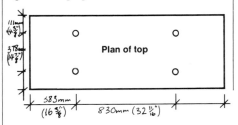

Plan of top

9 On the top face **N**, mark out the hole centres for the four upright poles **M** (see plan, left).

10 Drill right through with a 3mm (⅛") drill and then follow through with a 25mm (1") bit held in a brace. Bore through from the laminate side, taking care not to chip the plastic by ensuring you use a sharp bit.

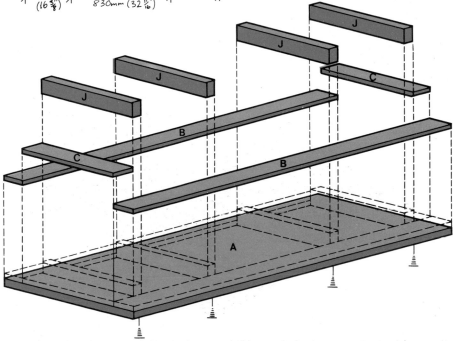

Exploded view of box

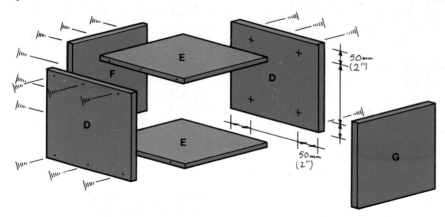

50mm
(2")

50mm
(2")

E

F

D

E

D

G

11 Wrap some 80 grit sandpaper round a piece of 19mm (¾") dowel and sand smooth the inside of the bored holes. Make them as smooth as possible as the poles must pass through them without scratching.

Assembling the two cabinets

12 Drill a series of clearance holes on the piece parts **D** and **F** as drawn above. These should all be 8mm (⁵⁄₁₆") from the outside edge of the following:
D — the 2 long edges
F — all round
Use a 4.5mm (³⁄₁₆") bit and a countersink bit.

13 Take part **E** and hold it in the vice with the long edge uppermost. Hold the reciprocal part **D** on to the edge and pilot drill through with a 3.0mm (⅛") pilot drill. Apply some PVA glue to the edge of **E** and secure with No. 2 × 32mm (1¼") screws. Ensure that the heads are below the surface.

14 Next apply **F** to **D/E** in the same fashion, making sure that the edges are flush.

15 Fit and apply **E** to **F/D**.

16 Lastly, apply **D** to **E/E/F**, screwing down from **F** first.

17 Leave the parts to dry, sand down and fill all screwhead holes with plastic filler (see TECHNIQUES p. 34 Filling holes with plastic filler). Sand flush and smooth.

18 Repeat the process to construct a second box.

19 Take the doors **G** and mark out the position of the adjustable hinges 70mm (2¾") from the top and bottom of the door. Follow the hinge maker's instructions and drill the hole so that the edge is 4mm (⁵⁄₃₂") from the edge (see TECHNIQUES p. 38 Fitting Adjustable Hinges.)

20 Set out the two boxes left and right, and on the 2 inside surfaces **D**, mark out and drill 4 clearance holes, 3mm (⅛") in each box, as illustrated above. Put both these boxes to one side.

21 Now mark out and drill 6 holes (4.5mm/³⁄₁₆") in each top for securing these boxes onto the bearers **J**, as illustrated right.

22 Degrease all the steel tubes with paraffin or a degreasing agent and wipe dry.

23 Take the 4 tube uprights **M** in turn and, working from the bottom, drill 4 times in each pole as follows. Drill a 4.5mm (³⁄₁₆") hole right through the tube at the first centre 357mm (14¹⁄₃₂") from the end of the tube. The next hole is 250mm (9²⁷⁄₃₂") further up, and the remaining 2 are drilled in the other direction, *ie*, at right angles (see diagram below).
You will need to centre punch each position before you start.

Direction of holes to be drilled in M from above

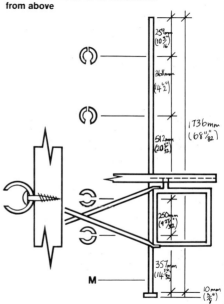

24 When the 4.5mm (³⁄₁₆") holes have been drilled in all 4 uprights, mark out in pairs the second holes to be drilled for the screw head (9mm/¹¹⁄₃₂" diameter). This means that when the 4 poles are in position, you will be able to screw sideways into the boxes from the centre and from front to back into the shelves at the top two positions. As you mark out and label, make sure that the smaller hole is the one which touches the box or the shelf.

25 Take the 2 other tubes **L** and mark out a line 40mm (1⁹⁄₁₆″) from both ends. Put these ends in turn in a metal-working vice so that the marked line aligns with the top of the jaws. Wind up the vice and crush the tube flat — pull towards you and bend the tube over to an angle of 25°. Check with a set square or a protractor. Repeat at the other end, but bend in the opposite direction (see diagram below).

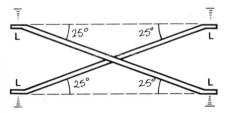

26 Now repeat the operation on the second tube. Drill the flattened ends with a 4.5mm (³⁄₁₆″) diameter drill bit.

27 Clean up the metal tube, file sharp ends smooth, degrease and prime with metal primer.

28 Take the dowel inserts and glue them into the bottom of the tube uprights **M** with glue and fixer adhesive, leaving 10mm (³⁄₈″) protruding as the foot. Secure at the side with a wire nail through a pre-drilled hole.

29 All metal parts should now be painted with the hammer finish grey paint, including the foot.

30 Take the shelves **H** and mark out the centre lines of the upright tubes. Spread glue on a 40mm (1⁹⁄₁₆″) edge of the triangular shelf supports **K** and apply them to the marked out lower edge of the shelf. The centre of the triangular block should be on the marked line. Pin to secure and leave to dry.

31 Check the marking out and drill a pilot hole in each triangle to line up with the positions on the tube.

32 Now is the time to paint the boxes and shelves with undercoat, top coat and, most important, clear satin lacquer over the top. (See TECHNIQUES p. 36 Finishing.) It is important for the final look of the piece to pick out the triangular shelf supports in black. Do this by painting carefully at the end. Make sure all the paint is completely dry before attempting final assembly.

33 Screw the uprights **M** in position on their respective boxes with No. 8 × 19mm (³⁄₄″) countersunk chipboard screws.

34 Asking someone to help you hold them, apply the diagonals **L** to the boxes centrally so that they touch at the crossover. Screw to secure into each box with 4 × No. 8 roundhead screws 19mm (³⁄₄″) long.

35 Thread the top over the tubes **M** and help it fall into the boxes. Screw through from the inside of the boxes with No. 8 countersunk 50mm (2″) screws.

36 Screw the shelves in position to the uprights and fit the doors to the boxes (see TECHNIQUES p. 38 Fitting Adjustable Hinges).

Fixing the cabinet and shelves to uprights M

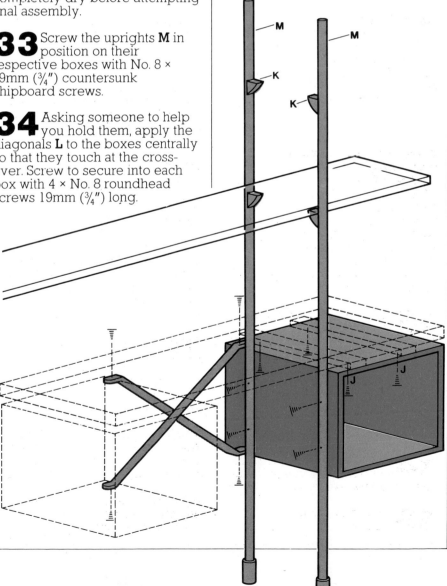

Display Shelving Unit

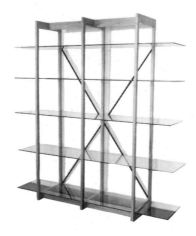

The design here relies on glass shelves and minimal construction to give a clean and unimposing solution to storage problems. The unit itself is probably best sited against a wall, and will look its best if not heavily laden. A weeping plant, a clock and a few treasured objects are better items for display than heavy books, which are better catered for by the storage unit featured on page 120.

Obviously, the glass shelves could be replaced with a board material, but for the uplifting look that glass gives, it is well worth paying extra. Be sure to have the edges polished smooth when you buy the glass to avoid the risk of cutting yourself.

Plans and dimensions

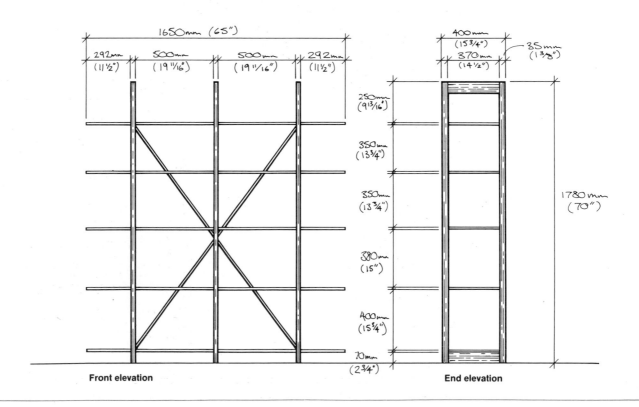

Front elevation

End elevation

You will need

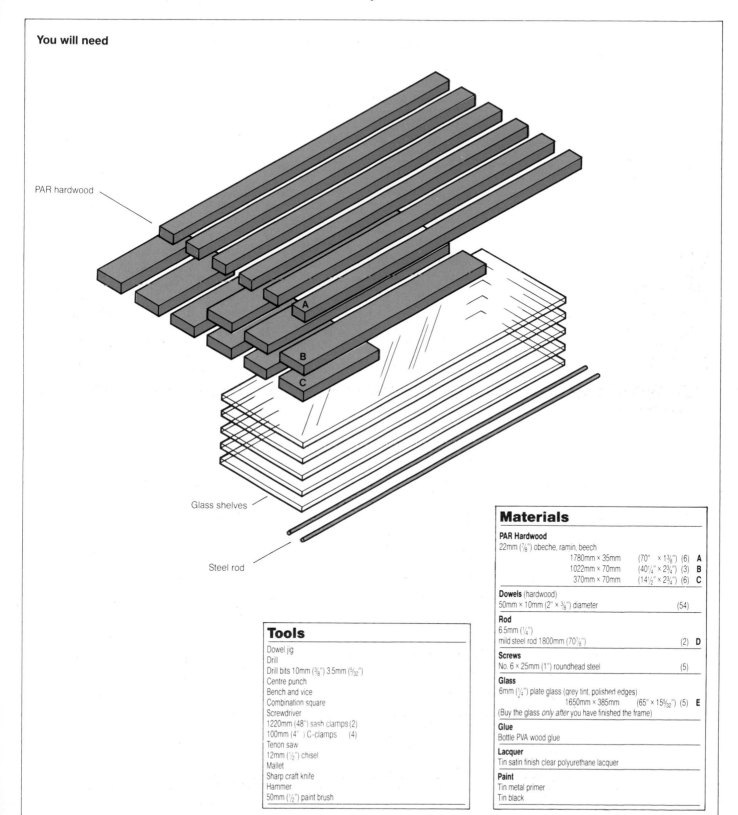

PAR hardwood

A

B

C

Glass shelves

Steel rod

Materials

PAR Hardwood
22mm (⅞") obeche, ramin, beech

1780mm × 35mm	(70" × 1⅜") (6)	**A**
1022mm × 70mm	(40¼" × 2¾") (3)	**B**
370mm × 70mm	(14½" × 2¾") (6)	**C**

Dowels (hardwood)
50mm × 10mm (2" × ⅜") diameter   (54)

Rod
6.5mm (¼")
mild steel rod 1800mm (70⅞")   (2) **D**

Screws
No. 6 × 25mm (1") roundhead steel   (5)

Glass
6mm (¼") plate glass (grey tint, polished edges)
          1650mm × 385mm   (65" × 15⁵⁄₃₂") (5) **E**
(Buy the glass *only after* you have finished the frame)

Glue
Bottle PVA wood glue

Lacquer
Tin satin finish clear polyurethane lacquer

Paint
Tin metal primer
Tin black

Tools

Dowel jig
Drill
Drill bits 10mm (⅜") 3.5mm (⁵⁄₃₂")
Centre punch
Bench and vice
Combination square
Screwdriver
1220mm (48") sash clamps (2)
100mm (4") C-clamps   (4)
Tenon saw
12mm (½") chisel
Mallet
Sharp craft knife
Hammer
50mm (½") paint brush

Instructions

1 Mark out all the dowel joints on the upright frames **A, C, A, C**. It will be evident which surfaces need to be drilled if you first lay out the frames on the floor.
Mark out all the hole centres, working from the same point; *ie*, start with the bottom end of **A** and mark upwards and then take the corresponding part **C**, starting with the bottom edge and working upwards (see plans below).

2 With the dowel jig, drill all these dowel holes to a depth of 26mm (1″) using a 10mm (⅜″) bit.

Frame **ACA**

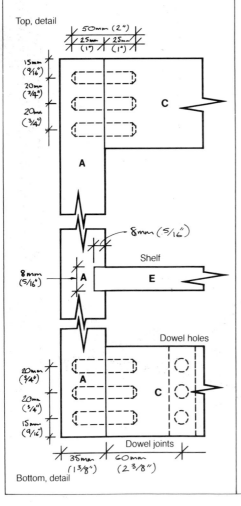

3 Try a 'dry' run to check the fit and label reciprocal parts identically. Then dismantle.

4 Clamp all 6 uprights together (dowel-hole side uppermost) with C-clamps and mark out the cutouts for the shelving (see large diagram, right).

5 Hold in the vice 2 at a time, perfectly lined up, and cut out the notches (see TECHNIQUES p. 32 Cutting Joints).

6 Glue up all 3 frames at the same time. Use newspaper to separate the frames in the clamps and slacken off once to wipe all the excess glue with a hot damp rag. Don't forget to use packing pieces. Leave to dry and clean up with sandpaper and block.

7 Mark out and drill the 2 outside frames for the 3 dowel joints. (The frames are all the same — just leave 1 of the 3 aside.)

8 Mark these dowel holes on all 3 parts **B** also (as drawn below).

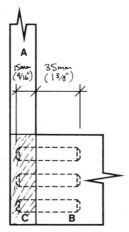

9 Drill all the holes using a dowel jig and a 10mm (⅜″) drill bit.

10 Clamp together all parts **B** and line up exactly.

11 Mark out centrally the halving joint and cut (see TECHNIQUES p. 32 Cutting Joints).

12 Take the centre frame and cut out the half lap notches as shown in the main illustration.

13 Try a 'dry' run to check that everything fits and that all the notches are cut. Then dismantle.

14 Glue up, clamping along the horizontals **B**. Use packing pieces and remember to wipe off any excess glue.

15 Leave to dry, clean up with sandpaper and then coat with clear lacquer. (See TECHNIQUES p. 36 Finishing.)

16 Take the two 6.5mm (¼″) rods and drill 3 holes, 3.5mm (⅛″) in diameter, in each — one exactly in the middle and at either end, each being 8mm (⁵⁄₁₆″) in from the end. Spot each centre with a centre punch before you drill and make sure they are all drilled on the same axis.

17 Paint the rods with metal paint — primer first — and hang up to dry, using string or wire passed through one of the end holes.

18 When dry, mark on the framework a centre point on the back edge of the mid-upright, 810mm (31⅞″) up from the bottom.

19 Drill a 2mm (³⁄₃₂″) pilot hole and, with a No. 6 screw, secure one rod through the second onto the wooden frame.

20 Rotate each rod in turn and fix in a similar fashion at a point where each hole crosses the centre line of its respective upright.

21 When the frame is complete, measure the positions of the glass shelves and check the dimensions against the list of materials. Make sure that your glass merchant understands that the glass has to slide through a finite measurement; *ie*, your narrowest dimension.

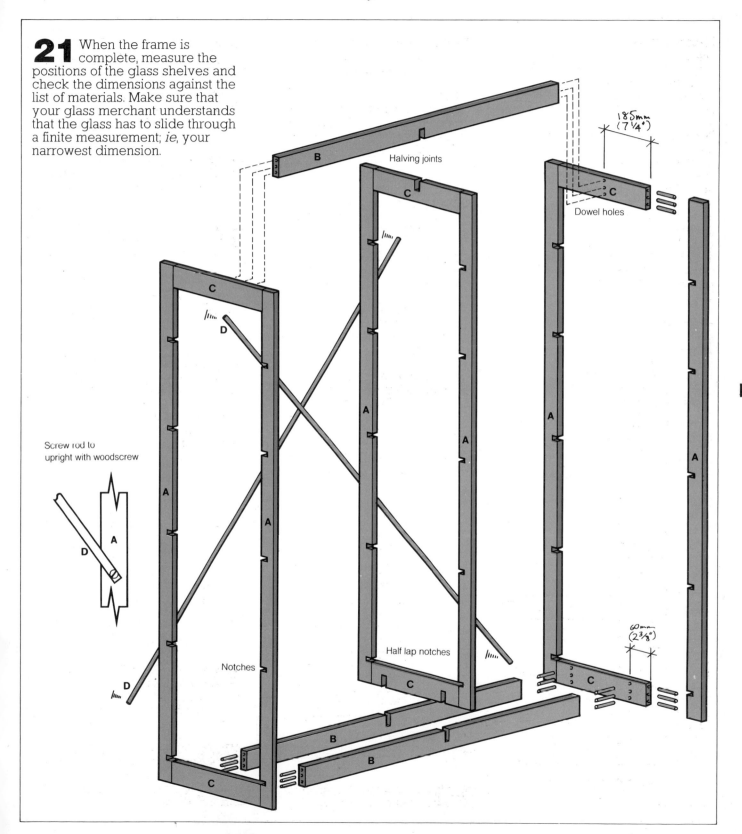

Halving joints

185mm
(7 1/4")

B

C

Dowel holes

C

D

Screw rod to
upright with woodscrew

A

A

A

A

A

A

D

A

A

Half lap notches

Notches

D

C

B

C

60mm
(2 3/8")

D

C

B

B

C

Fireplace Surround

Fireplaces are always a problem. In the past, many people ripped out an existing cast iron fireplace when modernising an old property. Nowadays it is much more acceptable to mix different styles, and modern furniture and accessories look perfectly at ease in old houses, providing the architectural features are painted white, so that one only sees relief and texture.

In the years that have passed since cast iron fireplaces were common, it seems to me that no one has designed a fireplace that is as efficient as were the old iron surrounds – the cast iron acting as a large radiator when it was well installed. So if you have them, leave your old cast iron fireplaces in their hearths. The ones you replace them with will probably be less efficient, and such original features add to the value of your property, because of their visual qualities. If faced with a dreary or gaudy thirty-year-old tiled fireplace, however, you will probably want to take it out fairly quickly.

The surround presented here is designed to fit in all styles of city house, and will most probably blend well with your existing fire back. But first of all you will have to remove your existing fireplace surround. This, like all demolitions, will be extremely dusty. Your chimney breast will need to be made good and probably replastered – at least in part.

Working from the rectangular opening of the fireplace, check and adjust the dimensions of the new surround before you start. Decorate the chimney breast, being sure to fill in all cracks first.

Plans and dimensions

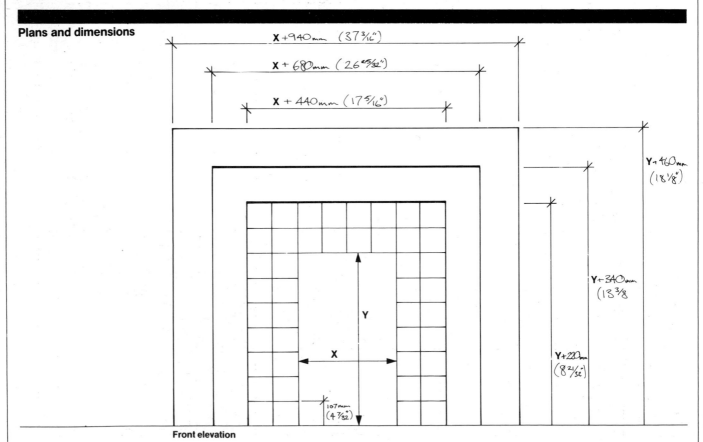

Front elevation

You will need

Tools

Drill
Drill bits: masonry bit for No 10 wall plugs
        3.5mm ($\frac{9}{64}$") pilot drill, 4.5mm ($\frac{3}{16}$"), 5mm ($\frac{7}{32}$")
        + countersink
Sanding block
Sandpaper 80 grit
        120 grit
Screwdriver
Hammer
Nail punch
Power jig saw with new blade
Pencil
Rule
100mm (4") C-clamps
Smoothing plane
75mm (3") paint brush

Medium Density Fibreboard

Cutting plan

Materials

Board
15mm ($\frac{5}{8}$") Medium Density Fibreboard

Panel 1
    (X + 940mm/37$\frac{13}{16}$") × (Y + 460mm/18$\frac{1}{8}$")   (1) **A**
    (Y + 460mm/18$\frac{1}{8}$") × (250mm/ 9$\frac{27}{32}$')   (2) **B**
    (X + 440mm/17$\frac{5}{16}$") × (240mm/ 9$\frac{7}{16}$")   (1) **C**

Panel 2
    (X + 940mm/37$\frac{3}{16}$") × (Y + 460mm/18$\frac{1}{8}$")   (1) **D**
    (Y + 340mm/13$\frac{3}{8}$") × (130mm/ 5$\frac{1}{8}$")   (2) **E**
    (X + 940mm/ 37$\frac{3}{16}$") × (120mm/26$\frac{3}{4}$")   (1) **F**

You will be able to cut parts B, C, E, F, or most of them, from the cutouts of A and D. It is not possible to advise on the best way of doing it in each individual case, as the fire opening size is variable. Work out the sizes of your piece part list and get your supplier to cut it for you. Even if you don't succeed in getting your smaller parts from this waste, they have been designed in smaller pieces to minimize any extra cost.

Screws
No 10 × 50mm (2") countersunk steel woodscrews   (7)
No 8 × 25mm (1") countersunk steel woodscrews   (20)

Glue
Bottle PVA wood glue

Wall Plugs
Plastic wall plugs for No 10 woodscrews   (7)

Nails
25mm (1") oval wire nails   (50)

Filler
Small tin two-pack metal body filler

Tiles
107mm (4") × 107mm (4") ceramic heatproof tiles to choice   (40)
(add 32 more if required as a floor covering)

Tile cement
1 tub

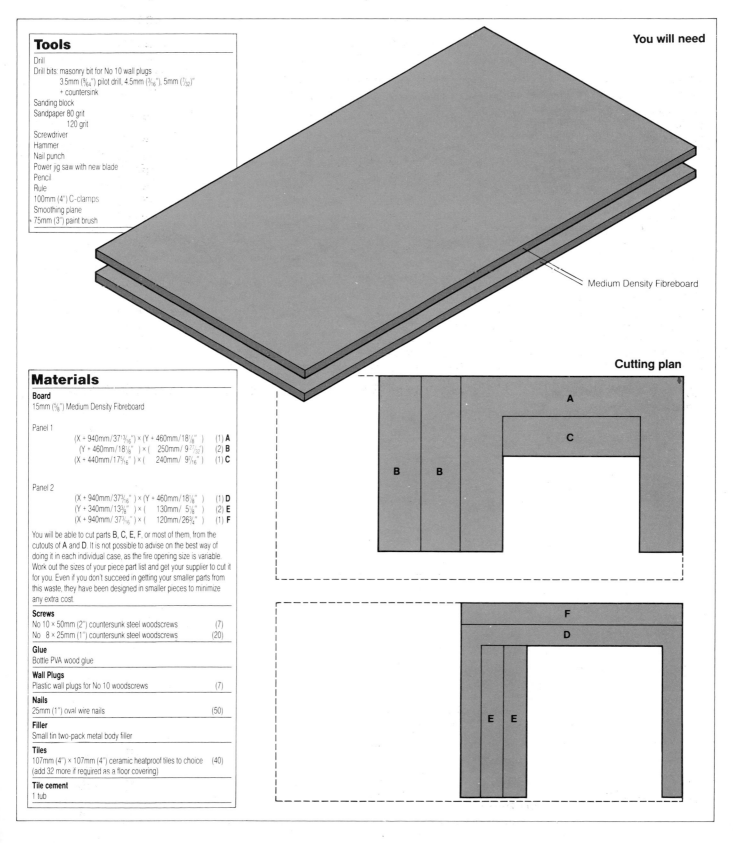

Preparation

Do all the masonry work to the chimney breast before you start to make this fire surround. Rip out the old fireplace and make good, replastering if necessary, so that you have a flat surface up to the fire back. Lay two rows of 107mm ($4\frac{7}{32}$") square heatproof ceramic tiles around the opening, and, if you don't already have a heat-proof hearth (see step 13), I would suggest laying four rows of the same tile out from the fireplace on a solid base. Now measure the opening and check the sizes against the formula below.

X = the width of the fire opening
Y = the height of the fire opening

Panel 1

interior cutout = X + 440mm
($17\frac{5}{16}$") wide
Y + 220mm
($8\frac{21}{32}$") high

Panel 2

interior cutout = X + 680mm
($26\frac{25}{32}$") wide
Y + 340mm
($13\frac{3}{8}$") high

Instructions

1 Calculate the sizes using the formula given and make a cutting list for your supplier based on the cutting diagram shown overleaf.

2 Get the supplier to cut to shape all parts **A** to **F**.

3 Try to get the supplier to remove the cutouts on pieces **A** and **D** also, but if not, do so at home. This should be done with a power jig saw and a new blade. Use a straight edge as a fence (see TECHNIQUES p. 33. Using a jigsaw) to the panel by the appropriate distance from the line to be cut. Be careful not to run over at the inside corners.

4 These parts can now be assembled into their respective panels **1** and **2**.

5 Drill clearance holes as drawn for No 8 countersunk screws. Remember to countersink.

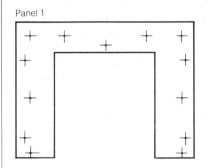

Panel 1

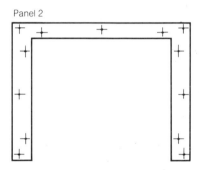

Panel 2

Layout showing position of screws
(dimensions vary according to individual openings)

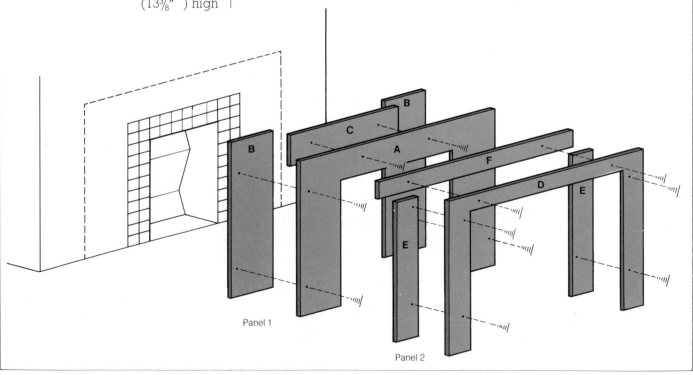

Panel 1

Panel 2

6 Starting with panel **1**, screw and glue parts **B** and **C** to **A**, remembering to pilot drill first. Clamp them together as you go, lining the edges up perfectly. Assemble panel **2** by screwing and glueing parts **E** and **F** to **D** in the same way.

7 Assemble panels **1** and **2** together with screws only. Finish the outside edges of both panels with a smoothing plane. The inside edges can be finished similarly, but use a chisel in the corners that cannot be planed. Finish with sandpaper and block.

8 Take apart and place panel **1** in position over the fire opening. Drill clearance holes for No 10 screws (5mm/$\frac{7}{32}$").

9 Drill through the clearance holes with the masonry bit. Insert the wall plugs into the wall behind the panel and then secure the panel in position with No 10 woodscrews.

10 Now apply glue to both faces to be brought together in panels 1 and 2 and secure as before with No 8 screws. If the panels do not close up properly, tack through with nails to secure.

11 Leave to dry and fill all holes and marks prior to decoration.

12 Paint the finished fire surround the same colour and texture as part of the wall; or, if you have a patterned wallpaper, take the background colour and use that.

13 If you do not have an existing hearth (see section on preparation), lay down a sheet of 10mm ($\frac{3}{8}$") plywood (X + 940mm/37" × 4 tile widths). Lay four rows of tiles to match the fire surround and then level back into the fire. Back with sand and cement. It is advisable to varnish the plywood prior to tiling. Laying the tiles on the plywood base will effectively raise their finished level to just above the carpet.

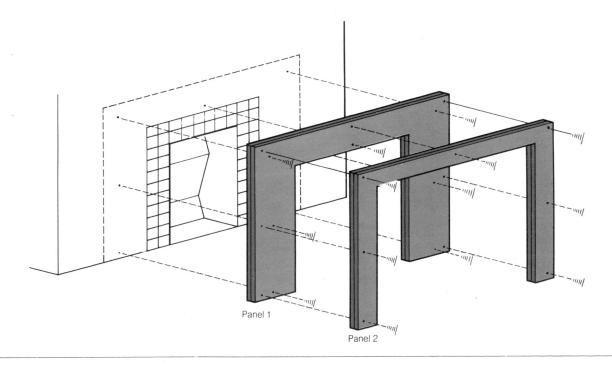

Panel 1

Panel 2

Dining Table

It is the use of black in this range that gives the group such a strong graphic image. The suite would, in my opinion, work less well in any other colour, and would also lose the contrast of the coloured panels. If you feel unable to live with black, however, a mid-grey would be a good second choice. The three designs are not as difficult to make as they may look, but I would advise people without any experience to tackle a simpler project first. The table and sideboard are straightforward enough, the design and detailing following strongly the characteristics of the chair, which itself has been strongly influenced by the difficulty in making shaped piece parts. To solve the problem I have eliminated shaped parts completely. The comfort and support afforded by a correctly curved back is here achieved by defining with care the seat and back angles. An upholstery cushion may also be fitted if desired.

Plans and dimensions

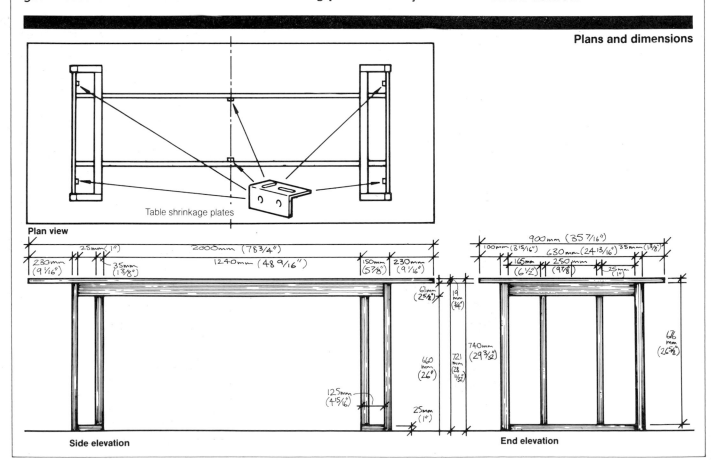

Table shrinkage plates

Plan view

Side elevation

End elevation

You will need

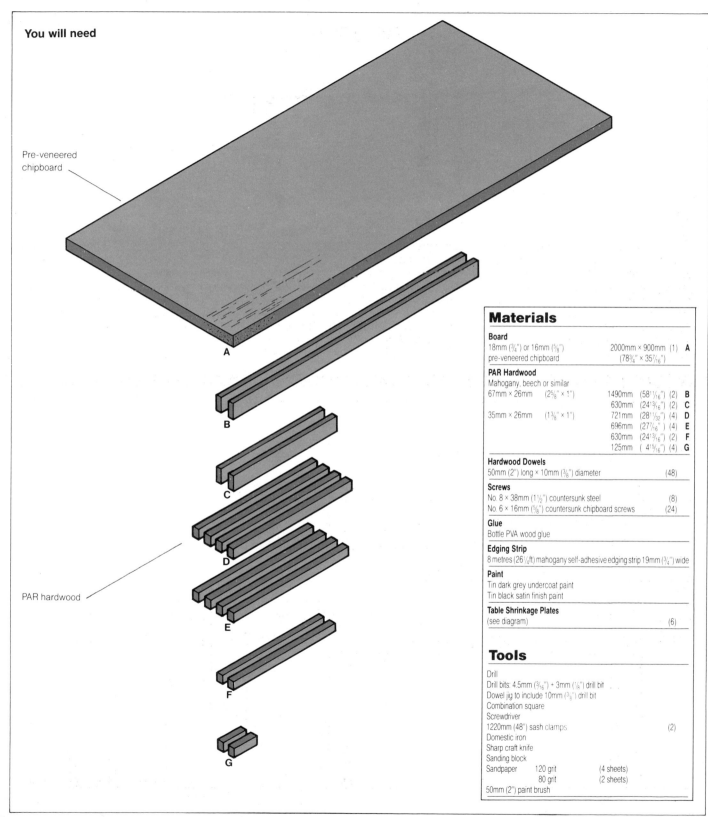

Pre-veneered
chipboard

A

PAR hardwood

B

C

D

E

F

G

Materials

Board

18mm (¾") or 16mm (⅝") pre-veneered chipboard	2000mm × 900mm (78¾" × 35⁷/₁₆")	(1)	**A**

PAR Hardwood

Mahogany, beech or similar

67mm × 26mm	(2⅝" × 1")	1490mm (58¹¹/₁₆")	(2)	**B**
		630mm (24¹³/₁₆")	(2)	**C**
35mm × 26mm	(1⅜" × 1")	721mm (28¹¹/₃₂")	(4)	**D**
		696mm (27⁷/₁₆")	(4)	**E**
		630mm (24¹³/₁₆")	(2)	**F**
		125mm (4¹⁵/₁₆")	(4)	**G**

Hardwood Dowels

50mm (2") long × 10mm (⅜") diameter	(48)

Screws

No. 8 × 38mm (1½") countersunk steel	(8)
No. 6 × 16mm (⅝") countersunk chipboard screws	(24)

Glue

Bottle PVA wood glue

Edging Strip

8 metres (26¼ft) mahogany self-adhesive edging strip 19mm (¾") wide

Paint

Tin dark grey undercoat paint
Tin black satin finish paint

Table Shrinkage Plates

(see diagram)	(6)

Tools

Drill
Drill bits: 4.5mm (³/₁₆") + 3mm (⅛") drill bit
Dowel jig to include 10mm (⅜") drill bit
Combination square
Screwdriver
1220mm (48") sash clamps   (2)
Domestic iron
Sharp craft knife
Sanding block

Sandpaper	120 grit	(4 sheets)
	80 grit	(2 sheets)

50mm (2") paint brush

Instructions

Marking out the dowel joints

1 Take the 2 long underails **B** and mark out the ends for 3 equal-spaced holes. Drill to the correct depth.

2 Repeat the process with the 2 short underails **C**. Then take the 2 long underails **B** and transfer the dowel hole positions to their reciprocal positions on **C** at a point 140mm (5½") from the end of **C**.

3 Continue round the frames, taking the outer legs **D** next, and mark out the top to take the 3 dowels from **C** on its narrow surface. Again, use **C** to mark out reciprocal hole positions.

4 Carry on from the outer legs **D** to the short front rail **G** and onto the long front rail **F**. The joint between **F** and the inner leg **E** is at a point 165mm (6½") in from the end of **F**.

Positioning dowel holes for drilling

PAR hardwood   D-G

PAR hardwood   B-C

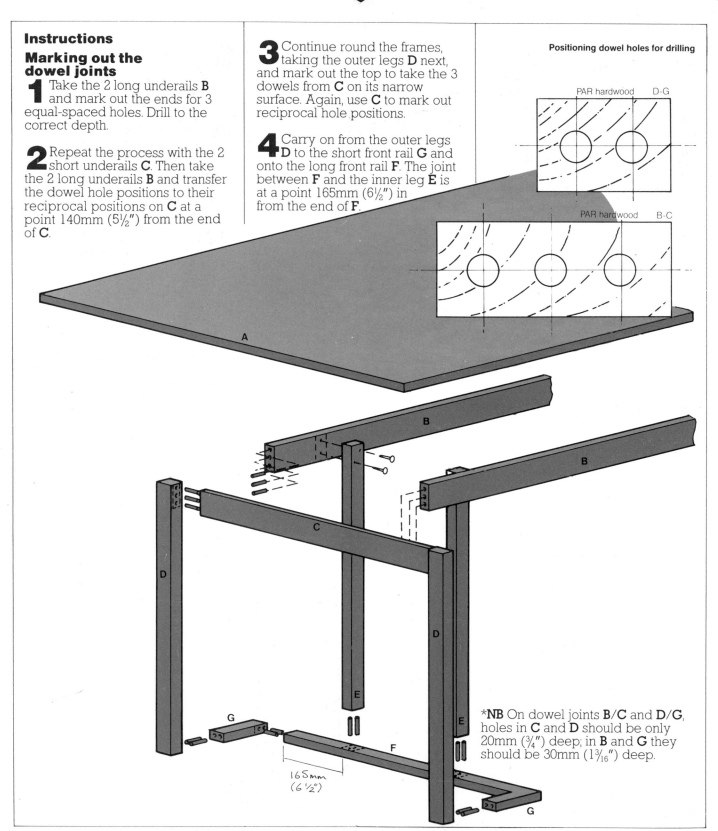

*NB On dowel joints **B/C** and **D/G**, holes in **C** and **D** should be only 20mm (¾") deep; in **B** and **G** they should be 30mm (1³⁄₁₆") deep.

165mm
(6½")

110

5 Take the inner legs **E** and drill two clearance holes 4.5mm (³⁄₁₆″) at the top of the legs (*ie*, not the dowel hole end). These should be marked out on the 35mm (1³⁄₈″) face and equally spaced.

6 Take the inner legs **E** and position the tops onto the long underail **B** at a point 100mm (4″) in from each end. Pilot drill through the legs with a 3mm (¹⁄₈″) bit.

7 Try a 'dry' assembly to make sure all the joints have been correctly drilled and that the holes are deep enough.

8 Glue up in the following order:

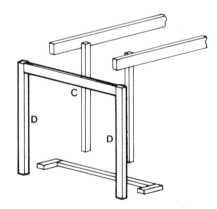

● **D** to **C** to **D**. Lay these frames as a pair in a single sash clamp separating with newspaper.

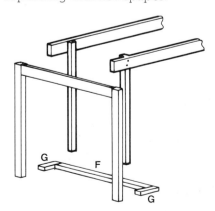

● **G** to **F** to **G**. Repeat as above.

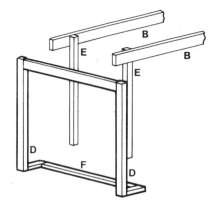

● Stand upright for final assembly. Clamp **G** to **D** and screw **E** to **B**. Drop into position on **F**, with dowels. The top frame should be clamped across from **E** to **C**. (See TECHNIQUES p. 35 Clamping) Wipe off all glue with a hot damp rag. Leave to dry.

9 Take the top panel **A** and, using a hot iron, edge it with the self-adhesive edging strip. Any burn marks will be covered later by black paint. After you have finished one edge, trim it with a sharp craft knife and sandpaper before you start the next one. When trimming with the knife, work in the same direction as when planing (see TECHNIQUES p. 36 Planing). Try a small section first.

10 Finish the frame and the top separately (see TECHNIQUES p. 36 Finishing).

11 Final assembly of the table is made by putting the table top upside down on the carpet and centralizing the frame on top of it. Screw the frame to the top with 6 table shrinkage plates that have been pre-attached to the under-frame in the appropriate positions (see plans and dimensions).

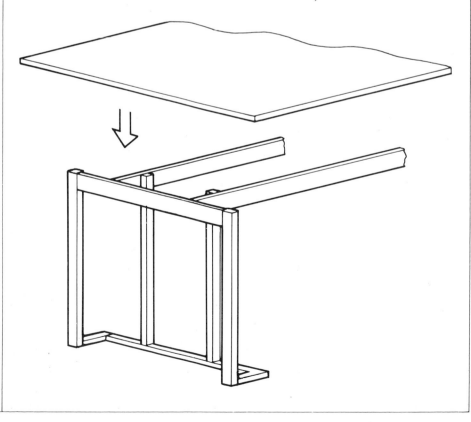

Dining Chair

While chairs require no particular skill to make, producing six separate pieces is a long business, no matter how simple the design, and will involve a substantial investment in materials; so be sure in your own mind that you are going to see the project through.

The design employs hardwood because softwood sections of timber would be much thicker, and therefore visually more clumsy. Because there are so many joints to complete, I have suggested the use of a dowel jig. Always choose a 10mm

(³⁄₈″) dowel where possible, as it has substantially more strength than the smaller alternatives, and buy your own dowel jig. You may think this an unnecessary expense, but it

will without doubt make the drilling twice as quick, twice as accurate, and, perhaps even more important, spare you from being irritated by the inaccuracy of bad drilling.

If you are making four or six chairs, treat the process like a production line. Carry out each operation described in the text on every piece of wood, and label each piece part with a letter of the alphabet — 24 off piece part '**A**' and so on. This is also the best way to order the materials, so that the supplier can give you accurately-cut identical piece parts.

Plans and dimensions

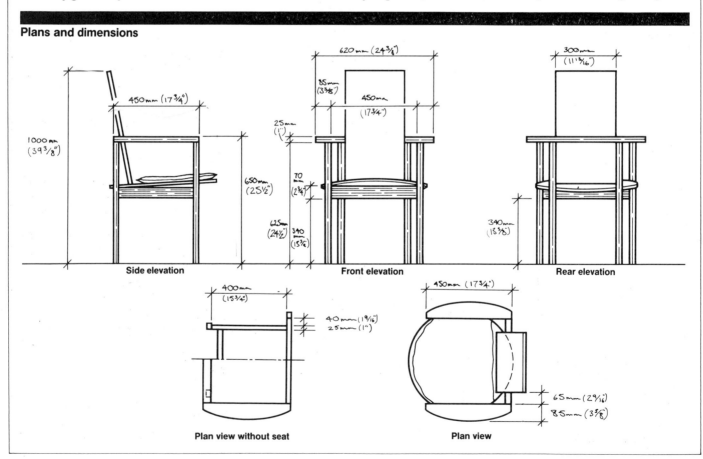

Side elevation

Front elevation

Rear elevation

Plan view without seat

Plan view

You will need

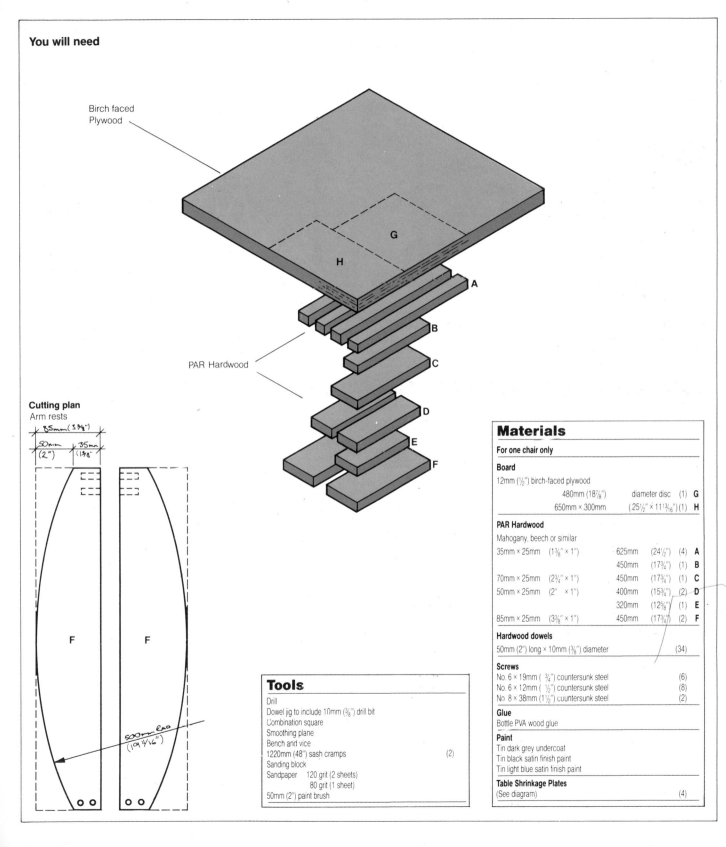

Birch faced Plywood

PAR Hardwood

G

H

A

B

C

D

E

F

Cutting plan
Arm rests

85mm (3⅜")

50mm (2")   35mm (1⅜")

F   F

500mm RAD (19 ¼/16")

Materials

For one chair only

Board
12mm (½") birch-faced plywood

480mm (18⅞")	diameter disc	(1)	**G**
650mm × 300mm	(25½" × 11¹³⁄₁₆")	(1)	**H**

PAR Hardwood
Mahogany, beech or similar

35mm × 25mm (1⅜" × 1")	625mm	(24½")	(4)	**A**
	450mm	(17¾")	(1)	**B**
70mm × 25mm (2¾" × 1")	450mm	(17¾")	(1)	**C**
50mm × 25mm (2" × 1")	400mm	(15¾")	(2)	**D**
	320mm	(12⅝")	(1)	**E**
85mm × 25mm (3⅜" × 1")	450mm	(17¾")	(2)	**F**

Hardwood dowels
50mm (2") long × 10mm (⅜") diameter	(34)

Screws
No. 6 × 19mm (¾") countersunk steel	(6)
No. 6 × 12mm (½") countersunk steel	(8)
No. 8 × 38mm (1½") countersunk steel	(2)

Glue
Bottle PVA wood glue

Paint
Tin dark grey undercoat
Tin black satin finish paint
Tin light blue satin finish paint

Table Shrinkage Plates
(See diagram)	(4)

Tools
Drill
Dowel jig to include 10mm (⅜") drill bit
Combination square
Smoothing plane
Bench and vice
1220mm (48") sash cramps   (2)
Sanding block
Sandpaper   120 grit (2 sheets)
            80 grit (1 sheet)
50mm (2") paint brush

Instructions

1 Take all the hardwood parts and mark out the positions of the dowels. Use the illustration to work out the positions and the dowelling jig to help you drill the holes in the right places. Also drill and countersink 4.5mm (³⁄₁₆″) clearance holes in the back rail **B**. **NB** Where the thickness of a piece part prevents you drilling to a full 25mm (1″) depth, drill to 20mm (³⁄₄″) and then drill to 30mm (1¼″) on the reciprocal part.

2 Take the 2 arms **F** and mark out the curve to the outside edge (this has been defined by the position of the dowels).
If you are making 6 chairs, it is best to make a template from cardboard and draw round it. You may find a household object (such as a circular table top) that you can use as a guide.
Cut the shapes roughly with a saw; *ie*, take a triangular shape off both ends and finish to the line with a smoothing plane. Finish-sand with 80 grit sandpaper and block.

3 Practise a 'dry' assembly before glueing, making sure you have enough packing pieces for cramping.

4 Glue up in the following order:
● **D** to **E** to **D** — clamp
● **C** to **D/D** — clamp
● Legs **A** to seat frame — cramp in position and use your eye to line up the legs so that they are parallel. Take care to get the rear joint to the inside of the back legs **A** (see diagram).
● Fit **F**, **B** and **F** to the completed frame below. The fronts of the arms can be weighted down, while a sash clamp is spanned across the arms at their widest point. You will need a spacer of 450mm (17¹¹⁄₁₆″) length to prevent the fronts of the arms being forced inwards.
NB Leave sub-frames to dry between each step.

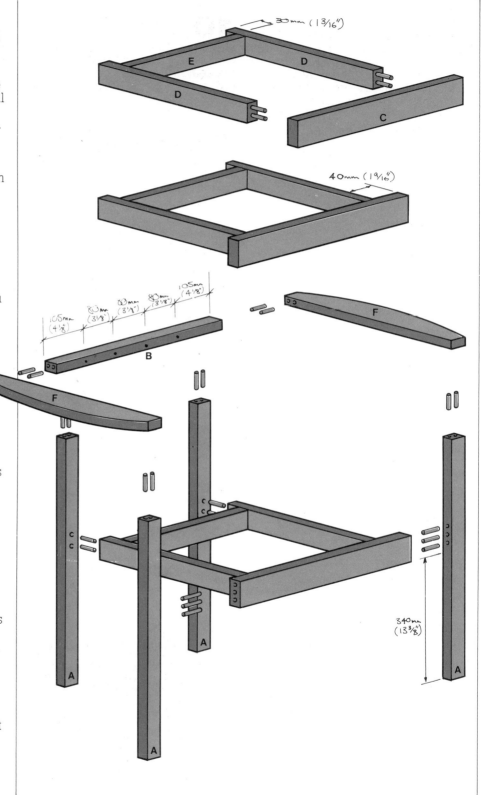

5 The easiest way to cut out the disc is with a power jig saw, but if you don't have one of these you will need to finish down to the line with a plane. Finish with sandpaper and block, adding a shallow radius to the front edge. Leave a crisp edge. Do this with a sharp plane.

6 Mark out the slot in the seat, as drawn below. This will always be at right angles to a line drawn through the centre of the disc. (See illustration on p. 153 Making a rudimentary compass.)

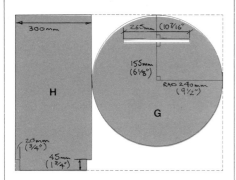

7 Cut out the slot by drilling a 10mm (3/8″) hole at one end to start and then cut out the hole with a power jig saw. If you don't have one, drill as many holes as possible with the drill, then break through them with a pad saw file and chisel. (It will, however, be much easier — and neater — to borrow a power jig saw.)

8 Take the back panel **H** and cut out the 2 notches (see diagram) before you finish sanding.

9 Paint the frame and the 2 panels separately. (See TECHNIQUES p. 36 Finishing.)

10 Final assembly of the chair is achieved by screwing table shrinkage plates (3) to the seat frame and securing the seat in position with 12mm (1/2″) screws (see diagram below).

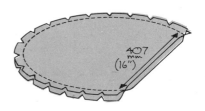

— Table shrinkage plates —

11 Secure the back panel from the outside face of the back rail with 2 × No. 8 wood screws. Pilot drill through the clearance holes, taking care not to break through. Fill the countersinks with filler and paint them black to conceal.

Upholstered pad for dining chair

For each pad you will need:

2 circles of chosen fabric (preferably a stone-coloured upholstery fabric) 514mm (20″) in diameter.

1 circular piece of 18mm (3/4″) resilient foam, 465mm (18 5/16″) diameter.

2 matching ribbons 350mm (13 3/4″) long (these will secure the pad to the seat by being threaded through the slit in the plywood seat at either side of the back panel).

1 Using a pair of compasses, draw out two circles on the underside of your length of fabric — one at 257mm (10 1/8″) radius and another at 242mm (9 1/2″) radius. Cut along the line of the larger of the two circles.

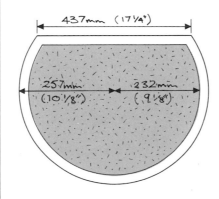

2 Place the two pieces of fabric face to face and pin. Sew along the second line to give a 15mm (5/8″) edge to the seam.

3 Create a flat edge by cutting off part of the circle and notch around the stitching as shown in the diagram below.

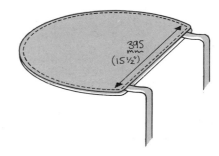

4 Turn the cushion inside out and insert the pre-cut foam piece.

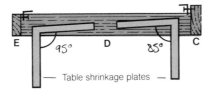

5 Close the open end by folding the material inwards and pinning. Stitch along the straight line 6mm (1/4″) from the outside edge, inserting and stitching through the ribbon ends as you go (see diagram). Continue around the whole perimeter to give a stitched border.

Sideboard

This sideboard completes the dining room suite. As you will see, the under-frame reflects that of the dining table and is designed to provide a serving surface for the table as well as to allow for storage of crockery and cutlery. Inside there are two compartments (you may wish to put in a shelf on adjustable sockets here). Again, as in other designs, the back is finished as well as the front so that the sideboard does not necessarily need to stand against a wall. For this piece of furniture, I have used a gap around the doors as a feature, both as a visual detail and also as a device to minimize the effect of tolerance incurred in adjusting the doors. Do read the section on adjustable hinges (p. 38) to understand fully how they work.

Plans and dimensions

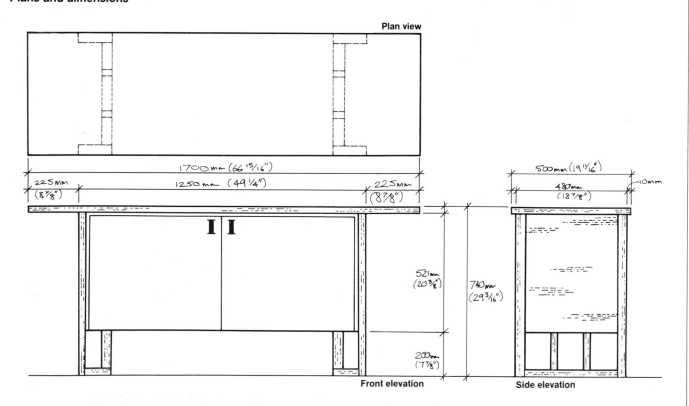

Plan view

1700mm (66 15/16")
1250mm (49 1/4")
225mm (8 7/8")
225mm (8 7/8")

500mm (19 11/16")
480mm (18 7/8")
10mm

521mm (20 3/8")
740mm (29 3/16")
200mm (7 7/8")

Front elevation

Side elevation

You will need

Pre-veneered chipboard

Medium Density Fibreboard

PAR hardwood

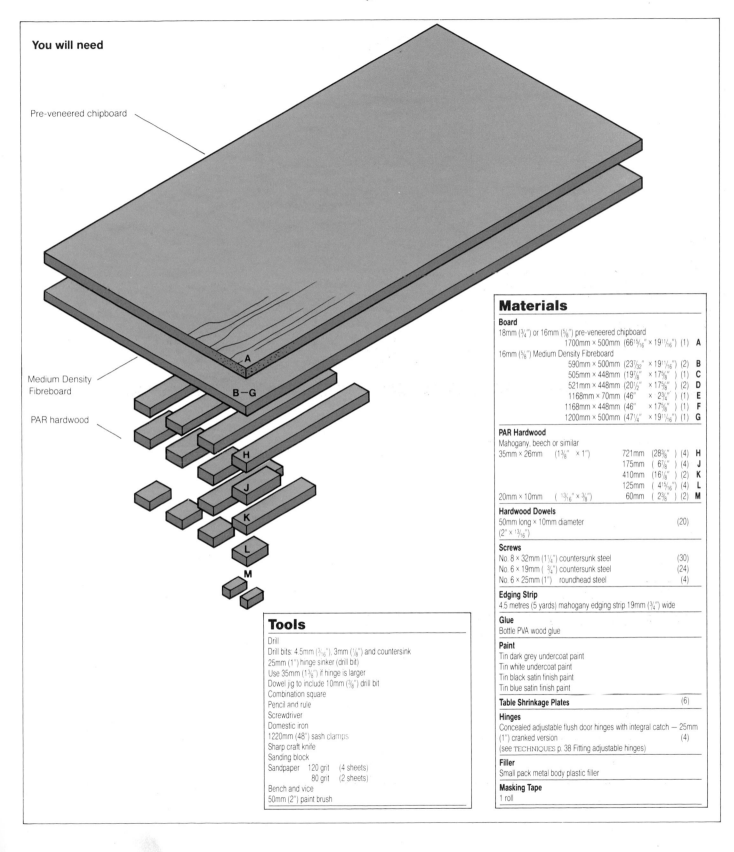

Materials

Board

18mm (¾") or 16mm (⅝") pre-veneered chipboard

1700mm × 500mm (66¹⁵⁄₁₆" × 19¹¹⁄₁₆")	(1)	**A**

16mm (⅝") Medium Density Fibreboard

590mm × 500mm (23⁷⁄₃₂" × 19¹¹⁄₁₆")	(2)	**B**
505mm × 448mm (19⅞" × 17⅝")	(1)	**C**
521mm × 448mm (20½" × 17⅝")	(2)	**D**
1168mm × 70mm (46" × 2¾")	(1)	**E**
1168mm × 448mm (46" × 17⅝")	(1)	**F**
1200mm × 500mm (47¼" × 19¹¹⁄₁₆")	(1)	**G**

PAR Hardwood

Mahogany, beech or similar

35mm × 26mm (1⅜" × 1")	721mm (28⅜")	(4)	**H**
	175mm (6⅞")	(4)	**J**
	410mm (16⅛")	(2)	**K**
	125mm (4¹⁵⁄₁₆")	(4)	**L**
20mm × 10mm (¹³⁄₁₆" × ⅜")	60mm (2⅜")	(2)	**M**

Hardwood Dowels

50mm long × 10mm diameter	(20)
(2" × ¹³⁄₁₆")	

Screws

No. 8 × 32mm (1¼") countersunk steel	(30)
No. 6 × 19mm (¾") countersunk steel	(24)
No. 6 × 25mm (1") roundhead steel	(4)

Edging Strip

4.5 metres (5 yards) mahogany edging strip 19mm (¾") wide

Glue

Bottle PVA wood glue

Paint

Tin dark grey undercoat paint
Tin white undercoat paint
Tin black satin finish paint
Tin blue satin finish paint

Table Shrinkage Plates	(6)

Hinges

Concealed adjustable flush door hinges with integral catch — 25mm
(1") cranked version (4)
(see TECHNIQUES p. 38 Fitting adjustable hinges)

Filler

Small pack metal body plastic filler

Masking Tape

1 roll

Tools

Drill
Drill bits: 4.5mm (³⁄₁₆"), 3mm (⅛") and countersink
25mm (1") hinge sinker (drill bit)
Use 35mm (1⅜") if hinge is larger
Dowel jig to include 10mm (⅜") drill bit
Combination square
Pencil and rule
Screwdriver
Domestic iron
1220mm (48") sash clamps
Sharp craft knife
Sanding block
Sandpaper 120 grit (4 sheets)
80 grit (2 sheets)
Bench and vice
50mm (2") paint brush

Instructions

1 Take the top panel **A** and, using a hot iron, edge it with the self-adhesive edging strip. Any burn marks will later be covered by black paint. After you have finished one edge, trim it with a sharp craft knife and sandpaper before you move on to the next. When trimming with the knife, work in the same direction as when planing. (See TECHNIQUES p. 36 Planing.) Finish all edges with sandpaper.
Put to one side.

2 Mark out and drill the dowel joints in exactly the same way as for the dining table (see p. 110).

3 Try a 'dry' assembly to make sure both frames fit together well. Label the joints and redrill deeper if necessary.

4 Glue up the frames as follows:
L to **K** to **L**. Lie the two assemblies as a pair in a single sash clamp separating with newspaper.
Wipe off the glue with a hot damp rag and leave all the under-frame parts to one side.

Cutting plan
Medium Density Fibreboard

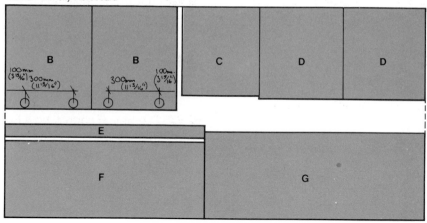

5 The MDF carcase is now to be screwed together, so mark out all the parts — **D**, **E**, **F**, **G** — for the clearance hole centres (4.5mm/³⁄₁₆″ diameter) to be drilled 8mm (³⁄₄″) in from the outside edges.
Taking **D**, mark out 3 equal-spaced holes on each side and 3 on the bottom only. Mark 2 more at the top front corner (see large diagram, right).
Taking **G**, drill 3 equal-spaced holes along either end, a total of 7 along one long edge only, and 3 more in the middle.
Taking **F**, drill 7 holes on the bottom panel. Make sure that the 3 in the centre are accurately positioned.
Taking **E**, drill 2 holes centrally marked on this front rail.

6 Countersink these holes from the direction in which they are to be screwed (see diagram).

7 Notch out centre panel **C** as drawn.

8 Hold the centre panel **C** upside down in the vice so that the bottom edge is flush with the bench top. Squeeze some PVA glue along the exposed edge and place the bottom panel **F** in position with the 3 countersinks uppermost. Holding the two panels flush and in position, drill through with a 3mm (¹⁄₈″) pilot drill. Screw to secure and wipe off excess glue.

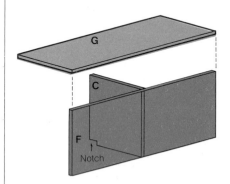

9 Place this assembly front downwards on the floor and screw on the back panel **G** in the same fashion, lining up the flush edge at all times. Leave 16mm (⁵⁄₈″) at each end for the end panels.

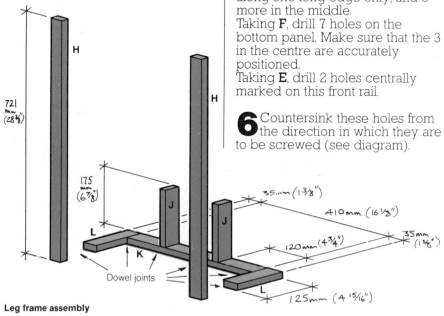

Leg frame assembly

10 Do the same for the end panels **D** and finally the front horizontal rail **E**. Wipe off all excess glue and leave to dry.

11 All the screw heads and countersinks on the outside of the cabinet must now be filled with plastic filler. Follow the maker's instructions carefully.

12 Take the two door panels and mark them out for the hinge positions. The placing of the hinges should be explained on the package in which they are bought, but if not, as a guide, drill the 25mm (1") diameter hole so that its edge is 2mm (1/16") from the edge of the door and its depth is 13mm (1/2"). These hole centres will correspond with their relative positions on the cabinet end panels.
(If you have been unable to buy a cranked hinge get an ordinary one and pack out from the inside surface of the end panel to the required thickness.) (See TECHNIQUES p. 38.) This will be evident if you set up the door with the hinge in it and put it onto the cabinet with the 10mm (3/8") step on the outside and then measure how big a spacer you need. You can of course work this out on paper (see diagram). Measure the space between the back of the hinge arm and the outside of the cup.
Remove the hinges and sand down the doors ready for painting.

Screwing leg frames to carcase

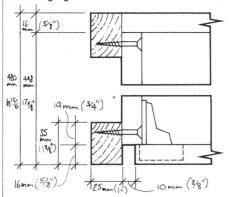

13 Drill clearance holes for the handles 3mm (1/8") in diameter in the top inside corners of the doors.

14 Paint the cabinet light blue inside and out, including the doors (see TECHNIQUES p. 36 Finishing).

15 The legs **H** should now be screwed to the carcase. Taking a scrap piece of 16mm (5/8") MDF, line up the legs at the front of the carcase so that the edge of the leg extends beyond the side panel by 16mm (5/8"). In this way it will eventually end up flush with the door front. Pilot drill (3mm/1/8" diameter) and screw to secure. Work around the cabinet; the back legs should line up flush with the outside of the back panel.

16 Turn the cupboard over and glue the dowel joints to the under-frame, **L** to **K** to **L** (see step 4), completing the leg frame with parts **J**. Clamp and leave to dry. Wipe off excess glue with a hot damp rag.

17 Turn the cupboard back the right way up and screw through the bottom panel into uprights **J**.

18 Sand down the leg frames and paint them black, taking care to keep a good sharp edge where the legs meet the cabinet. Use masking tape for this. Paint the top and handles also.

19 Hang the doors, measuring up from the bottom of the cabinet.

20 Screw the top down onto the carcase with table shrinkage plates and apply the small black wooden door handles **M**.

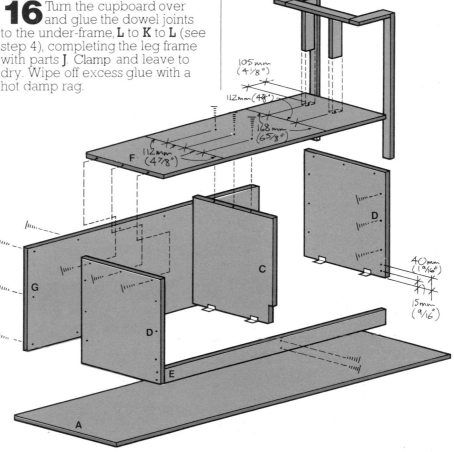

Storage Unit

This unit was designed to solve basic storage problems. It is about as simple as you can get, but includes the option of a shaped lip to provide more interest. Clean and simple solutions such as this will look elegant if extra care is taken at the finishing stage. It won't take very long to put together, so don't begrudge the time spent in the proper presentation and finishing of the panels.

Choice of colour will depend on your taste, but I would suggest keeping to neutrals such as greys or blacks. Not only are they easier to fit into colour schemes, but they also tend to enhance the objects that you place on the shelves.

Adding a profiled solid lip is entirely up to you. If the unit is to be free-standing, then a lip should be applied back and front. If it is to stand against a wall, then obviously the front edges only need be done. (See TECHNIQUES p. 36 Edge Profiling.)

Plans and dimensions

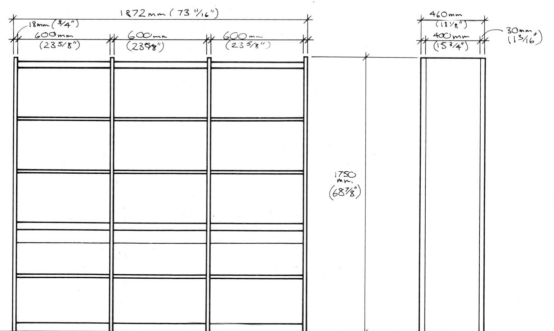

Front elevation   Side elevation

1872 mm (73 ¹¹/₁₆")
18mm (³/₄")
600mm (23 ⁵/₈")
600mm (23 ⁵/₈")
600mm (23 ⁵/₈")
460mm (18 ¹/₈")
400mm (15 ³/₄")
30mm (1 ³/₁₆")
1750 mm. (68 ⁷/₈")

You will need

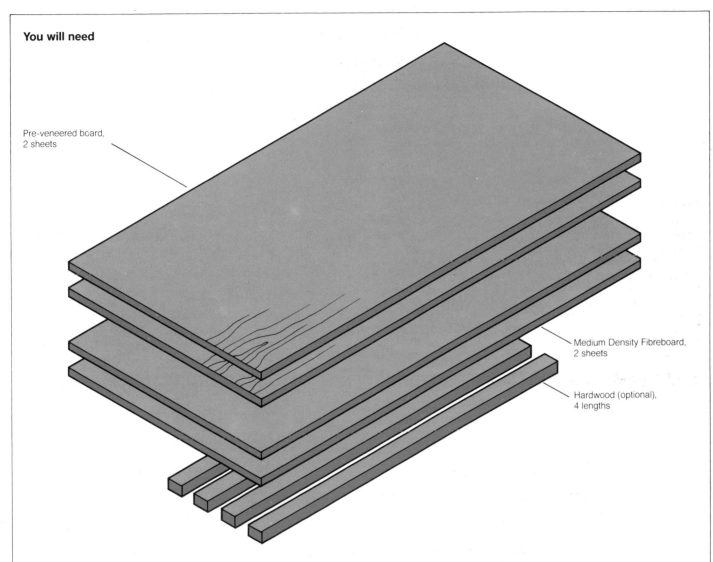

Pre-veneered board,
2 sheets

Medium Density Fibreboard,
2 sheets

Hardwood (optional),
4 lengths

Tools

Drill bit (size to match shelf sockets)
3mm (⅛") drill
1220mm (48") sash clamps   (4)
Screwdriver (slot head)
Hammer and nail punch
Sanding block
Sandpaper   80 grit   (2 sheets)
              120 grit   (2 sheets)
Smoothing plane
Tenon saw
Bench and vice
Dowelling jig and dowels 8mm (⁵⁄₁₆")
Pencil
Rule
75mm (3") paintbrush

Materials

Board
16mm (⅝") pre-veneered board, oak finish
(18mm (¾") is preferable if available)
1750mm × 400mm   (68⅞" × 15¾")   (4) **A**
16mm (⅝") Medium Density Fibreboard
600mm × 340mm   (23⅝" × 13⅜")   (9) **B**
598mm × 340mm   (23⁹⁄₁₆" × 13⅜")   (9) **C**
600mm × 45mm   (23⅝" × 1¾")   (15) **D**
600mm × 250mm   (23⅝" × 9⅞")   (3) **E**

Hardwood (optional lips)
ramin/obeche
1760mm × 30mm × 20mm (69.2" × 1.18" × 0.78")   (4/8) **F**

Edging
Self-adhesive edging strip
3.5mm (⁵⁄₃₂") for short edges
(15mm (⅝") if solid lips are not used)

Adjustable Shelf Supports Socket and plug   (108)

KD Fittings
(see illustration)
Brown plastic KD fittings   (36)

Screws (for KD fittings)
No. 8 × 25mm (1") countersunk steel   (144)

Nails
32mm (1¼") panel pins   (80)

Glue
PVA wood glue

Filler
Wood stopper

Paint
Dark grey undercoat
Satin finish grey topcoat

Sundries
A few softwood glue blocks
25mm × 25mm × 45mm (1" × 1" × 1¾")   (45)
38mm × 38mm × 45mm (1½" × 1½" × 1¾")   (9)

Cutting plan

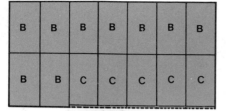

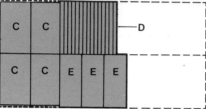

Instructions

1 Take 6 shelf panels **B** and glue on their respective downstand lips **D** with some PVA glue, leaving the top edge proud by 1mm (1/32"). Tack through to secure with panel pins. Sink below the surface with a nail punch, remembering to fill the holes with a stopper before finishing. As an extra support, apply glue blocks rubbed with glue along the inside. Wipe off excess glue with a hot damp rag. Put to one side. These 6 panels will form the top horizontal and the plinth.

2 When the glue is dry, clean up the exposed top edge with a smoothing plane and finish with both grades of sandpaper, being sure to use a cork block and keep the edges smooth but crisp.

3 Repeat the process on the 3 mid-horizontals, putting the larger downstand **E** to the rear edge. Be sure to use some substantial (38mm × 38mm/1½" × 1½") glue blocks here.

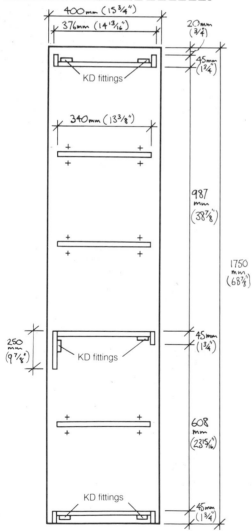

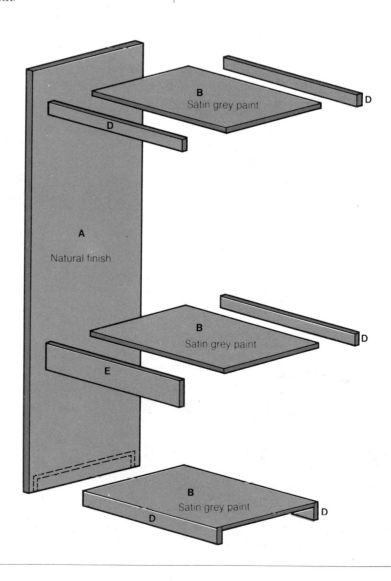

4 Take each of the upright panels **A** in turn and lie them flat for marking out. Mark end panels on the side only, leaving the show veneer (oak) to the outside.

5 Starting from the bottom edge, lightly mark the position of the bottom shelf. This should be flush with the bottom of the panel and equidistant from either side.

6 Then mark the mid-horizontal positions which, at the front, are 608mm ($23\frac{15}{16}$") above the bottom panel (see drawing, left).

7 The top panel is positioned 20mm ($\frac{25}{32}$") down from the top edge. All horizontals are positioned equidistant from either side.

8 When you have marked all these panels, the positions for the adjustable shelf sockets can also be marked on — the central position being exactly halfway between the fixed horizontals. All shelf stud positions are 85mm ($3\frac{11}{32}$") in from either side.

Adjustable shelf sockets

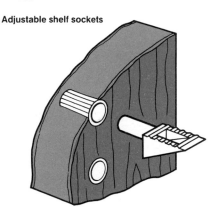

9 Drill the panels **A** for these sockets. On the outside panels, be careful not to drill right through. If, on the centre panels, you do decide to drill through, be sure to have a piece of scrap wood to drill on, so that the veneer does not break out.

If you intend to add profiled edges, now is the time to do it. So:-

10 Take the lengths of hardwood and mark the profile out on either end, continuing the lines down the length of the piece of lipping. (See TECHNIQUES p. 36 Edge Profiling.) Hold the length in a vice and plane down to the line. Repeat the process on all the lips.

Lip profile

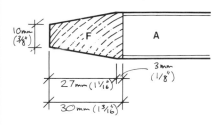

11 The profiled lip is then glued and clamped to the long edge of the upright panel **A**. Be sure that the lip is proud on both sides of the panel before you leave it to dry, so it can be planed flush afterwards. Use PVA glue and employ dowels and a dowelling jig to line up the lips properly (see TECHNIQUES p. 33).

12 When dry, plane the edges flush, setting the plane to a fine cut so as not to penetrate the veneered surface.

13 Cut the ends flush and finish sand with 80 grit sandpaper.

14 Edge the short edges with veneered strip (hot press with a domestic iron).

15 The long edges should also be veneered if lips are not used.

16 Position the **KD** fittings as drawn (see plan, left) and secure with No. 8 screws using, of course, a pilot drill (3.0mm/$\frac{1}{8}$").

KD Fittings, section through

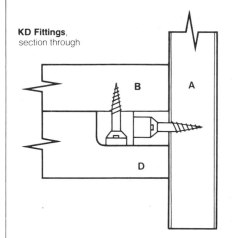

KD Fittings from beneath

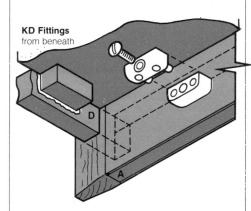

123

17 Try a 'dry' run in assembling the unit on its back to check for accuracy. If you have made any mistakes you will be able to re-position a fitting some way from its original position, as none will be seen. Then take the units apart and prepare them for finishing.

18 Apply the paint finishes as directed in the main illustration, left (see TECHNIQUES p. 36 Finishing). If you wish to finish the solid lips with a natural varnish, mask off the area before you apply the paint.

19 Leave the panels to dry thoroughly (24 hours) before you re-assemble.

Work Desk

If you have ever wanted a desk at home, but have no room for a separate 'office', this design could provide the answer for it will not look out of place in your living room. Its novel construction is based on the two carcases which are suspended from, and at the same time reinforce, the top-to-leg panel joint. The table is also braced by four stout shelf brackets concealed behind the carcases. The result is an uncluttered and simple appearance that produces more than just a desk, and as such it will look at home in a domestic environment.

Two drawer units offer two drawers each for storage of letters and stationery. Both are capable of receiving a file drawer and instructions for this are included, but you will need to buy a pair of metal telescopic drawer runners. These will ensure that the drawers extend fully for good access to the suspended files.

If the desk is destined for your lounge, you may wish to consider an alternative to the colour scheme specified, although the piece will always appear to advantage if the top and leg panels are both manufactured in the veneered chipboard.

Plans and dimensions

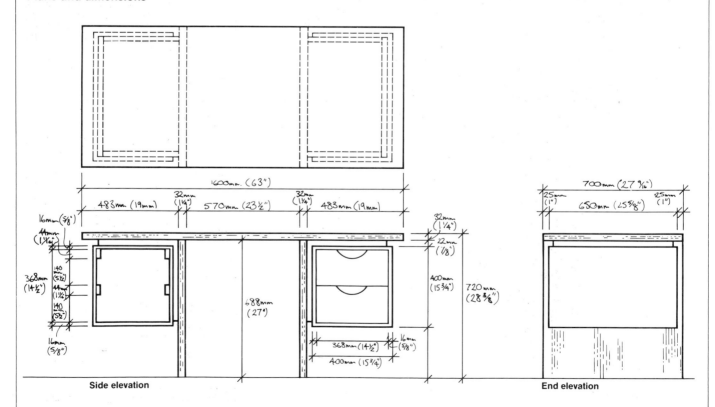

Side elevation

End elevation

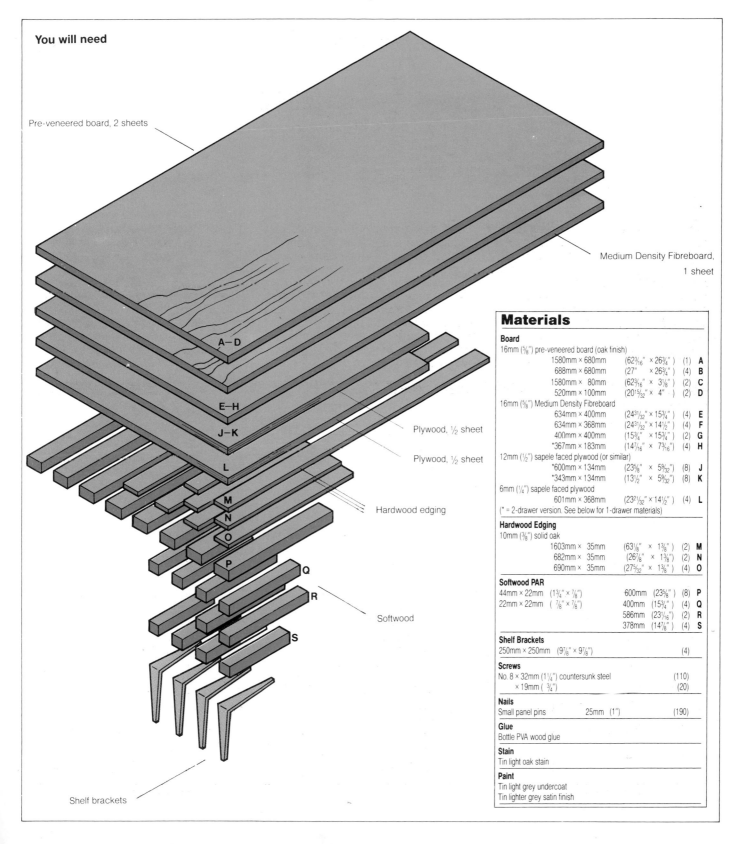

You will need

Pre-veneered board, 2 sheets

Medium Density Fibreboard, 1 sheet

A–D

E–H

J–K

L

Plywood, ½ sheet

Plywood, ½ sheet

M

N

O

Hardwood edging

P

Q

R

Softwood

S

Shelf brackets

Materials

Board

16mm (⅝") pre-veneered board (oak finish)

1580mm × 680mm	(62³⁄₁₆″ × 26¾″)	(1)	**A**
688mm × 680mm	(27″ × 26¾″)	(4)	**B**
1580mm × 80mm	(62³⁄₁₆″ × 3⅛″)	(2)	**C**
520mm × 100mm	(20¹⁵⁄₃₂″ × 4″)	(2)	**D**

16mm (⅝") Medium Density Fibreboard

634mm × 400mm	(24³¹⁄₃₂″ × 15¾″)	(4)	**E**
634mm × 368mm	(24³¹⁄₃₂″ × 14½″)	(4)	**F**
400mm × 400mm	(15¾″ × 15¾″)	(2)	**G**
*367mm × 183mm	(14⁷⁄₁₆″ × 7³⁄₁₆″)	(4)	**H**

12mm (½") sapele faced plywood (or similar)

*600mm × 134mm	(23⅝″ × 5⁹⁄₃₂″)	(8)	**J**
*343mm × 134mm	(13½″ × 5⁹⁄₃₂″)	(8)	**K**

6mm (¼") sapele faced plywood

601mm × 368mm	(23²¹⁄₃₂″ × 14½″)	(4)	**L**

(* = 2-drawer version. See below for 1-drawer materials)

Hardwood Edging

10mm (⅜") solid oak

1603mm × 35mm	(63⅛″ × 1⅜″)	(2)	**M**
682mm × 35mm	(26⅞″ × 1⅜″)	(2)	**N**
690mm × 35mm	(27⁵⁄₃₂″ × 1⅜″)	(4)	**O**

Softwood PAR

44mm × 22mm	(1¾″ × ⅞″)	600mm	(23⅝″)	(8) **P**
22mm × 22mm	(⅞″ × ⅞″)	400mm	(15¾″)	(4) **Q**
		586mm	(23¹⁄₁₆″)	(2) **R**
		378mm	(14⅞″)	(4) **S**

Shelf Brackets

250mm × 250mm (9⅞″ × 9⅞″) (4)

Screws

No. 8 × 32mm (1¼") countersunk steel	(110)
× 19mm (¾")	(20)

Nails

Small panel pins	25mm (1")	(190)

Glue

Bottle PVA wood glue

Stain

Tin light oak stain

Paint

Tin light grey undercoat
Tin lighter grey satin finish

Materials list continued

Varnish
Tin clear polyurethane lacquer satin finish

Filler
Small tin medium oak wood stopper

*If you wish to make one filing drawer — substitute the items marked with a * from the original materials list with these:

Board
12mm (½") sapele faced plywood
600mm × 260mm	(23⅝" × 10¼")	(2)	**T**
319mm × 260mm	(12⁹⁄₁₆" × 10¼")	(2)	**U**

16mm (⅝") Medium Density Fibreboard
367mm × 367mm	(14⁷⁄₁₆" × 14⁷⁄₁₆")	(1)	**V**

Metal
2mm (¹⁄₁₆") aluminium strip
319mm × 40mm	(12⁹⁄₁₆" × 1½")	(2)	**W**

Runners
2 telescopic drawer runners
40mm (1½") × 12mm (½") 500mm-550mm (19¹¹⁄₁₆"-21⅝")

Tools

100mm (4") C-clamps	(4)
Hammer	
Nail punch	
Smoothing plane	
Sanding block	
Sandpaper 120 grit (4 sheets)	
80 grit (4 sheets)	
Combination square	
Screwdriver	
Drill	
Drill bits: 3mm (⅛"), 4.5mm (³⁄₁₆") and countersink	
Bench and vice	
Power jig	
Half round file	
12mm (½") paint brush	

Instructions

Making the desk framework

1 Take the top panel **A** and put the face side (oak veneer) face down. Take the 2 long linings **C** and, having glued 1 face, place it glue side down on the long edge of the top panel. Nail to secure and ensure that all edges line up flush.

2 Repeat the process for the 2 short linings **D**, and finally the second long lining **C**.

3 Take the leg panels **B** and glue the reverse faces together. C-clamp them in perfect alignment and pin through to secure. Do both panels.

Cutting plans

Pre-veneered board, 16mm (⅝")

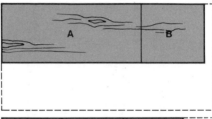

Medium Density Fibreboard, 16mm (⅝")

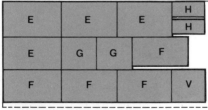

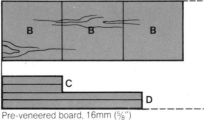

Pre-veneered board, 16mm (⅝")

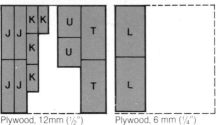

Plywood, 12mm (½") Plywood, 6 mm (¼")

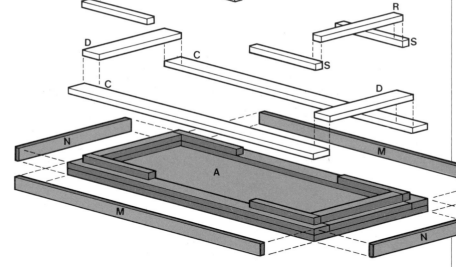

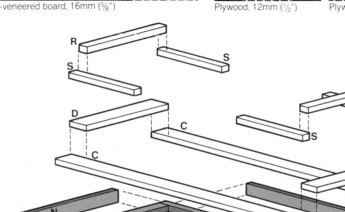

4 Take the short oak edgings **N**. Glue and pin to secure on both short edges of top panel **A**. Ensure some slight overlap along all edges. Trim the ends flush and apply the 2 long edges **M**. Leave to dry and then plane and sand flush. Sink pin heads below the surface of the wood and fill. Repeat the process on the long edges of the two leg panels **B/B**. The long edges are the 688mm (27") dimension which should be the grain direction.

5 Apply the spacers **Q** on both completed leg panels, flush at the top and set in from the sides by 68mm (2¹¹⁄₁₆"), as shown in the diagram right.

6 Mark out on the underlinings **C** the internal positions of the leg panels; ie, a centrally-spaced position of 570mm (22⁷⁄₁₆").

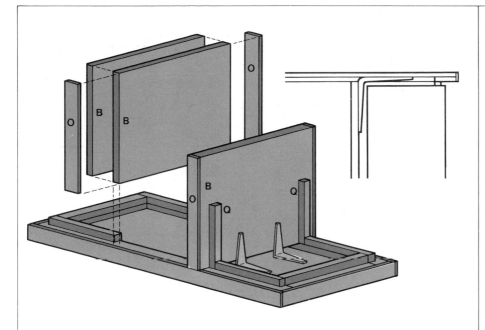

Making the drawer cabinets

10 Drill out the clearance holes 4.5mm (³⁄₁₆″) around the edges of the panels **G** and **E** as shown below, 8mm (⁵⁄₁₆″) from the edge (see TECHNIQUES p. 40 Tricks of the trade, Marking out).

11 Hold part **F** in the vice and apply part **E**. Glue the edge and screw in to pre-drilled pilot holes.

12 Next apply **G** then **F** then **E** to complete box. Repeat steps 10, 11 and 12 on second cabinet and leave to dry.

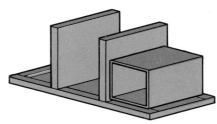

7 Screw the shelf brackets at the top ends of the leg panels, extending beyond the top edge by 16mm (⁵⁄₈″). Use a spare piece of 16mm (⁵⁄₈″) board for lining-up purposes. Drill a 3mm (¹⁄₈″) pilot hole and secure with No. 8 × 32mm (1¼″) wood screws.

8 The leg panels **B/B** can now be placed in position on the top panel and secured.

9 Apply spacers **S** and **R** to the underside of the top panel. Glue and screw. The basic desk part is now finished. Clean up with sandpaper, fill all nail holes, finish sandpapering and apply satin and clear finishes (see TECHNIQUES p. 36 Painting and Finishing).

13 Drill clearance holes in **F** and **E** for attaching the cabinet to the desk.

Assembling drawer cabinets

Assembling drawers

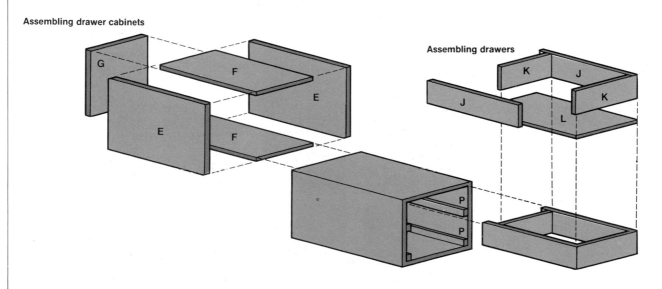

14 Paint the boxes, finishing with a clear satin lacquer.

Making the drawers

15 Check the finished width of the drawers by placing the pre-cut parts inside the cabinet in their intended position; *ie*, **K** between both sides **J**. You *must* allow 2.5mm (³⁄₃₂") clearance. If not, trim to size or re-cut.

16 Drill 5 clearance holes in the front panels **K** for attaching front panels **H**.

17 Hold **K** end up in the vice. Glue and nail **J** to it.

18 Nail and glue the bottom panel **L** to **K/J**; then to the second **K**; then to **J**.

19 Repeat steps 15–18 on remaining 3 drawers and leave to dry. Apply glue block to rear joint.

20 Take the front panels **H** and cut out the curve. This will become the drawer pull. Use a power jig saw, half round file and sandpaper. Paint grey and finish.

Fitting the drawers

21 Take each box in turn and turn it upside down. Apply the top drawer runners **P**; nail and glue, leaving 18mm (¹¹⁄₁₆") between the front end and the front edge of the cabinet.

22 Slide one drawer (upside down) on top of the 2 applied runners **P**. Lay small pieces of card along the edges of the drawers (*ie*, as spacers) and then apply the second pair of runners in exactly the same way, not forgetting the 18mm (¹¹⁄₁₆") space at the front end. When all runners have been attached and the drawers are fitted, label each one to its position (*ie*, on the cabinet interior).

23 Turn the desk the right way up and align the drawer fronts **H** by C-clamping each one in turn through the drawer pull hole. Pull out and screw through from inside the drawer. Always pilot drill (3mm/⅛") and check fit after each screwing operation. Make sure each drawer has been assembled in its allocated position.

24 Leave to dry and re-assemble.

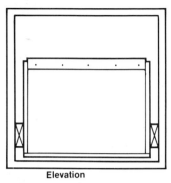

Elevation

25 When making the single drawer version, the drawer tray is assembled in exactly the same manner, but is obviously narrower in order to include the telescopic runners. Check the internal width before assembling as before.
The filing pockets should be supported by two aluminium plates which are screwed to the drawer front and back.

Making a single filing drawer

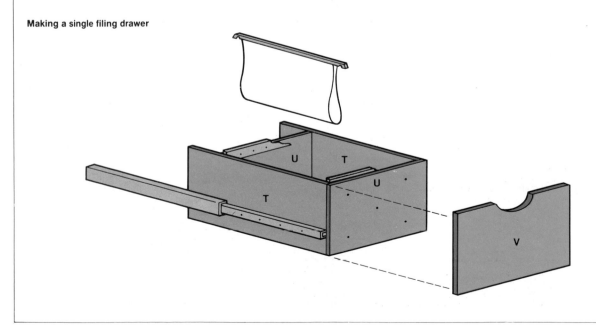

Bathroom Cabinet and Shelf

Having often been asked to design furniture for bathrooms, experience shows that built-in cupboards can meet consumer resistance if their installation involves renewing the bathroom sanitary ware. Unless you are prepared to rip out your basin, bath and other fixtures, for most of us putting cupboards in a bathroom will be confined to just that. So here is a design that will not only complement your existing basin but also involves no more in the way of installation than just screwing it to the wall.

The cupboard includes a centre shelf, while one of the doors features a double-hinged mirror that will swing round to reflect a side view of your head. Beneath is a shelf with a groove detail running along its length, incorporating a position for your toothbrush mug, whisky glass, or whatever!

The two drawers below are a useful addition, though not essential to the design. They are not difficult to make, just a little time-consuming.

When you come to screw the cabinet to the wall, mark out all the holes first, then drill the wall and plug the holes. If you drill into a cavity wall, be sure to use cavity fixing. Don't try to attach the cupboards to the wall without secure fixings.

Plans and dimensions

650mm (25¹⁹⁄₃₂")
324mm (12¾") · 324mm (12¾")
600mm (23⅝") · 582mm (22²⁹⁄₃₂")
150mm (5⅞")
30mm (1³⁄₁₆")
40mm (1⁹⁄₁₆")
282mm (11⅛")
150mm (5⅞")
16mm (⅝")

Front elevation

950mm (36²⁵⁄₃₂")
150mm (5⅞")
18mm (1¹⁄₁₆")
100mm (3¹⁵⁄₁₆")
1mm (⅛")
81mm (3³⁄₁₆")
245mm (9⅝")

177mm (7")
185mm (7¼")

Side elevation

You will need

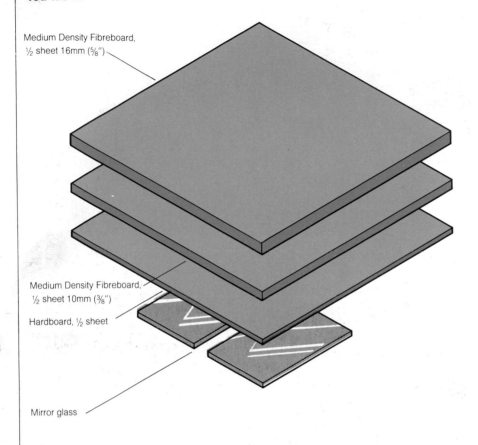

Medium Density Fibreboard,
½ sheet 16mm (⅝″)

Medium Density Fibreboard,
½ sheet 10mm (⅜″)

Hardboard, ½ sheet

Mirror glass

Materials

Board

16mm (⅝″) Medium Density Fibreboard

584mm × 150mm (23″ × 5²⁹⁄₃₂″)	(2)	**A**
650mm × 177mm (25¹⁹⁄₃₂″ × 6³¹⁄₃₂″)	(1)	**B**
618mm × 150mm (24¹¹⁄₃₂″ × 5²⁹⁄₃₂″)	(1)	**C**
618mm × 130mm (24¹¹⁄₃₂″ × 5⅛″)	(1)	**D**
642mm × 324mm (25⁹⁄₃₂″ × 12¾″)	(2)	**E**
950mm × 195mm (37¹³⁄₃₂″ × 7¾″)	(1)	**F**

10mm (⅜″) Medium Density Fibreboard

245mm × 81mm (9⅝″ × 3³⁄₁₆″)	(2)	**G**
175mm × 57mm (6⅞″ × 2¼″)	(4)	**H**
175mm × 17mm (6⅞″ × 2¹⁄₃₂″)	(4)	**J**
227mm × 45mm (8¹⁵⁄₁₆″ × 1¾″)	(2)	**K**
100mm × 30mm (3¹⁵⁄₁₆″ × 1³⁄₁₆″)	(4)	**L**
100mm × 20mm (3¹⁵⁄₁₆″ × ²⁵⁄₃₂″)	(4)	**M**
227mm × 150mm (8¹⁵⁄₁₆″ × 5²⁹⁄₃₂″)	(2)	**N**

3mm (⅛″) Hardboard

650mm × 640mm (25¹⁹⁄₃₂″ × 25³⁄₁₆″)	(1)	**O**
955mm × 30mm (37¹⁹⁄₃₂″ × 1³⁄₁₆″)	(2)	**P**
955mm × 22mm (37¹⁹⁄₃₂″ × ⅞″)	(5)	**Q**

Hinges
(chrome finish)
38mm (1½″) × 22mm (⅞″) (6)

Shelf Brackets
125mm (5″) × 100mm (4″) (2)

Triangular Corner Brackets
50mm (2″) × 50mm (2″) (2)

Screws
No. 8 × 32mm (1¼″) countersunk woodscrews (26)
No. 8 × 38mm (1½″) countersunk woodscrews (6)
No. 6 × 18mm (¾″) countersunk woodscrews (16)
No. 6 × 16mm (⅝″) countersunk woodscrews (50)

Nails
25mm (1″) oval wire nails (50)
12mm (½″) veneer pins (30)

Wall Plugs
or cavity fixings
For No. 8 × 25mm (1½″) screws (8)

Filler
Tin plastic metal body filler

Mirror
Cut to size to fit the doors
(582mm) × (324mm) × 4mm (2)
(22²⁹⁄₃₂″) × (12¾″) × ⁵⁄₃₂″

Mirror Pads
or glue for glueing mirror to doors

Glue
Bottle PVA wood glue

Magnetic Catch (2)

Paint
Tin light grey primer/undercoat
Tin white paint
Tin grey paint
Tin black paint
Tin clear varnish, satin finish

Cutting plan

Medium Density Fibreboard

A	A
B	
C	
D	
E	**E**
F	

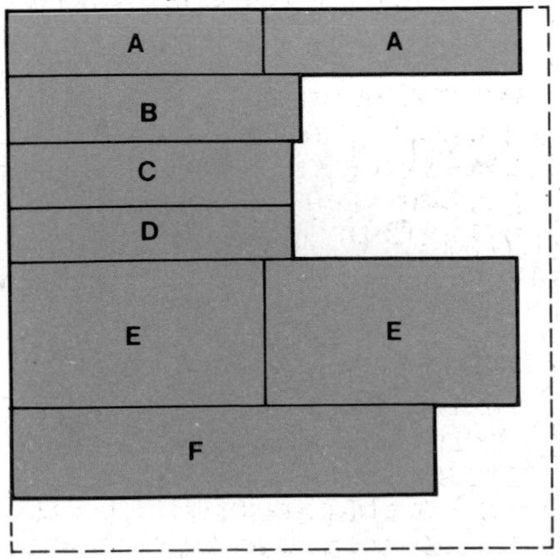

Tools

Drill (electric)
Masonry bit (for No. 8 woodscrews + plug)
Drill bits 4.5mm (³⁄₁₆″) countersink
3.5mm (⁵⁄₃₂″)
3.0mm (⅛″)
2.0mm (³⁄₃₂″)
Pencil, rule (tape), spirit level
Hammer
Small nail punch
Screwdriver
Sanding block
Sandpaper 80 grit (4 sheets)
120 grit (4 sheets)
Smoothing plane
75mm (3″) paint brush
Bench and vice
Combination square
Electric jig saw
12mm (½″) chisel
Half round file
Pincers

Instructions

The cabinet

1 Take the bottom panel **B** and apply a radius to one long edge (see TECHNIQUES p. 36 Edge profiling). This will now be the front edge. Put to one side.

2 Drill the cabinet sides **A, A** and bottom **B** to take countersunk No. 8 screws, 8mm ($^5/_{16}$″) in from the edge as directed in the illustration right. Check with a screw to make sure the head is below the surface. Don't forget the screws for the mid-shelf **D** This shelf can go wherever you like, to accommodate tall shampoo bottles, for example.

3 Hold panel **D** vertically in the vice (end up) and place one panel **A** over it. Line up the clearance holes in the middle of panel **A** with the centre line of the end edge of panel **D**. Ensure that the shelf **D** is at right angles to **A** (*ie*, that the shelf will end up horizontal). See also that **D** is lined up with one edge of **A**, which will now become the back edge.

4 Drill through into **D** with a pilot drill (3.0mm/$^1/_8$″), then glue the edge and screw home with a No. 8 × 32mm (1$^1/_4$″) countersunk screw. Wipe off the glue with a hot wet rag.

5 Repeat step 4 at the opposite end, completing an H-shape, A/D/A.

6 Pilot drill, glue and screw down panel **B** (bottom) onto both panels **A**. Line up the back edge, letting the profiled long edge protrude at the front. Make sure all other edges line up well. Wipe off glue.

7 Insert **C** (top) into the framework and secure in the same way with glue and screws.

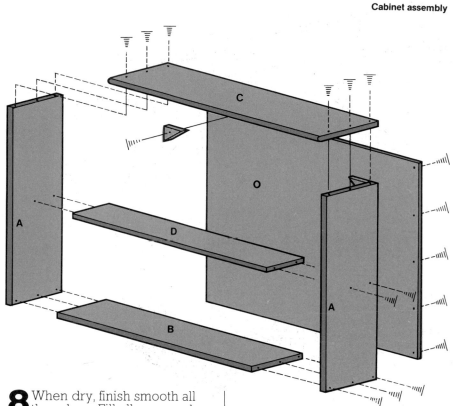

Cabinet assembly

8 When dry, finish smooth all the edges. Fill all gaps and screw heads with plastic filler, leave to dry and sand to a smooth finish. (See TECHNIQUES p. 36 Sanding.) A smoothing plane can be used, but only on the MDF exposed edges.

9 Screw on the triangular corner brackets into the top and side panels with No. 6 × 16mm ($^5/_8$″) screws. These must be exactly flush with the back edge.

10 Lay the cabinet down on its front and place the back panel **O** in position. Use this opportunity to square up the construction and, after drilling clearance holes around the edge (5mm/$^3/_{16}$″ in from the edges), screw down into pre-drilled pilot holes (2.0mm/$^1/_{16}$″) in the back of the cabinet framework. From inside the cabinet drill clearance holes right through the corner brackets and back panel.

The doors

11 Take both panels **E**, which are to be the doors. The left hand door is left plain. But the right hand door is to have a second hinged panel. To make the hinged panel, mark out the smaller rectangle (282mm × 150mm/11$^1/_8$″ × 5$^{15}/_{16}$″) as shown. Place the hinges in position on this panel and, keeping them parallel, mark out accurately the positions of the screw holes. Do this for both hinges, drill pilot holes and screw the hinges down onto the panel.

12 Remove the screws and hinges and saw out the smaller panel. Using an electric jig saw (see TECHNIQUES p. 33), work in from the long edge and turn the corners as tightly as your jig saw will allow.

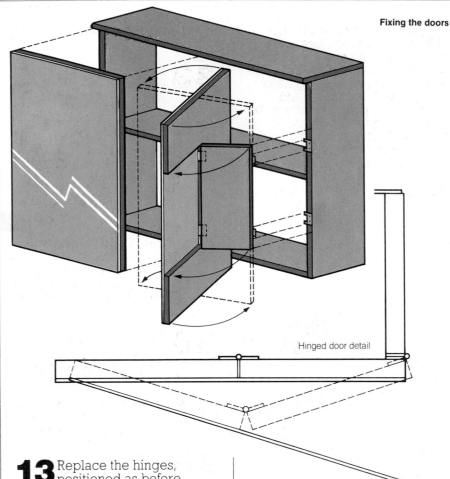

Fixing the doors

Hinged door detail

20 Remove the strips (with a 12mm (½") wood chisel) from the shelf in order to cut the described circle with a saw. Finish with a half-round file.

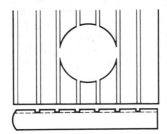

21 Replace the strips with veneer pins, but this time apply glue to the backs of the strips.

22 When finished, wipe off all the excess glue and weight the shelf while it dries.

23 When dry, profile the front edge to match the top panel of the cabinet (see TECHNIQUES p. 36 Edge Profiling). Fill any gaps on the front edge.

The drawers

24 Glue and tack J to H along its top edge as drawn.

25 Glue and tack G to H/J through the front (line up the side edges of G flush with H).

26 Insert N and tack through from H/J.

27 Complete the assembly by glueing in K and tacking to secure.

28 Repeat 24–27 on second drawer.

29 Drawer supports M and L can now be drilled for clearance holes. Then glue and screw them onto the bottom of the shelf. Do this by placing the drawers centrally in position and marking the point where J meets the shelf bottom surface. Secure with 32mm (1¼") screws.

13 Replace the hinges, positioned as before.

14 Hang the doors by laying the cabinet flat on its back and placing the hinge in position on the edge of the side panel A. Do this by drawing a line 10.5mm ($^{13}\!/_{32}$") in from the outside edge. Secure all the hinges to the cabinet in the same way with two screws per hinge.

15 Offer up the doors to the respective hinges and, leaving a 1mm ($^{1}\!/_{32}$") gap down the length (use a spacer), mark one hole only per hinge and pilot drill.

16 Screw the door onto the hinge with one screw to each hinge (if you have the position wrong, you will have two other chances to get it right).

17 Close the doors and check their position. If either doesn't fit, go back to step 15 and repeat it, using one of the unused holes in the hinge. Insert all the screws into the hinges. The cabinet is now ready for painting.

The grooved shelf

18 Take panel F and, working from the front edge, lay down the hardboard strips P and Q with veneer pins only. Use a 5mm ($^{7}\!/_{32}$") spacer and work to the back.

19 Take the proposed tooth mug and scribe centrally on the 3 middle strips a circle that is 5mm ($^{7}\!/_{32}$") larger overall than the mug.

30 All components can now be painted (see TECHNIQUES p. 36 Finishing). Make sure all parts are sanded smooth and filled where necessary. Paint the cabinet white, leaving the door fronts bare apart from a 10mm (⅜") border.
The grooved shelf is painted grey and the drawers black. Finally, apply a single coat of clear satin varnish.

31 When dry, apply the mirrors. It is best to take the doors to the glass merchant and ask him to fit them. Have the edges polished. Apply glue or sticky tabs to the doors and carefully drop the mirror onto the unpainted door panels. Get a friend to help you line them up. *Do not apply glue or pads to the small second hinged panel.*

32 Fit the magnetic catches to the top panel **C**.

Hanging the units

The grooved shelf

33 Using a spirit level, draw a horizontal line 300mm (11¹³⁄₁₆") above your basin.

34 Measure the width of your basin and mark the centre line. Transfer this onto the horizontal line and then mark along the same line two points 350mm (13¾") apart (or 175mm (6⅞") either side of your central point).

35 With the top of your shelf bracket (the 125mm/4¹⁵⁄₁₆" length) lining up with your horizontal line, mark the holes where you need to drill the wall.

36 Using the masonry bit, drill and then plug the wall. Secure the shelf brackets with 38mm (1½") No. 8 screws.

37 The cabinet will be fitted on the same centre line, 150mm (5¹⁵⁄₁₆") above the shelf.

38 Ask a friend to hold it in position while you scribe through with a pencil the positions of the two screws from the top inside corners. Drill.

39 Plug and secure as in 36.
For easier fixing the cabinet weighs a lot less and is more manoeuvrable without the doors on.
If the wall is a cavity wall, be sure to use cavity bolts to secure the units. If you suspect that the fixings are not secure enough, *do not attempt to hang these units.*

40 Line up the shelf centrally and screw from below with 16mm (⅝") × No. 6 screws. Finally, insert the drawers.

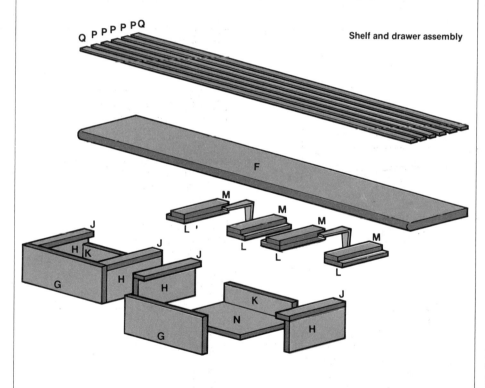

Shelf and drawer assembly

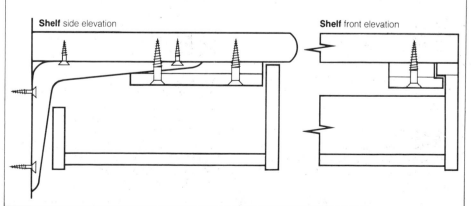

Shelf side elevation

Shelf front elevation

Bunk/Twin Beds

This design can be made in its entirety or separately. Make one bed first — and the second one when you need it! Put them on top of one another and fit the ladder and guard rail. Take them apart and use them as twin beds — the design will accommodate all these functions. The complete unit will, of course, look equally at home in a children's bedroom or in the spare room and

its strong construction, if implemented well, will last for years. Choice of colour is obviously up to you. If feeling adventurous, you could even paint the dowels in several different colours. The boltheads could be painted to match the

dowels and the best way to do this would be to assemble the frame and paint it just before you give the bolts the last few turns; *ie*, while they are not touching the wood. Leave for 24 hours before you screw home.

Note that the bed is designed around a 1900mm × 915mm ($74\frac{7}{8}'' \times 36''$) mattress, so if you are using a different size you may have to adjust the dimensions.

Plans and dimensions

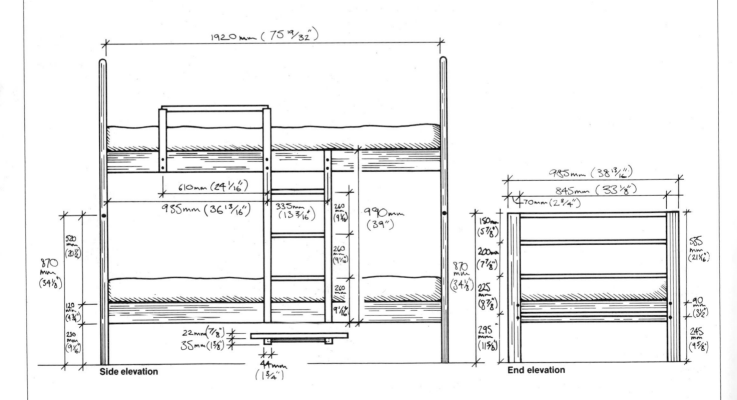

Side elevation

End elevation

You will need

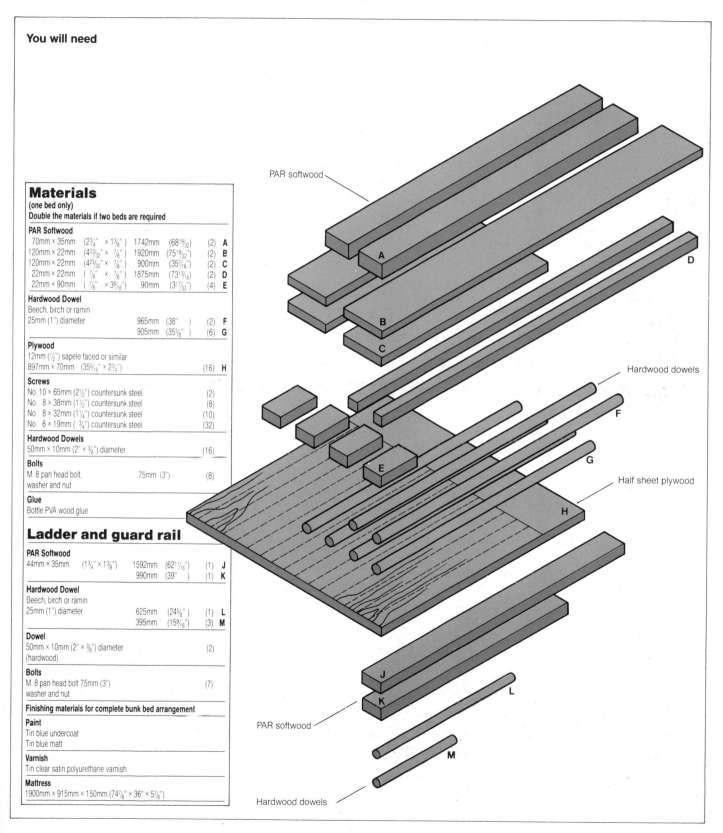

Materials

(one bed only)
Double the materials if two beds are required

PAR Softwood

70mm × 35mm	(2¾″ × 1⅜″)	1742mm	(68¹⁹⁄₃₂″)	(2)	**A**
120mm × 22mm	(4²³⁄₃₂″ × ⅞″)	1920mm	(75¹⁹⁄₃₂″)	(2)	**B**
120mm × 22mm	(4²³⁄₃₂″ × ⅞″)	900mm	(35⁷⁄₁₆″)	(2)	**C**
22mm × 22mm	(⅞″ × ⅞″)	1875mm	(73¹³⁄₁₆″)	(2)	**D**
22mm × 90mm	(⅞″ × 3⁹⁄₁₆″)	90mm	(3¹⁷⁄₃₂″)	(4)	**E**

Hardwood Dowel

Beech, birch or ramin

25mm (1″) diameter	965mm	(38″)	(2)	**F**
	905mm	(35⅝″)	(6)	**G**

Plywood

12mm (½″) sapele faced or similar

897mm × 70mm	(35⁵⁄₁₆″ × 2¾″)	(16) **H**

Screws

No. 10 × 65mm (2½″) countersunk steel	(2)
No. 8 × 38mm (1½″) countersunk steel	(8)
No. 8 × 32mm (1¼″) countersunk steel	(10)
No. 6 × 19mm (¾″) countersunk steel	(32)

Hardwood Dowels

50mm × 10mm (2″ × ⅜″) diameter	(16)

Bolts

M. 8 pan head bolt,	75mm (3″)	(8)
washer and nut		

Glue

Bottle PVA wood glue

Ladder and guard rail

PAR Softwood

44mm × 35mm	(1¾″ × 1⅜″)	1592mm	(62¹¹⁄₁₆″)	(1)	**J**
		990mm	(39″)	(1)	**K**

Hardwood Dowel

Beech, birch or ramin

25mm (1″) diameter	625mm	(24⅝″)	(1)	**L**
	395mm	(15⁹⁄₁₆″)	(3)	**M**

Dowel

50mm × 10mm (2″ × ⅜″) diameter	(2)
(hardwood)	

Bolts

M. 8 pan head bolt 75mm (3″)	(7)
washer and nut	

Finishing materials for complete bunk bed arrangement

Paint

Tin blue undercoat
Tin blue matt

Varnish

Tin clear satin polyurethane varnish

Mattress

1900mm × 915mm × 150mm (74⅞″ × 36″ × 5⅞″)

PAR softwood

Hardwood dowels

Half sheet plywood

PAR softwood

Hardwood dowels

Tools

Tenon saw
Brace
25mm (1") diameter twist bit
100mm (4") C-clamp (2)
Drill
Drill bits: 10mm (³/₈") 4.5mm (³/₁₆")
8mm (⁵/₁₆") 3mm (¹/₈") 5mm (³/₁₆")
Screwdriver
Spanner
Dowel jig
1220mm (48") sash clamps (2)
Combination square
Sandpaper 120 grit (4 sheets)
80 grit (4 sheets)
Sanding block
12mm (½") paint brush
Bench and vice

Instructions

1 Take the leg sections **A** and grip in the vice by the flat wide surfaces (*ie*, edge up). Mark out the centre line and with the brace and bit (check the bit size against the dowel section, 25mm/1") drill right through. Get a friend to watch you do it, and make sure you are drilling through on a perfectly vertical axis. The bottoms of the legs must be bored through as well. This is done by butting up the remaining flat ends and gripping them in the vice so that they line up perfectly. Then drill as before. Put some scrap wood underneath to keep the hole crisp as you drill through.

Drilling dowel holes in leg sections

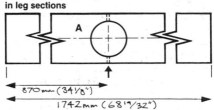

2 Saw the leg sections into 2 pairs and mark out the positions of the other dowels (see plans and dimensions). Bore out all these blind holes to a depth of 30mm (1³/₁₆") exactly (some tape wrapped around the bit will act as a guide).

3 Drill out the dowels **F** for 10mm (³/₈") dowels (see diagram), using 20mm (³/₄") spacing.

4 Finish sand all dowel parts **F** and **G** and paint finish. Do not paint the last 25mm (1") on **G** or the area around the dowel holes on **F** as these areas will be glued. (See TECHNIQUES p. 36 Finishing.)

5 Glue these frames together (see TECHNIQUES p. 35 Glueing), sash-clamping along the dowels.

6 The top dowel is applied after these frames have been dried and after they have been drilled to receive the connecting 10mm (³/₈") dowels (see details below).

Connection at top of leg, detail

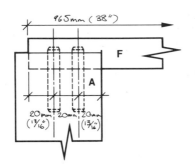

7 Drill 4 × 8mm (⁵/₁₆") diameter clearance holes straight through these end frames (for the connecting bolts). Follow the dimensions specified in the illustration.

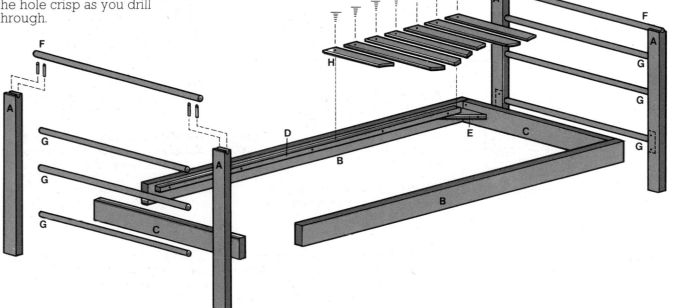

8 Now put the bed frame together. Mark out and drill the dowel holes on the ends of the support rails **B** and **C** using a 10mm (³/₈″) bit and a dowelling jig. Penetrate 15mm (¹⁹/₃₂″) deep into **B** and 35mm (1³/₈″) deep into **C**.

9 Put some glue into the holes and clamp the frame together with sash clamps

Bed frame to end frame connection

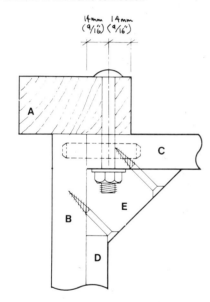

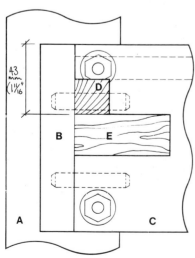

10 While the glued frame is setting, apply the pre-drilled corner braces **E** in position. Apply glue to the 2 short edges and rub into each corner; secure with 2 × 38mm (1½″) No. 8 screws per corner. Make sure these braces are 43mm (1¹¹/₁₆″) from the top edges of the side rails. Check with a combination square. Leave to dry.

11 Take the 2 support rails **D** and drill equally spaced 4.5mm (³/₁₆″) diameter clearance holes along their lengths. Apply some glue to the back edge and screw each one in position inside **B**, resting at each end on corner blocks **E**.

12 On both ends of the bed frame, mark out the clearance holes on parts **C**. Check the position by placing each end frame over **C**. Drill through and try a 'dry' run to make sure that the whole frame goes together.

13 Take the frame apart and finish all parts with clear lacquer, including the blue dowels.

14 Re-assemble, the final step being to drill all the plywood slats and screw them down, equally spaced, along the length of the bed frame with No. 6 × 19mm (³/₄″) screws.

Making the ladder

15 To make the ladder, take the length of PAR softwood **J** and mark out the hole to be drilled 360mm (14³/₁₆″) from one end.

16 Bore right through the piece of wood and then cut in two along the line already marked as in step 1.

17 Take the shorter length and drill through 2 × 8mm (⁵/₁₆″) diameter (¹/₈″) clearance holes as illustrated. Put to one side.

Ladder and guard rail

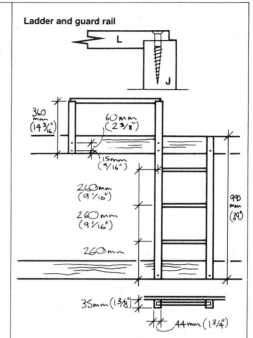

18 Take the other two parts **J** and **K** and, while held together, mark across all the ladder rung dowel holes at the centres specified in the illustration above.

19 Bore out these blind holes to a depth of 30mm (1³/₁₆″) exactly.

20 Put dowels **M** into ladder uprights and clamp to the assembled bunk bed set. Line up exactly and drill 8mm (⁵/₁₆″) clearance holes right through.

21 Clamp small upright **J** in position and drill 8mm (⁵/₁₆″) holes as in step 20.

22 Horizontal dowel **L** is not glued, but just screwed in position through the dowel. Use a 65mm (2½″) No. 10; a 5mm (³/₁₆″) clearance hole and 3mm (¹/₈″) pilot hole. This means that the whole assembly can be taken apart.

23 Dismantle the ladder and guard rail and finish as before. (See TECHNIQUES p. 36 Finishing.)

Child's Bunk Bed and Activities Unit
(for 5-year-olds upwards)

All children like a place of their own to play in, while parents, too, appreciate any means of concentrating their youngster's activities in one well-defined area. This design provides the answer. It incorporates a bed, small wardrobe, desk and a shelf, making it as versatile as the size and shape will permit.

The bed, of course, is on top, but not so high that it will prevent you from looking at junior in it (and, of course, low enough for bed-making not to be a mountaineering exercise). There is a ladder at the end for junior to use, and safety rails to prevent dreams becoming nightmares.

The construction is solid and will stand a considerable degree of wear and tear, while the design will give your child a place in which to organise a variety of activities on those rainy days.

This particular design enables you to put the bed in a corner (left hand or right hand) or, if you wish, in the middle of the bedroom with the head against a wall.

Plans and dimensions

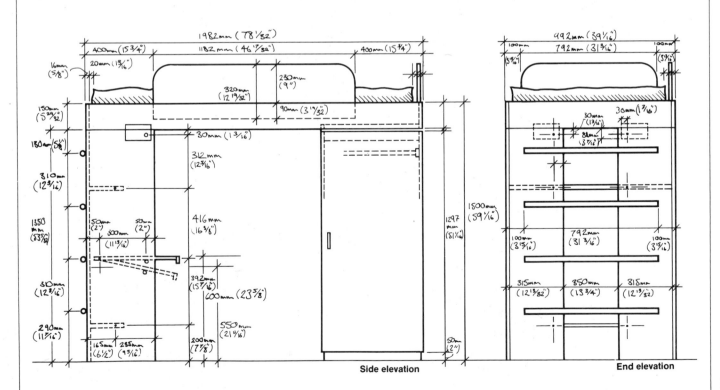

Side elevation

End elevation

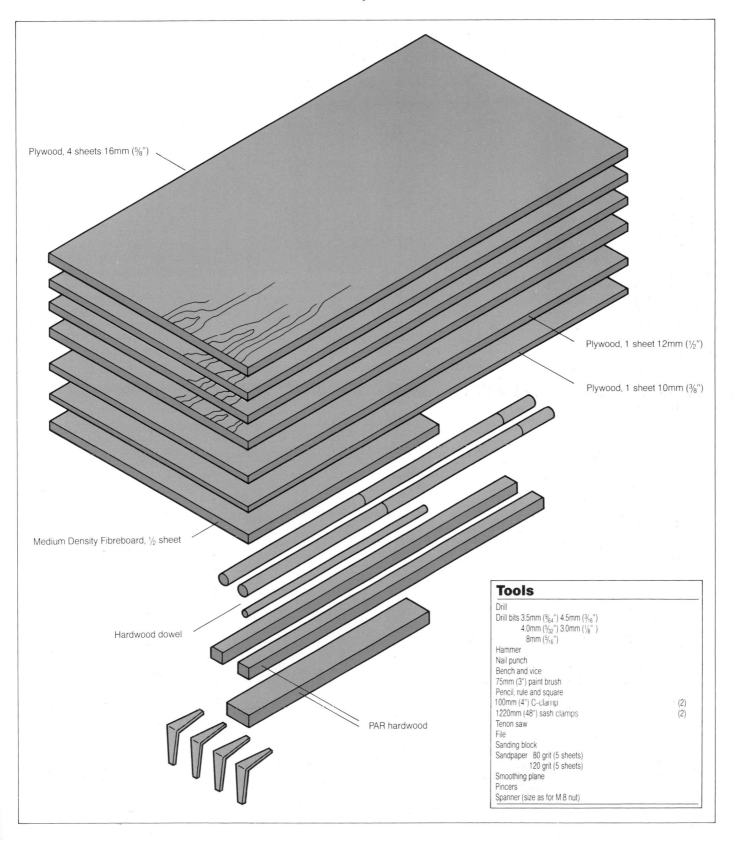

Plywood, 4 sheets 16mm (⅝")

Plywood, 1 sheet 12mm (½")

Plywood, 1 sheet 10mm (⅜")

139

Medium Density Fibreboard, ½ sheet

Hardwood dowel

PAR hardwood

Tools

Drill
Drill bits 3.5mm (⁹⁄₆₄") 4.5mm (³⁄₁₆")
        4.0mm (⁵⁄₃₂") 3.0mm (⅛")
        8mm (⁵⁄₁₆")
Hammer
Nail punch
Bench and vice
75mm (3") paint brush
Pencil, rule and square
100mm (4") C-clamp   (2)
1220mm (48") sash clamps   (2)
Tenon saw
File
Sanding block
Sandpaper 80 grit (5 sheets)
           120 grit (5 sheets)
Smoothing plane
Pincers
Spanner (size as for M.8 nut)

Materials

Board

16mm (⅝") birch-faced plywood

960mm × 150mm	(37¹³/₁₆" × 5²⁹/₃₂")	(2)	**A**
1982mm × 150mm	(78½" × 5²⁹/₃₂")	(2)	**B**
1350mm × 400mm	(53⁵/₃₂" × 15¾")	(2)	**C**
1350mm × 315mm	(53⁵/₃₂" × 12¹³/₃₂")	(2)	**D**
1297mm × 600mm	(51¹/₁₆" × 23⅝")	(1)	**E**
150mm × 88mm	(5²⁹/₃₂" × 3¹⁵/₃₂")	(6)	**F**
568mm × 88mm	(22⅜" × 3¹⁵/₃₂")	(2)	**G**
1350mm × 976mm	(53⁵/₃₂" × 38⁷/₁₆")	(2)	**H**

12mm (½") birch-faced plywood

1300mm × 568mm	(51¾" × 22⅜")	(1)	**J**
976mm × 568mm	(38⁷/₁₆" × 22⅜")	(1)	**K**
568mm × 50mm	(22⅜" × 1")	(2)	**L**
944mm × 50mm	(37⁵/₃₂" × 1")	(1)	**M**

10mm (⅜") birch-faced plywood

1182mm × 320mm	(46¹⁷/₃₂" × 12¹⁹/₃₂")	(1)	**N**
792mm × 320mm	(31³/₁₆" × 12¹⁹/₃₂")	(1)	**O**
960mm × 70mm	(37¹³/₁₆" × 2¾")	(16)	**P**

16mm (⅝") Medium Density Fibreboard

960mm × 500mm	(37¹³/₁₆" × 19¹¹/₁₆")	(1)	**Q**
960mm × 250mm	(37¹³/₁₆" × 9²⁷/₃₂")	(2)	**R**

PAR Hardwood

22mm × 22mm (⅞" × ⅞")

	1950mm	(76¾")	(2)	**S**

45mm × 22mm (1¾" × ⅞")

	965mm	(38")	(1)	**T**

Hardwood Dowel

Birch or beech

792mm × 35mm	(31³/₁₆" × 1⅜")	(4)	**U**
980mm × 12mm	(38¹⁹/₃₂" × ½")	(1)	**V**

Shelf Brackets
125mm × 100mm (5" × 4") (4)

Hinges
Chrome plated steel cranked hinge
50mm × 50mm × 16mm × 16mm (2" × 2" × ⅝" × ⅝") (2)
(see illustration)

Magnetic Catch
White and chrome (1)

Handle
Red D· handle or similar to choice (1)

Filler
Small tin cream stopper

Screws
No. 6 × 19mm (¾") countersunk woodscrew	(46)
No. 6 × 16mm (⅝") countersunk woodscrew	(48)
No. 8 × 25mm (1") countersunk woodscrew	(16)
No. 8 × 32mm (1¼") countersunk woodscrew	(33)
No. 8 × 38mm (1½") countersunk brass finish woodscrew and cup	(10)
No. 8 × 46mm (1¾") countersunk brass finish woodscrew and cup	(24)

Bolt
M.8 (8mm/⁵/₁₆" diameter) roundhead bolt
50mm (2") (6)
6 washers and 6 hex nuts

Nails
Oval wire nails
25mm (1") (100)

Glue
PVA wood glue

Mattress 1900mm × 900mm × 150mm (74¹³/₁₆" × 35¹/₁₆" × 5²⁹/₃₂")

Wardrobe Rail
565mm (22¼"), plus brackets

Cutting plans

16mm (⅝") plywood

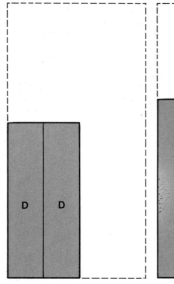

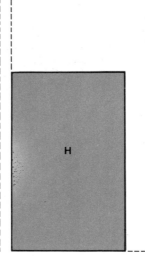

16mm (⅝") plywood

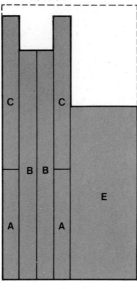

12mm (½") plywood

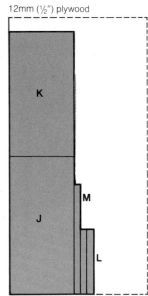

10mm (⅜") plywood

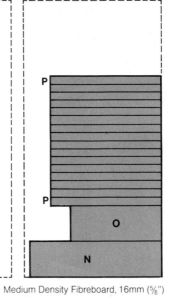

Medium Density Fibreboard, 16mm (⅝")

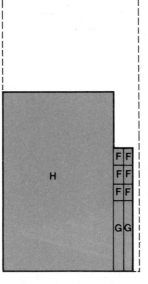

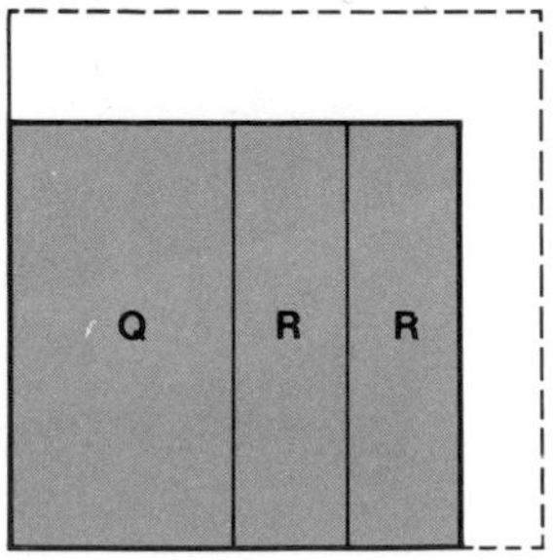

Varnish
Clear satin finish lacquer

Red Stain
Small tin red stain

Instructions

1 Check all the piece parts against the cutting layout and label them **A–V**. If any are wrong or missing, cut again.

2 Take the bed rails **B** and the battens **S**. Having drilled 12 clearance holes along the length of each batten, glue and screw them to the bed rail **B**, parallel to and 28mm (1³⁄₃₂") from, the bottom edge (ie, the worst).

3 Now assemble the bed rail frame by butting the long rail **B** onto the short rail **A**. Glue and tack through with 25mm (1") nails. Wipe off any trace of excess glue (this is *most* important). Continue round the frame until it is complete, then leave to dry after checking that it is square. (Do this by measuring across the diagonals, which should be exactly the same.) Leave to dry.

4 Fix one shelf bracket to each corner with 7 No. 6 × 16mm (⁵⁄₈") screws.

5 Sand the corners flush (start with 80 grit and finish with 120 grit paper). Punch in the nail heads and fill with stopper.

6 Take the support slats **P** and drill a 3.5mm (⁹⁄₆₄") hole at each end centrally and 10mm (³⁄₈") in from the end. Now, working from both ends and from the middle, screw these 16 slats into the bed frame, spacing them equally. The gaps will be about 48–50mm (1⁷⁄₈"–2") wide, depending on the accuracy of the cut on the slats. Use a spacer.

7 Cut and shape the radius on the guard rails **N** and **O**. Use a jig saw and sandpaper (80 grit). Keep your edges crisp and finish with 120 grit sandpaper. Drill 4 clearance holes in each rail as illustrated below (4.5mm/³⁄₁₆") and put to one side.

8 On the bed frame screw and glue the bed brackets **F** in position through pre-drilled clearance holes. Use No. 8 × 25mm (1") screws and locate these brackets firmly up against the slat support battens **S**.

The desk end assembly

9 Take the side panel **C** and butt it up to the end panel **D** in exactly the same way as for the bed frame. Glue both faces and tack through. Panel **C** goes *over* the end of panel **D**. Make sure the tops and bottoms are flush. Clean off all the excess glue.

10 Do the same on the other panels **C** and **D**.

11 Mark out and drill clearance holes (4.5mm/³⁄₁₆″) for all the screws on these two panels (see drawing). No countersinking is required.

12 Lay the 2 corner assemblies **C/D** on their back (with panels **D** flat on the ground). Take the lower shelf panel **R** and offer it into its position. Pilot drill (3.0mm/¹⁄₈″) through panel **C** and repeat on the other side. The pilot drill should enter the shelf panel **R** centrally.

13 Glue all 3 touching edges of shelf panel **R** and secure in position with 2 screws and cups.

14 Repeat the glueing process on upper shelf **R**.

15 Turn the assembly over and, after lining up the shelves with their clearance holes in panels **D**, screw through to secure in the same way.

16 Take the ladder dowels **U** and drill one pilot hole (3.0mm/¹⁄₈″) in each, 66mm (2¹⁹⁄₃₂″) in from one end. Then from the inside of the assembly, screw each of the dowels in position through the first hole with a No. 8 × 46mm (1¾″) screw and cup.

17 Starting with the top dowel, swing it into the horizontal position. Pilot drill through and secure as directed in 16 through all of the holes. Repeat for all 4 dowels, using 6 screws per dowel.

18 For the desk position, drill 2 blind holes in each of the panels **C** from the inside (see plans and dimensions). These should be about 10mm (³⁄₈″) deep. Cut the length of dowel **V** to exact length of 980mm (38⁹⁄₁₆″) and spring it into position. Be careful not to drill right through. These two positions enable you to adjust the desk height as your child grows, or to tilt the desk at an angle.

19 Prepare the desk top by glueing the strip of hardwood **T** to the desk top panel **Q**. Use 2 sash clamps to hold in position and make sure the top of the hardwood edge is just slightly above the top panel. Wipe off glue, leave to dry and then sandpaper smooth. A smoothing plane can be used here.

20 Offer the desk top into its position and pilot through panel **C** into the side of the desk top. This pilot hole must be below the centre line of the panel **Q** edge.

The wardrobe

21 Take the plinth panel **K** and glue and tack along the short edges of downstands **L**. Glue and insert the downstands **M** and tack to secure in the same way (using the 25 oval wire nails).

22 Turn the plinth over and glue blocks (about 50mm × 20mm × 20mm (2″ × ¾″ × ¾″) around all the joins. Leave to dry after cleaning off the excess glue.

23 Lay the plinth on its edge and offer up the back panel **J** into position 600mm (23⅝″) back from the front edge. This is best done by measuring and marking out the position of panel **J** and its respective line of nails. Glue this end and tack through from under the plinth to secure.

24 Take one of the panels **H** and mark out the positions of **K** and **J** on it. Apply glue to the edge of **J** and to **M**. Lay panel **H** in position and tack through to secure. Wipe off excess glue.

25 Repeat with second panel **H**.

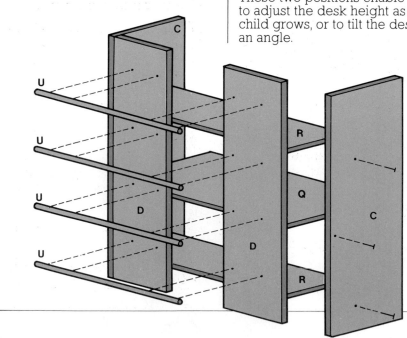

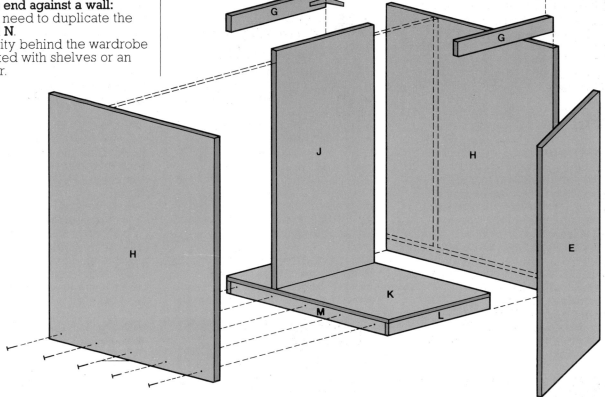

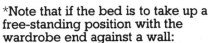

*Note that if the bed is to take up a free-standing position with the wardrobe end against a wall:

- You will need to duplicate the guard rail **N**.
- The cavity behind the wardrobe can be fitted with shelves or an extra door.

26 Take the 2 horizontal rails **G** and span them across the front and back of the wardrobe at the top. The ends of this rail should be glued before it is tacked in position to secure, letting it protrude above both panels **H** by 25mm (1"). Panel **G** at the back should be stepped back from the edge of **H** so that it will fix the location for the bed frame.

27 Stand both support assemblies upright, and with the help of a friend, lift the bed frame onto them. Make sure everything is square and will fit together properly.

28 Take an 8mm (5/16") diameter drill and bore from the outside through the panels **C**, **D** and **H** into the brackets **F**. Now bolt through and test for rigidity.

29 Take the cranked hinges and screw them into position on the carcase side with No. 6 × 19mm (3/4") screws. Climb inside the wardrobe and get someone to hold the door accurately lined up in its closed position. Mark the hole centres. Pilot drill and fix. Check that the door closes properly.

30 Take off the guard rails **N** and **O** and the ladder dowels **U** and stain them red (see TECHNIQUES p. 36 Finishing). Leave to dry.

31 Finish everything in clear varnish.

32 Reassemble and fit the door handle, magnetic catch and the wardrobe rail with the screws provided.

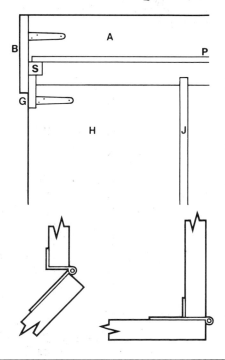

Basic Bed

Designers are increasingly interested in the exploitation of all kinds of materials for their own intrinsic qualities. That is to say, they are exploring ways in which to use materials chosen for their natural colour, finish and texture, without the need to add a finish of veneer or lacquer.

The material, in this case chipboard, is therefore visualized not as an inner core, but as the right material and finish for the design in mind. It will not dirty easily, and so needs no resistant lacquers applied to the surface.

This is an ideal design to try for someone moving into a new flat, for example, or for anyone who needs to make a base for their mattress quickly and cheaply. (If your mattress is a different size from that stipulated, the dimensions can be adapted according to the formula given.) It may be considered a temporary solution, or, with its stylish but basic use of chipboard, you may feel it has a more permanent place in your home. Either way, a duvet will add a much better finish than blankets (as well as being more practical).

Plans and dimensions

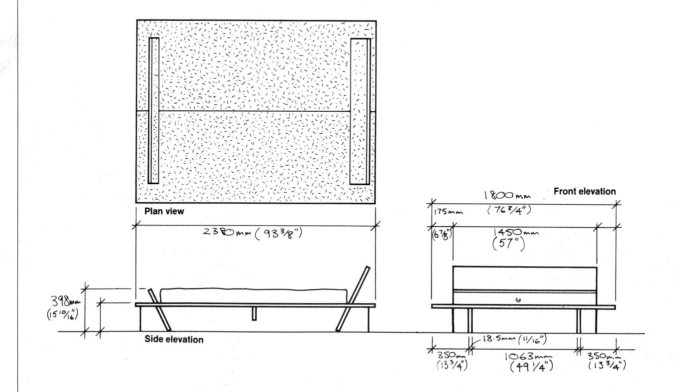

Plan view

2380mm (93³/₈")

398mm (15¹⁰/₁₆")

Side elevation

1800mm (76³/₄")

175mm (6⁷/₈")

1450mm (57")

Front elevation

18.5mm (11/16")

350mm (13³/₄")

1063mm (49¹/₄")

350mm (13³/₄")

The design demands very little of its maker, but do take care in cutting out the boards. Just because you are using a cheap material you can't afford to be slapdash. The reverse is generally true, as bad cutting looks worse on inferior quality materials. Keep your work crisp.

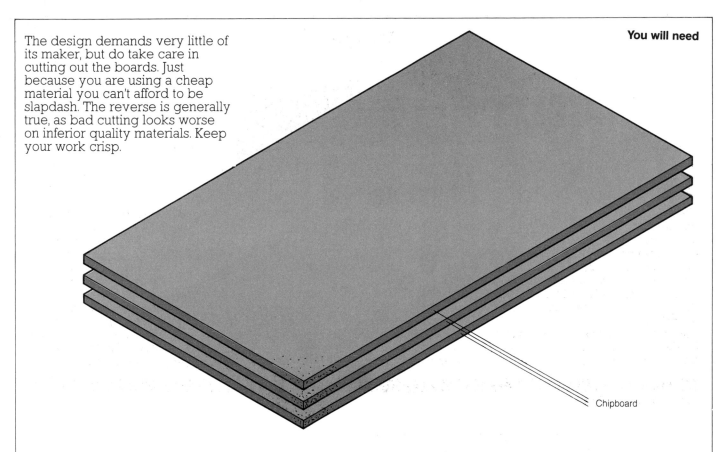

Chipboard

OTHER MATTRESS SIZES

This bed has been designed to take a double mattress of width 1370mm (4'6"), but the design can be adapted for use with a larger or smaller double mattress - or even as a single bed. All you need to do is amend the dimensions on some (but not all) of the piece parts, assuming that the width is the only dimension that changes ie, all mattresses are 1900mm (6'3") long.

So, using this equation, rewrite your cutting sheet (mattress width is written as MW).

$$A = 2380mm\ (93^{11}/_{16}") \times \frac{(MW + 215mm/8^{15}/_{32}")}{2}$$

B = no change
C = (MW + 80mm/3⅛") × 700mm (27⁹/₁₆")
D = (MW + 80mm/3⅛") × 450mm (17¹¹/₁₆")
E = (MW - 150mm/5¹⁵/₁₆") × 230mm (9")

The 30mm (1³/₁₆") slots in **A**, **C** and **D** should be roughly a quarter the length of **C** and **D**.

All other measurements stay the same.

Materials

Board
18mm (¾") chipboard

2380mm × 900mm	(93⅜" × 35⁷/₁₆")	(2)	**A**
2280mm × 230mm	(89⅜" × 9")	(2)	**B**
1450mm × 700mm	(57" × 27½")	(1)	**C**
1450mm × 450mm	(57" × 17¾")	(1)	**D**
1220mm × 230mm	(48" × 9")	(1)	**E**
610mm × 100mm	(24" × 4")	(2)	**F**

Screws
No. 8 × 32mm (1¼") countersunk steel woodscrews   (10)

Tools

Electric jig saw

Sharp new jig saw blades

Square

Screwdriver

Mallet

Sandpaper   80 grit (2 sheets)

Sanding block

Drill

Drill bits 4.5mm, 3mm, (³/₁₆", ⅛"), countersink

Chisel

Pencil

Rule

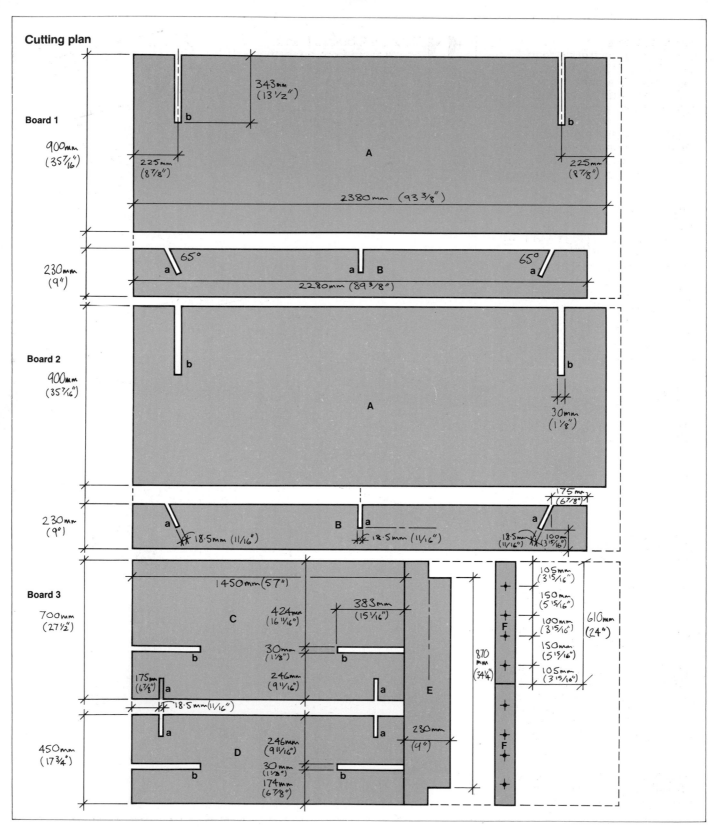

Cutting plan

Instructions

Check your mattress size at 1905mm (6′ 3″) × 1370mm (4′ 6″).

1 Check the sizes of the chipboard parts against the materials list.

2 Lay out all the parts and label them by letter according to the diagram. Carefully mark out the positions of all the slots **a** and **b**.

3 Note that some slots are 18.5mm (¾″) wide (**a**) and others are 30mm (1⅛″) wide (**b**). The wider slots will need to accept angled panels.

4 Cut out the slots very carefully with an electric jig saw. Work right up to the line and don't try and cut *a*) too fast or *b*) two boards at once. Clean up the joint squarely with a chisel and mallet.
It is important to cut these slots accurately and cleanly.

5 Sand off the sharp edges with sandpaper and block.

Assembly

6 Slide part **D** into the slots of both parts **B**.

7 Slide part **C** into the slots at the opposite end of parts **B**.

8 Slot the cross-piece **E** into the middle slots of **B**.

9 Slide into this assembly from either side the 2 base parts **A**. Just before you close up the **A**s together, mark out 2 hole centres, directly in line with part **E**, to secure parts **A** to **E**. Take apart and drill.

10 Reassemble and secure with 2 screws, No. 8 × 32mm (¼″) through **A** into **E**.

11 Take the 2 braces **F** and screw them from beneath up into the bases **A** outside the head and tailboard. You will need to turn the bed up on its side for this. Do it gently and use a pilot drill of 3mm (⅛″) diameter.

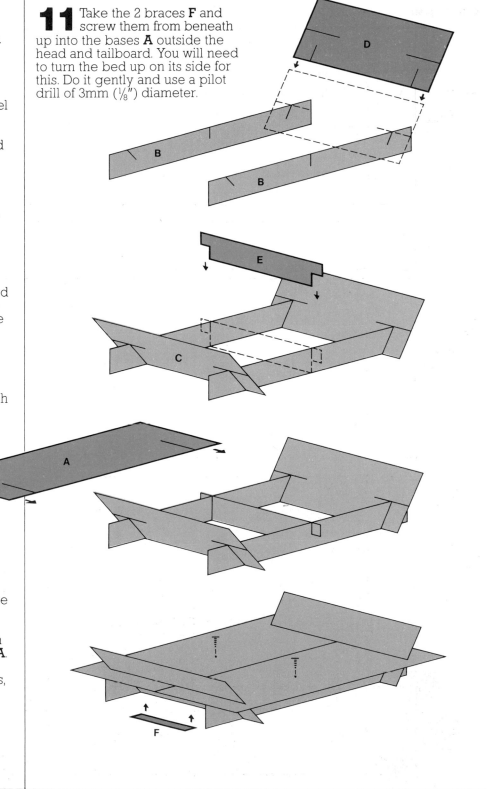

Free Standing Fabric Screen

Screens have enjoyed a revival over the past few years, particularly among people adopting the 'one room living' approach to interior design. Not only can they be seen as a way of hiding and concealing parts of a room, but also as a means of dividing up a large area. Using a decorative screen in this way will add interest to any contemporary interior.

This screen has been designed for easy and quick construction. Work methodically and neatly, as your workmanship will be more visible on this than on other projects. The material will be of your own choice; bright and graphic designs will work well but, if you are unsure, choose a neutral-coloured plain fabric — a grey or a colour similar to the wall finishes.

The hinges do not need to be cut in, but will look a lot neater if they are. Having achieved success with this version, you might be keen to make a screen with more than three sections. This is possible, of course — you could even make a screen to cross the entire width of your room — but remember that it will be more stable if not in one long straight line.

Plans and dimensions

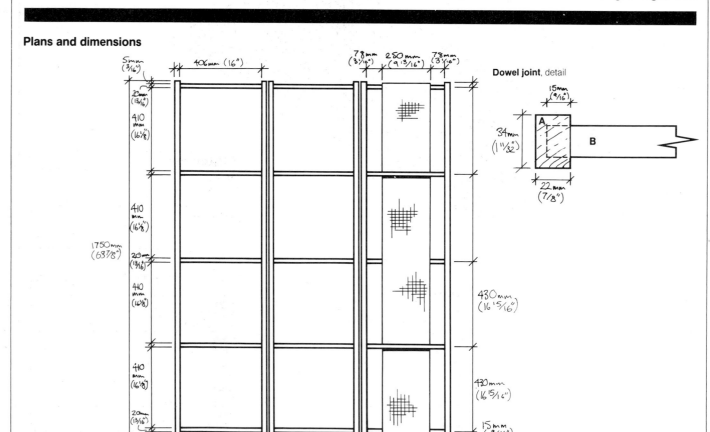

Dowel joint, detail

Front elevation

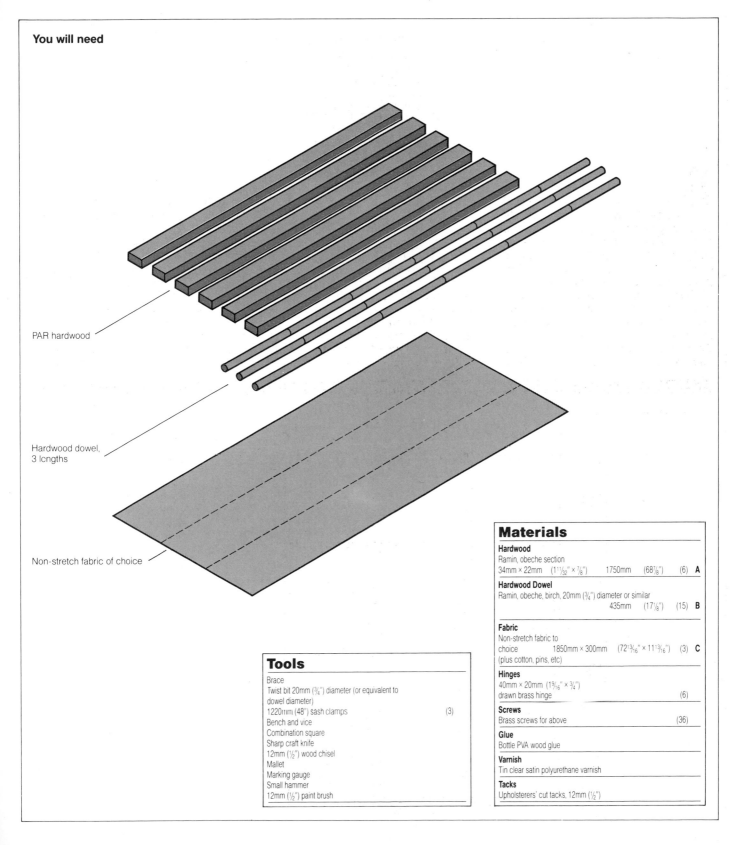

You will need

PAR hardwood

Hardwood dowel,
3 lengths

Non-stretch fabric of choice

Materials

Hardwood
Ramin, obeche section
34mm × 22mm (1¹¹/₃₂" × ⅞") 1750mm (68⅞") (6) **A**

Hardwood Dowel
Ramin, obeche, birch, 20mm (¾") diameter or similar
435mm (17⅛") (15) **B**

Fabric
Non-stretch fabric to
choice 1850mm × 300mm (72¹³/₁₆" × 11¹³/₁₆") (3) **C**
(plus cotton, pins, etc)

Hinges
40mm × 20mm (1⁹/₁₆" × ¾")
drawn brass hinge (6)

Screws
Brass screws for above (36)

Glue
Bottle PVA wood glue

Varnish
Tin clear satin polyurethane varnish

Tacks
Upholsterers' cut tacks, 12mm (½")

Tools

Brace
Twist bit 20mm (¾") diameter (or equivalent to
dowel diameter)
1220mm (48") sash clamps (3)
Bench and vice
Combination square
Sharp craft knife
12mm (½") wood chisel
Mallet
Marking gauge
Small hammer
12mm (½") paint brush

Instructions

1 Take all the uprights **A** and mark out all the hole centres as shown (see plans and dimensions).

2 Find the centre of each of these lines and drill with the brace and bit all the blind holes, 15mm (⁹⁄₁₆″) deep. Clamps the wood to your bench top rather than hold it in the vice. Check that your drill or twist bit is the same diameter as your dowel and make sure the point of the bit does not break through.

3 Sand the dowel rails **B** and assemble each frame in turn, clamping across the dowel joints. Take care to clean off all excess glue with a hot damp rag. Leave to dry. *Do not* glue the bottom rung in each case. Keep it in position, but dry jointed.

4 Hold a pair of frames low in the vice around the area to be hinged, separating each part with a spacer of thickness 2mm (¹⁄₁₆″) (anything handy will do, providing it is 2mm (¹⁄₁₆″) thick).

5 Place the first hinge in position and mark round it with a sharp pencil. Mark the remaining 2 hinge positions in the same way.

6 Take out one frame and remark the hinge position with a square. Lay the square across the end of the hinge position and draw the sharp knife across, cutting into the wood.

7 Use a sharp marking gauge to describe the long edge position of the hinge. Carefully remove the wood with a mallet and sharp chisel.

8 Carry on removing wood until the hinge fits snugly into the cutout.

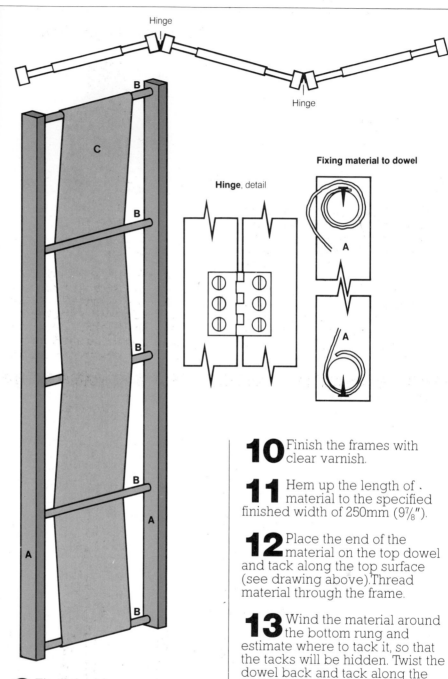

Hinge

Hinge

Hinge, detail

Fixing material to dowel

9 Fit all the hinges, remembering to pilot drill all the holes or use a bradawl. For extra neatness when securing these hinges, screw in steel screws first (brass screws are soft and can easily be damaged). Line up the screw heads with the vertical rail.

10 Finish the frames with clear varnish.

11 Hem up the length of material to the specified finished width of 250mm (9⅞″).

12 Place the end of the material on the top dowel and tack along the top surface (see drawing above). Thread material through the frame.

13 Wind the material around the bottom rung and estimate where to tack it, so that the tacks will be hidden. Twist the dowel back and tack along the length to secure the material and trim. Wind the dowel back until the material is taut, then pin through both ends of the vertical rail **A** to secure the dowel in position.

14 Repeat with the other 2 frames.

Dressing Stand with Mirror

If you are at all like me, you'll find a dressing stand like this very useful. I tend to empty all my pockets onto the nearest available space and throw all my clothes over the closest empty chair.

This item has two shelves, a full length mirror, a rail for ties and such like, and a place for your hat at the top. The whole unit is free-standing and just sits in the middle of your bedroom.

You'll find the stand is not a difficult thing to make and won't take very long either, but don't rush it. Cut accurately and neatly, and take time over the finishing, paying particular attention to preparation and cutting back between coats. The crucial

step is being sure not to put the shelves over the pole until the latter is completely dry.

The choice of colour is up to you, but I have devised a scheme which is not too demanding, while also being composed of shades that are currently fashionable. If you do manage to find some dowel made of hardwood, it would be worth considering leaving a natural finish on these two piece parts.

Plans and dimensions

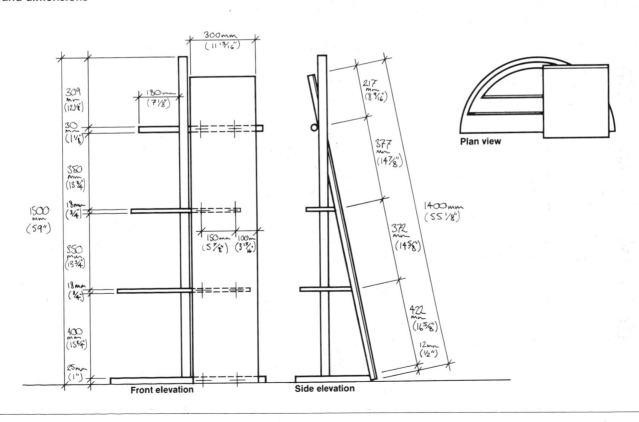

Plan view

Front elevation **Side elevation**

You will need

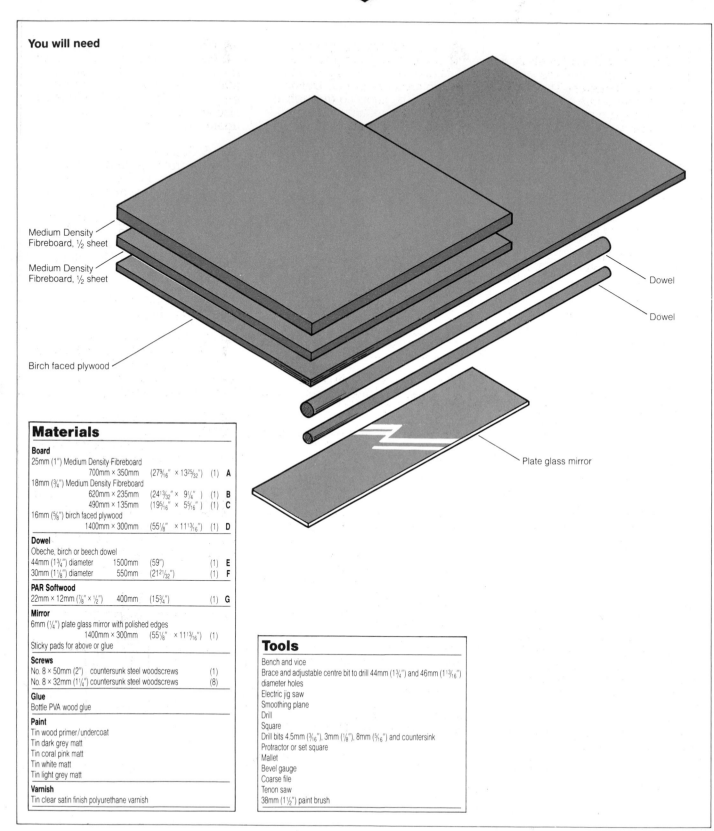

Medium Density Fibreboard, ½ sheet

Medium Density Fibreboard, ½ sheet

Birch faced plywood

Dowel

Dowel

Plate glass mirror

Materials

Board
25mm (1") Medium Density Fibreboard
   700mm × 350mm (27⁹⁄₁₆" × 13²⁵⁄₃₂") (1) **A**
18mm (¾") Medium Density Fibreboard
   620mm × 235mm (24¹³⁄₃₂" × 9¼") (1) **B**
   490mm × 135mm (19⁵⁄₁₆" × 5⁵⁄₁₆") (1) **C**
16mm (⅝") birch faced plywood
   1400mm × 300mm (55⅛" × 11¹³⁄₁₆") (1) **D**

Dowel
Obeche, birch or beech dowel
44mm (1¾") diameter 1500mm (59") (1) **E**
30mm (1⅛") diameter 550mm (21²¹⁄₃₂") (1) **F**

PAR Softwood
22mm × 12mm (⅞" × ½") 400mm (15¾") (1) **G**

Mirror
6mm (¼") plate glass mirror with polished edges
   1400mm × 300mm (55⅛" × 11¹³⁄₁₆") (1)
Sticky pads for above or glue

Screws
No. 8 × 50mm (2") countersunk steel woodscrews (1)
No. 8 × 32mm (1¼") countersunk steel woodscrews (8)

Glue
Bottle PVA wood glue

Paint
Tin wood primer/undercoat
Tin dark grey matt
Tin coral pink matt
Tin white matt
Tin light grey matt

Varnish
Tin clear satin finish polyurethane varnish

Tools

Bench and vice
Brace and adjustable centre bit to drill 44mm (1¾") and 46mm (1¹³⁄₁₆")
diameter holes
Electric jig saw
Smoothing plane
Drill
Square
Drill bits 4.5mm (³⁄₁₆"), 3mm (⅛"), 8mm (⁵⁄₁₆") and countersink
Protractor or set square
Mallet
Bevel gauge
Coarse file
Tenon saw
38mm (1½") paint brush

Instructions

1 Mark out on the 3 panels **A**, **B** and **C** the hole centres (45mm/1¾″ diameter). They are all on the centre line of the length of the panels and at the appropriate distance in from the long edge (see drawing below).

Cutting diagram

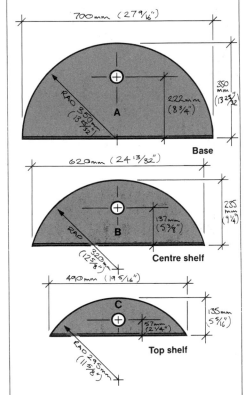

2 Bore through parts **C** and **B** with the bit set at 2mm (¹⁄₁₆″) larger diameter than the pole **E** (try out on a scrap piece first to check the diameter). Be careful not to break up the bottom surface as you come through — a piece of scrap clamped to the back will stop this.

3 Bore through part **A** with the bit set to exactly the same diameter as the pole **E**. Finish the inside of all the holes with 80 grit sandpaper.

4 Make a compass by taking part **G** and drilling an 8mm (⁵⁄₁₆″) diameter hole in one end to take an ordinary pencil. Define the radius by tapping through at the other end a 25mm (1″) oval wire nail.

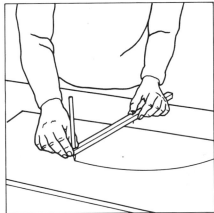

5 Draw out the radii on all 3 panels and cut to the line with an electric jig saw.

6 Hold in the vice each panel in turn and file smooth the rough edge. Take care to keep the edge square to the panel. Finish with 80 grit sandpaper.

7 On all the straight edges of panels **A**, **B** and **C**, draw on a complete bevel; ie, at either end draw a line 11.5° off the vertical. Connect these two lines with a line running along the upper face edge of each panel. Plane down to this line, checking the angle with a bevel gauge as you go.

8 Finish with sandpaper (80 grit) and take off the sharp edges on all surfaces with 120 grit sandpaper.

9 Take the pre-cut mirror backing panel **D** and drill the clearance holes (4.5mm/³⁄₁₆″) for the retaining screws. Countersink.

10 Now paint all the panels white, including undercoat (see TECHNIQUES p. 36 Finishing). Make sure that the paint does not enter the hole (this will reduce its size and prevent easy sliding against the pole.)

11 Paint the upright pole **E** in coral pink, leaving bare the last 20mm (¾″) of the pole. Drill and countersink a clearance hole (4.5mm/³⁄₁₆″ diameter) exactly 202mm (7¹⁵⁄₁₆″) from one end of the horizontal dowel **F** (this is to secure it to the upright pole **E**). Paint the whole of **F** in dark grey.

12 Paint the mirror back **D** in light grey.

13 When completely dry, take the pole **E** and hold it in the vice at an angle which leaves the bottom end at a manageable height.

14 Saw a **V**-shaped cut in the end of **E** with a tenon saw. Make it no more than 5mm (³⁄₁₆″) wide. Now cut a wedge in some scrap pine.

15 Glue the unpainted end of the pole and apply glue inside the hole in **A**. Push the panel **A** onto the pole **E**, until **E** is flush with the bottom of the panel **A**.

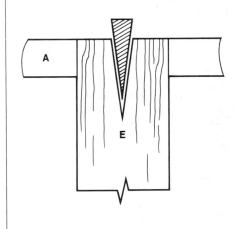

16 Apply glue to the V-cut, then hammer the wedge into the cut with the mallet.

17 Check that the panel is square to the pole in all directions and leave to dry.

18 When dry, saw off the excess wedge still protruding and sand smooth.

19 Fix a hook and eye screw into pole **E**, 400mm (15¾") from the base **A**.

20 Slide **B** over **E** and help it into position resting on the hook and eye.

21 Fix another hook and eye screw into pole **A**, 350mm (13²⁵⁄₃₂") from the top of **B**.

22 Slide **C** over **E** and help it into position on to the hook and eye screw.

23 Taking the panel **D**, rest its bottom end against the base of **A** and square up **B** and **C** through the clearance holes in **D**. Secure the horizontal panels with a roundhead screw through the hook and eyes.

24 To fix panel **D** to the horizontal panels, pilot drill and secure with No. 8 × 32mm (1¼") screws.

25 Line up the horizontal dowel **F** with its central clearance hole in position on the pole. Cramp in position, checking that it is horizontal. Pilot drill and secure with 2 No. 8 × 32mm (1¼") screws into the dowel and 1 No. 8 × 50mm (2") screw into the pole.

26 Finish the entire dressing stand with clear lacquer (see TECHNIQUES p. 36 Finishing) and leave to dry.

27 Finally, glue the mirror to the backing panel with glue or sticky pads. If the backing panel is not flat, slacken off the retaining screws and pack out before applying the mirror.

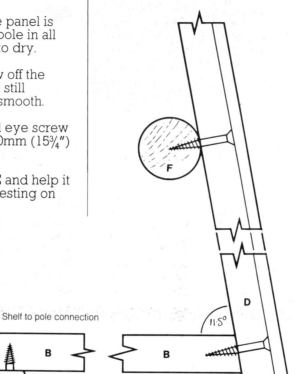

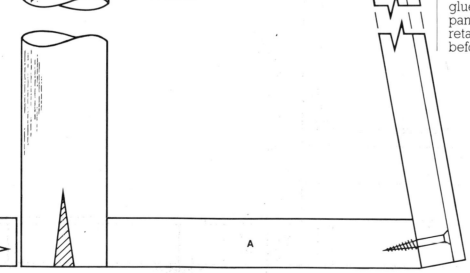

Shelf to pole connection

Hook and eye screws

11.5°

Bed with Integral Table

Beds are once more being considered as more than just divans with a cover which reaches down to the floor. In fact, the popular use of duvets has meant that putting a cover over the top of the bed can look quite ugly. A much more attractive effect can be obtained by using a simple duvet and cover over a mattress supported on a bed base such as shown here. This version has a profiled solid wood edge and legs painted in colour by way of contrast.

The simple four-legged platform will support the mattress adequately, giving a firm but not a solid feel. Use a good mattress and turn it from time to time. A further refinement can be added by fixing one or two side tablets. Although small, they provide a perfect resting place for cups and glasses, books and clocks. A table can be fitted to one side only, or to both.

This design is one of the simpler projects in the book, being an example of basic screw-together technology. When you have finished, add that final touch by buying a brightly-coloured duvet cover or top blanket. But do check before you start that you can move an item of this size up the stairs and into the bedroom!

Plans and dimensions

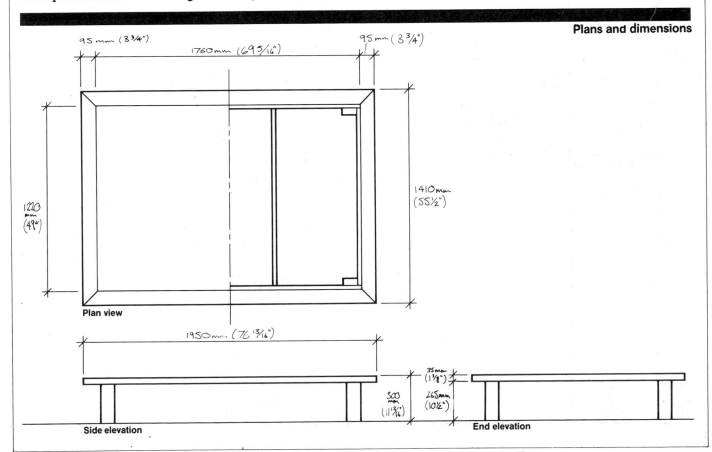

95 mm (3 3/4") 1760mm (69 5/16") 95 mm (3 3/4")

1410mm (55 1/2")

1220 mm (48")

Plan view

1950 mm (76 13/16")

35mm (1 1/8")

265mm (10 1/2")

300 mm (11 3/16")

Side elevation

End elevation

You will need

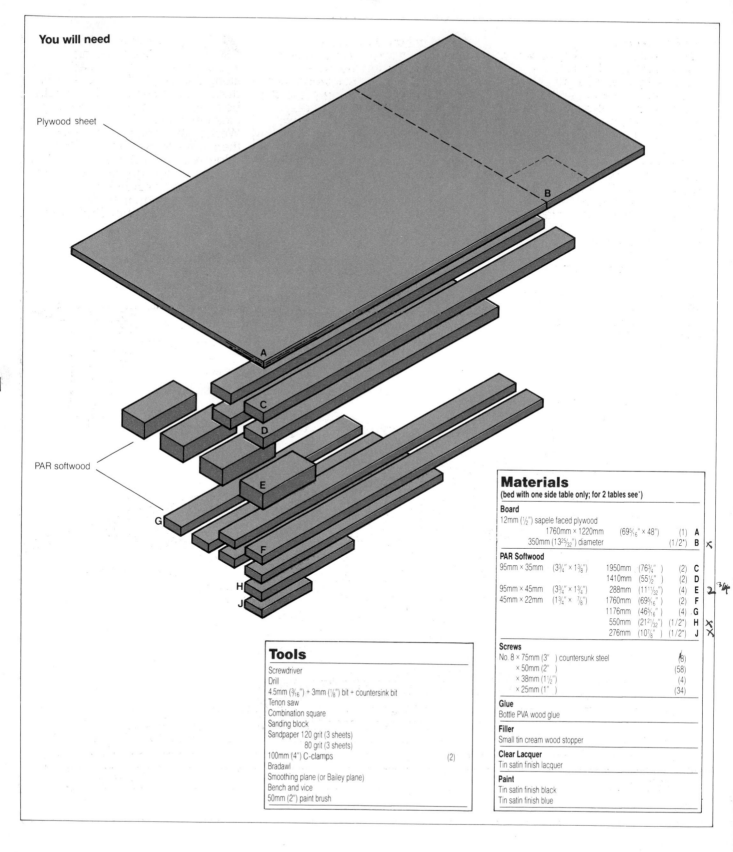

Plywood sheet

PAR softwood

Tools

Screwdriver
Drill
4.5mm (³⁄₁₆") + 3mm (¹⁄₈") bit + countersink bit
Tenon saw
Combination square
Sanding block
Sandpaper 120 grit (3 sheets)
        80 grit (3 sheets)
100mm (4") C-clamps   (2)
Bradawl
Smoothing plane (or Bailey plane)
Bench and vice
50mm (2") paint brush

Materials
(bed with one side table only; for 2 tables see*)

Board

12mm (½") sapele faced plywood

1760mm × 1220mm	(69⁵⁄₁₆" × 48")	(1)	A
350mm (13²⁵⁄₃₂") diameter		(1/2*)	B

PAR Softwood

95mm × 35mm	(3¾" × 1³⁄₈")	1950mm	(76¾")	(2) C
		1410mm	(55½")	(2) D
95mm × 45mm	(3¾" × 1¾")	288mm	(11¹¹⁄₃₂")	(4) E
45mm × 22mm	(1¾" × ⁷⁄₈")	1760mm	(69⁵⁄₁₆")	(2) F
		1176mm	(46⁵⁄₈")	(4) G
		550mm	(21²¹⁄₃₂")	(1/2*) H
		276mm	(10⁷⁄₈")	(1/2*) J

Screws

No. 8 × 75mm (3") countersunk steel		(8)
× 50mm (2")		(58)
× 38mm (1½")		(4)
× 25mm (1")		(34)

Glue

Bottle PVA wood glue

Filler

Small tin cream wood stopper

Clear Lacquer

Tin satin finish lacquer

Paint

Tin satin finish black
Tin satin finish blue

Instructions

1 Take the 12mm (½") plywood **A** and sand down all the rough edges with 80 grit sandpaper. Mark out and drill all the clearance holes for screwing down into the rail supports. These should be 11mm (⁷⁄₁₆") from the edge of the board and then the remaining two rows of holes should be marked out equidistant along the length of the board (see diagram below). Countersink all these holes and mark this face as the top side. Also drill a minimum of 8 × 25mm (1") diameter holes in the plywood base for ventilation.

2 Take the (outside) support rails **F** and **G** and drill the clearance holes for the softwood lips (4.5mm/³⁄₁₆") as shown in the diagram below.

3 All the rail supports **F** and **G** are now screwed and glued to the top **A**, using the two G-clamps to hold the soft wood rails in position. Run a squiggly line of PVA glue along the line of the screw holes. Bring the rail down onto the plywood base, clamp at both ends and screw through the panels, making sure as you go that the rail is flush with the edge of the board.
Complete the 2 long rails **F** first and the 4 transverse rails **G** afterwards. Trim rails to length if necessary.

4 Apply the edge profile to the lips **C** and **D** by planing against a pencil line scribed along the length of the lip. This is drawn from a radius which should be scribed on the end of each lip (see detail below).
Work to this long line first and then move to the middle of the edge, removing all the waste material as you go, until you have the required rounded shape. Finish with sandpaper. (See TECHNIQUES p. 36 Edge Profiling.)

Details of lip and support rails

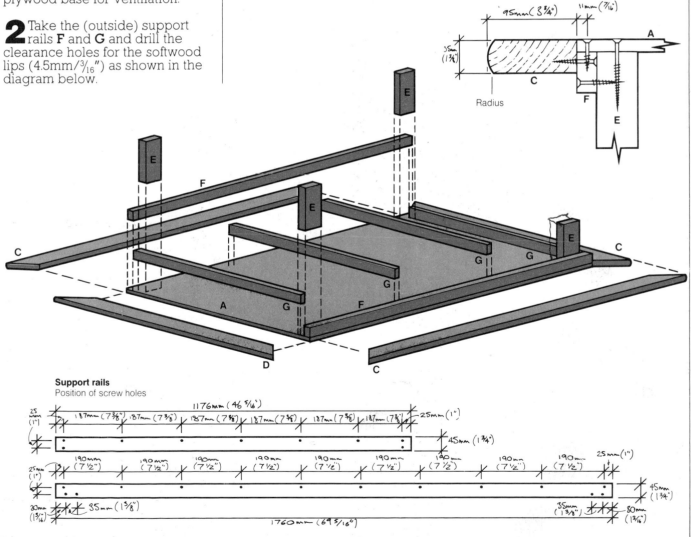

Support rails
Position of screw holes

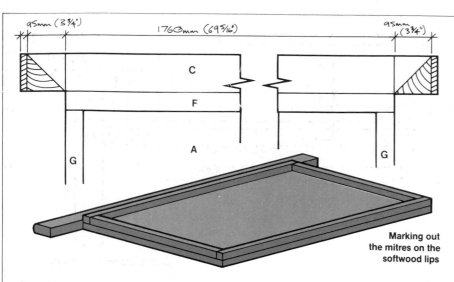

95mm (3¾")
1760mm (69⁵⁄₁₆")
95mm (3¾")

C

F

A

G

G

**Marking out
the mitres on the
softwood lips**

Mitre joints can be strengthened by cutting 2 slots across the joints with a tenon saw. Then well glued pieces of veneer are slid into the slots, left to dry and cleaned up (see illustration below).

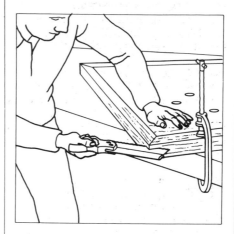

5 Put the top panel **A** top side down on the floor and pick up the 4 softwood lips **C** and **D**. Offer each lip in turn to its respective position, and label 1, 2, 3 and 4, so that their position is fixed. These lips are in total 190mm (7½") longer than the side they butt up to, and we now have to mark out the mitre joint. So, 95mm (3¾") in from one end, mark a pencil line square across the lip. Position this line against the respective corner of the panel, and then at the other end of **A** mark across onto the lip where the panel finishes. Square across. Now take the mitre square and mark a 45° line outwards from the two lines you have already marked towards the end of the lip as shown in the diagram above.

6 Repeat step 5 on all 4 lips and then cut the mitres with a tenon saw. Imagine the bed as a giant picture frame, and make sure that lines are angled the right way before you begin to cut. Clamping the lips to a work top with a C-clamp will keep them fixed while you saw. A good idea is to mark the mitre all the way round so that you keep the saw square as you cut. If you leave excess on the mitre, this must be removed with a plane before the joint is put together.

7 Now screw and glue the lips to the panel. Place the panel **A** with the supports upwards on a table or bench (builders' trestles will do), so that you can walk round it. Clamp a piece of wood to the lower face of the panel to provide a rest for the lip. Place the lip on this piece of wood and clamp it in place with the second C-clamp so that the mitre lines up with the corner of the panel. Put a screw into the first hole and tap it with a hammer. Take the lip off and drill a 3mm (⅛") pilot hole where marked. Now run a line of PVA glue down the lip; replace the lip in position and screw home with a 50mm (2") No. 8 screw.
Working along the lip, pilot drill with a bradawl and screw through every hole, securing the lip and making sure that the top faces are flush.

8 Work around the bed in the same way. Clamp the mitres to make sure they are flush and that they line up. Apply glue to the mitres themselves, not forgetting to clean off all the excess with a hot wet rag. Leave to dry.

9 The legs are profiled in exactly the same way as the edge lips. Mark out the radius on the ends and plane between the lines until the radii are achieved. Finish with sandpaper.

Leg with profiled edge

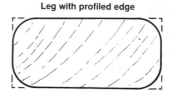

10 The legs are glued and screwed in position with 2 × 50mm (2") No. 8 screws through the long support rail **F**, with a 50mm (2") No. 8 screw through the other rail **G** and finally through the top with 2 × 75mm (3") No. 8s (don't forget to make the clearance holes through the plywood before screwing).

11 Prepare the bed base ready for sanding, starting with 80 grit and finishing with 120 grit. Gaps and defects can be filled with wood colour filler.

Side table

12 Cut out the side table support rails **H** and **J** as drawn below and drill 4.5mm (³/₁₆") clearance holes at the square end. The half lap joints should be cut square and finished with a sharp chisel (see TECHNIQUES p. 32 Cutting Joints). Finish by sanding both parts.

13 The easiest way to cut out the disc **B** is with a power jig saw. Otherwise you will need to finish down to the line with a plane. Finish with sandpaper and block, adding a shallow edge radius if required.

14 Glue the cruciform support **H/J** together and apply PVA glue to its top face. Then place this face down onto the disc and leave to dry under a weight of some sort.

15 Finish the whole assembly with your desired paint finish. (See TECHNIQUES p. 36 Finishing.)

16 Fit tablet to bed and scrape off finish where parts meet. Apply glue to these areas and screw home to secure, having first pilot drilled the holes.

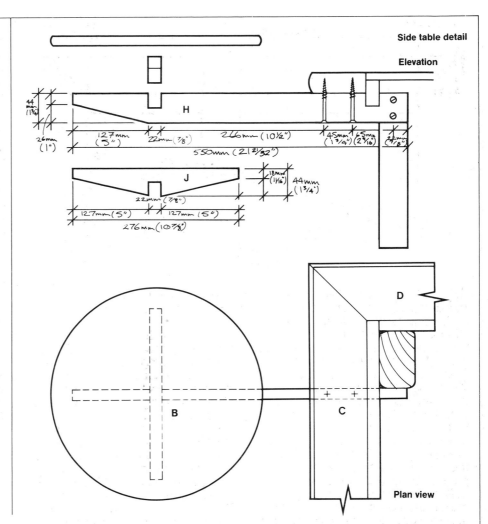

Side table detail

Elevation

Plan view

159

Conversion tables
Inches to millimetres
Basis: 1 in = 25.4 mm (exactly).
All values in this table are exact.

inch	millimetre		inch			inch			inch		
1/64	0.015 625	0.396 875	17/64	0.265 625	6.746 875	33/64	0.515 625	13.096 875	49/64	0.765 625	19.446 875
1/32	0.031 250	0.793 750	9/32	0.281 250	7.143 750	17/32	0.531 250	13.493 750	25/32	0.781 250	19.843 750
3/64	0.046 875	1.190 625	19/64	0.296 875	7.540 625	35/64	0.546 875	13.890 625	51/64	0.796 875	20.240 625
1/16	0.062 500	1.587 500	5/16	0.312 500	7.937 500	9/16	0.562 500	14.287 500	13/16	0.812 500	20.637 500
5/64	0.078 125	1.984 375	21/64	0.328 125	8.334 375	37/64	0.578 125	14.684 375	53/64	0.828 125	21.034 375
3/32	0.093 750	2.381 250	11/32	0.343 750	8.731 250	19/32	0.593 750	15.081 250	27/32	0.843 750	21.431 250
7/64	0.109 375	2.778 125	23/64	0.359 375	9.128 125	39/64	0.609 375	15.478 125	55/64	0.859 375	21.828 125
1/8	0.125 000	3.175 000	3/8	0.375 000	9.525 000	5/8	0.625 000	15.875 000	7/8	0.875 000	22.225 000
9/64	0.140 625	3.571 875	25/64	0.390 625	9.921 875	41/64	0.640 625	16.271 875	57/64	0.890 625	22.621 875
5/32	0.156 250	3.968 750	13/32	0.406 250	10.318 750	21/32	0.656 250	16.668 750	29/32	0.906 250	23.018 750
11/64	0.171 875	4.365 625	27/64	0.421 875	10.715 625	43/64	0.671 875	17.065 625	59/64	0.921 875	23.415 625
3/16	0.187 500	4.762 500	7/16	0.437 500	11.112 500	11/16	0.687 500	17.462 500	15/16	0.937 500	23.812 500
13/64	0.203 125	5.159 375	29/64	0.453 125	11.509 375	45/64	0.703 125	17.859 375	61/64	0.953 125	24.209 375
7/32	0.218 750	5.556 250	15/32	0.468 750	11.906 250	23/32	0.718 750	18.256 250	31/32	0.968 750	24.606 250
15/64	0.234 375	5.953 125	31/64	0.484 375	12.303 125	47/64	0.734 375	18.653 125	63/64	0.984 375	25.003 125
1/4	0.250 000	6.350 000	1/2	0.500 000	12.700 000	3/4	0.750 000	19.050 000	1	1.000 000	25.400 000